Architecture
in Times of Need

Architecture in Times of Need

Make It Right
Rebuilding New Orleans'
Lower Ninth Ward
With Contributions by
Brad Pitt

Edited by Kristin Feireiss

PRESTEL
Munich · Berlin · London · New York

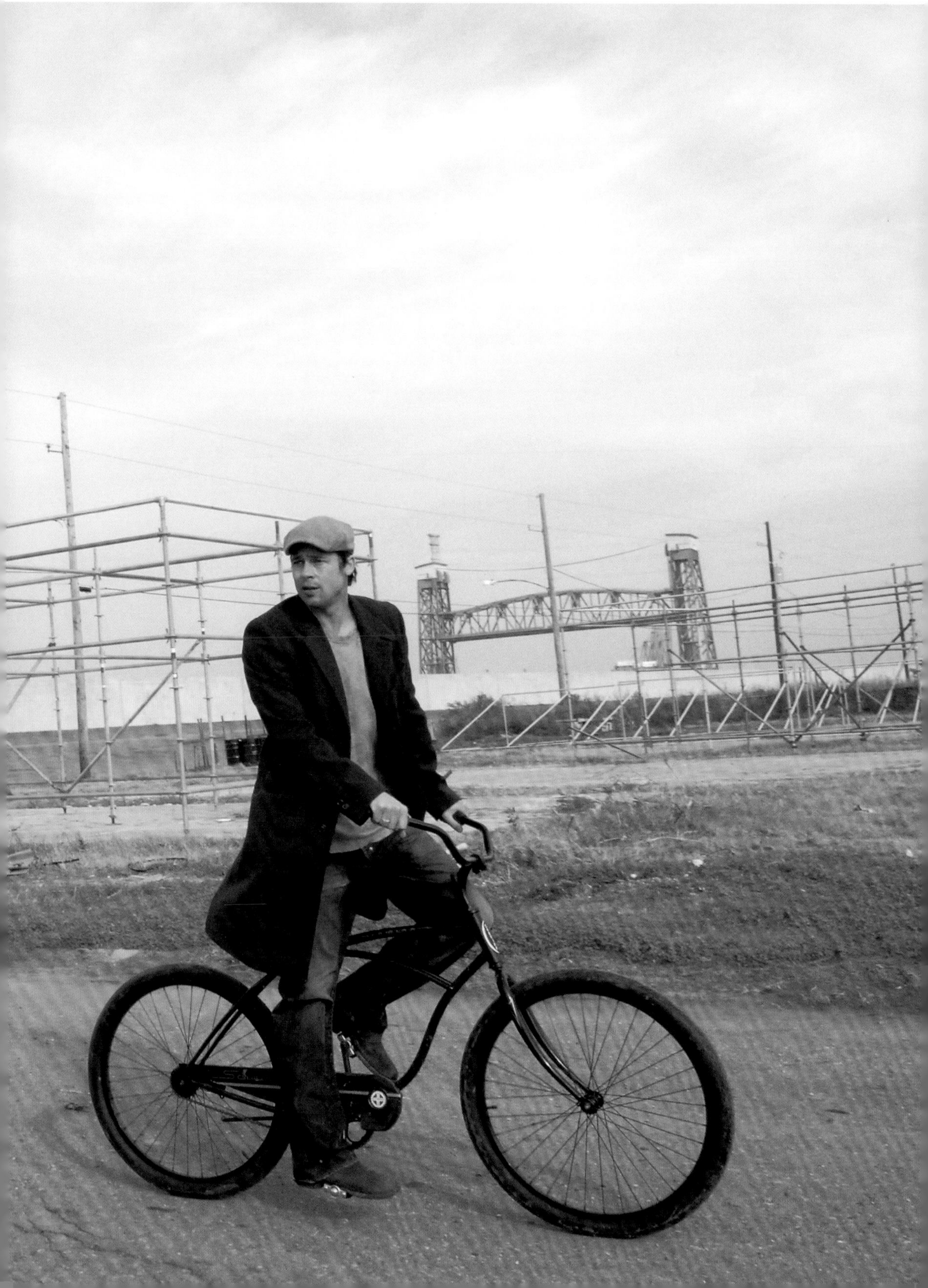

Brad Pitt

Foreword

Katrina has been called the greatest natural disaster in U.S. history, but that description is incorrect. Some have said, "Well that's what happens when you live on the coast," but even that is wrong. Let's be clear, Katrina was man-made.

I am loath to say anything bad about an engineer; I find it such a noble profession. But in this case, decades of reckless handling of the levees combined with a negligent lack of political effort to rectify issues that were common knowledge would ultimately kill more than 1,800 people. More than 1,000 of those deaths were in the Lower Ninth Ward alone. (It's impossible to calculate the true death toll given the numerous related deaths from fragile health, broken hearts, and a tripling in suicides, but experts place this number much higher.) There is no need to go into the horror stories now, but the most sickening thought is that this all could have been avoided. Make no mistake, this is an issue of social justice, and a responsibility exists to right this wrong.

Our first response in a crisis should be to help those who are the most vulnerable and at this we failed—failed miserably. Most would say we continued this failure throughout the recovery effort. But what began as frustration with government's inertia became insight into New Orleans as a microcosm of many of the world's problems: the marginalization of a people, the malpractice of providing low-quality housing for low-income people, even the victimization of oil greed. (If New Orleans had been receiving their fair share of profits from offshore drilling, they would have been able to autonomously secure their levees properly.)

You can argue New Orleans is a victim of climate change given the increase in frequency and ferocity of storms ... a victim of business practices that cut shipping canals at the expense of the wetlands, once the natural storm barrier for New Orleans. You can argue they have suffered the injustice of antiquated building practices which respect the profit margin and not its inhabitants, suffered the injustice of a political machine that doesn't protect its people equally. And if the levees had just been built right the first time, with respect for the people who lived amongst them ... if they'd just practiced a little preventive medicine and spent a little more, well then we wouldn't be faced with the tens of billions it is costing to fix it today. But that didn't happen. And we do have to fix it. And not make the same mistakes again.

This thinking would inform the Make It Right project. We couldn't bring back the residents' heirlooms, photographs, or their lost loved ones, but maybe we could build a bridge home for those struggling to rebuild their lives before all opportunity atrophied and their lots fell prey to speculators. Maybe we could offer a more humane building standard. Maybe we could turn tragedy into victory. We would begin in the historical Lower Ninth Ward because of its iconic significance, and because it had the most difficult shot at coming back.

And so our mandate became this: we would create homes that were sustainable and build with clean materials for a just quality of life. We would create homes that would not contribute carbon but could operate pollution-free. We would build for safety and storm resiliency. We'd create new jobs in the process and we wouldn't stop until we could achieve all of this affordably. (One of the first criticisms I ran up against was that "poor people don't give a shit about green tech." I argued the exact opposite for it was they who would benefit most.) We'd call on some of our great architectural minds to innovate these solutions and, in turn, advance the discussion, practice, and evolution of green tech, thus creating a template that could be replicated at the macro level. We would engage and rely on the community to define the function of their neighborhood and adhere to their guidance, protecting New Orleans' rich culture. We'd hit the streets, raise some cash, and become a catalyst to get families home. We would take what was wrong and make it right.

There'd be numerous complications along the way: misinterpretations of intent, complex loan structures, protection of architects' designs, and worries about gentrification, to name just a few. If someone would have detailed the immense hurdles we'd encounter, it might have appeared too daunting a task to take on. By that same token, had we not believed so naively in the possibility, we would not be experiencing the unquantifiable sensation we're witnessing now—a neighborhood resurrecting itself from the rubble, and the penultimate joy of families returning home. MIR has exceeded my expectations.

I would like to thank the editor Kristin Feireiss for her efforts to coordinate the multitude of contributions that make up MIR and for bringing all these stories together in this book.

Kristin Feireiss

Editor's Foreword

The idea for this book emerged in November of 2007 in the Lower Ninth Ward of New Orleans during the inauguration of the Pink Project, an installation of abstracted pink houses which marked the locations of the former homes of the citizens who lived near the infamous levee break on the Industrial Canal. These homes were destroyed during the flooding caused by Hurricane Katrina on August 29, 2005, a day on which many of the neighborhood's residents perished.

This unique and exciting spatial installation, the Pink Project—initiated by Brad Pitt and executed together with GRAFT Architects—sought to refocus public interest on the ongoing human catastrophe resulting from the lack of substantive public help two years after Katrina, and to motivate individuals and institutions from all over the world to donate to the Make It Right (MIR) initiative.

From newspapers to blogs to television, the reaction was overwhelmingly positive. All of a sudden this remarkable humanitarian project was well known all over the United States, and even spread to Europe and other parts of the world. But it also became evident that only a very few people working on the inside really knew what this complex and ambitious project was all about.

Make It Right is different from any other humanitarian activity. It is not only about collecting money—using rich people's resources to address poor people's needs— but it is about a powerful long-term concept, a complex operational process, and an ambitious design strategy. It is the search for answers to the problems of global warming within architecture's most repetitive module—the family residence. MIR does not showcase a new sustainability concept for a corporate headquarters, but rather deals with the normally neglected, the usually restrictive issues of the world: low-income, affordable, and sustainable houses, the housing of the masses—the architecture of daily life.

After Katrina the sense of urgency that matched the size of the catastrophe was overwhelming and called for an immediate solution and instant relief. But MIR decided not to give in to the temptation to rush forward and merely provide cookie-cutter, temporary shelters. Instead it set its sights on the long-term goal of giving the former inhabitants back their homes, their dignity, and a chance for the future. With this in mind this initiative is not only about newly built houses with the highest sustainable standards, it is about restarting and re-establishing a neighborhood with green public spaces for all generations to live among and enjoy.

Certainly this publication wishes to serve as a blueprint for nonprofit organizations and engaged individuals, but it also tries to give an emotional introduction to New Orleans, the spirit and magic of this fascinating city and its inhabitants. The volume gives room to the people of the Lower Ninth Ward who suffered badly during and after Hurricane Katrina and who never gave up; it explains how to rebuild a neighborhood with a strong aesthetic idea and a clear sustainable goal under the pressures of time.

This book also gives insight into the obstacles that had to be overcome while developing trust and establishing a dialogue between Make It Right, the community members, the landowners of the Lower Ninth Ward, and government representatives. It pays tribute to the role of the initiator of MIR, Brad Pitt, and his operational team who organized fundraising efforts and managed a complex and fair roadmap for financial support.

Complicated and critical questions that were encountered during the entire process of this endeavor are also addressed in this publication: Was it the right choice to rebuild a community that lies in a natural floodplain; what setbacks were to be endured; what fights were fought between the participants; what disappointments were to be overcome?

A central part of this book is dedicated to the design proposals of some of the most well-known, exciting, and innovative architects spanning all generations, who continue to give their very best for only a symbolic compensation—and finally to the built results: the new homes.

In late spring 2007, following the completion of an initial research and development phase, MIR started the first "generation" of house designs by inviting thirteen architects from around the world. After a period of thorough design charrettes, value engineering, and prototype testing, the first houses were occupied by their new (and mostly former) owners. This occurred around the third anniversary of Katrina in August 2008.

Building on feedback from the community and evaluating experiences, it became clear that additional house typologies should be added to the portfolio to better serve the neighborhood's needs. In spring of 2009 a second group of architects was invited to expand the "catalogue" of MIR house designs, while also giving the architects from the first phase the choice to voluntarily participate.

Only time will tell if this intense engagement on the part of MIR, which seeks to address a long neglected issue while cracking the code of high design sustainability in affordable homes, will be successful in the long run. What will become of these ideas in the next decades; how many initiatives will be built upon the shoulders of MIR?

It is impossible to thank all the contributors who have participated in the making of this book. But without the intensive dialogue and the continuous drive that GRAFT invested, the process of making this book could not have happened. It is the right moment to thank the graphic designers Heimann und Schwantes for their engagement. There were also many spontaneous encounters for which I wish to express my gratitude—like with Mavis Yorks, who decided to take a break from her daily profession to live as a photographer on site in the Lower Ninth Ward, documenting every day, from the catastrophe to the growing of hope.

Since we started more than two years ago working on this publication, which can be seen as an architectural book but at the same time as a manual on how to make it right elsewhere, the first twenty homes have already been occupied or are well under construction in the Lower Ninth Ward; eighty more will hopefully be completed by the end of 2009.

Mark Wigley, architectural theorist and Dean of the Architecture Department of Columbia, New York, is right when he says, "I think it's the job of an architect to be optimistic, to invent new forms of optimism, to contaminate us all with the possibility that we could live differently."

Charles E. Allen, III, President of HCNA

Silver Linings

If there is one thing among many things that the people of New Orleans have learned and grown to appreciate in the aftermath of Hurricane Katrina is those little things called silver linings. Those little things are the positive outcomes from very negative situations. Hurricane Katrina and the man-made failure of levees in the wake of this storm were without a doubt one of the most destructive and negative set of experiences experienced by any people anywhere in the world. But, in Katrina's aftermath and the post-disaster recovery period that continues to unfold, we the people of New Orleans, and in particular the Lower Ninth Ward, have come to count and appreciate our silver linings. For all of us in this community, coming to know Brad Pitt, the Cherokee Investment Family, and all working in the context of the Make It Right project family has indeed been a silver lining of an experience. And, most importantly, Make It Right has come to bring a collection of our Lower Ninth Ward organizations together in a collective we now call the Lower Ninth Ward Stakeholders Coalition. The coalition meets every Wednesday of every week to consult and work with the Make It Right partners to further shape the most ambitious and necessary multimillion-dollar community housing and redevelopment project ever under- taken in our nation's and perhaps the world's history. And we fully realize that the ground we are treading on is very important and being watched by everyone in the world.

But, back to the silver lining part of all this. I firmly consider our coalition to be not only a wonderfully committed group of fellow community leaders but more importantly and affectionately they are family members. They are family members who squabble and disagree just as all families do over various issues. But, let's face it, that's how families get along. What holds the family together always are those common threads, expe- riences, and lineage from which the family cannot under any circumstances be unbound. And, I wouldn't trade this family for anything. We disagree, deliberate, struggle, advance, and excel together. And, what matters is that we ultimately excel. Excel we have done thus far. And, I have absolutely no doubt in my mind that we will continue to excel. And, we will do it together! So, every now and then, one must stop and count the silver linings—those wonderful, ever-splendid, and miraculous intangibles that get us through the hard times of our lives. This publication is dedicated to the memory of all the many people of the Lower Ninth and New Orleans who perished directly or indirectly due to Hurricane Katrina.

Douglas Brinkley

Pink Houses and Green Futures

O Katrina! Thousands of Lower Ninth Ward residents during the hurricane found themselves stuck in the brutal floodwaters of August 29, 2005 as booming gusts of wind ripped off rooftops. Boom! Boom! Crash! Somehow the Industrial Canal levee had breached and a mad-attic rush of muddy water flooded into Creole cottages and old-timey shotgun edifices within minutes, slapping the bottoms of chandeliers. Homes were popped from their foundations, spinning dervishly like Kansas farms in *The Wizard of Oz.* The doors of the earth had opened up and swallowed everything in sight. A washing out had occurred. The legendary Fats Domino lived in the neighborhood and his little yellow mansion drowned. Somebody, assuming he had died, spray-painted "R.I.P. Fats" on the side. With camera-eyes trained on the rank desultoriness, the national media declared the entire Lower Ninth an unsalvageable wasteland. Once the tailwinds passed and the sun shined forth, hordes of dragonflies buzzed over the abandoned neighborhood languishing in a caked-mud dustbowl of bewilderment. The gig seemed up. No more manicured lawns or Sunday church bells or Popeye's Fried Chicken.

But actor Brad Pitt and his band of Make It Right eco-activists didn't throw in the towel. Ignoring these premature mortuarial conclusions, they insisted that the grim post-disaster Lower Ninth blues could be reharmonized into a brazen new gospel bounce under the banner of sustainable rebuilding. Following Katrina about a hundred rainless days seemed to have transpired and the earth cracked nothingness. Then things started to get better in the Lower Ninth. Durable levees were constructed to help protect the neighborhood. Traffic lights blinked and water pumps groaned to life. Volunteers streamed into the devastated neighborhood and families returned. Time was slowly starting to heal the stricken area. Eventually hunks of the collapsed levee wall calcified. The human spirit—as exemplified in Make It Right—gloriously did not. Instead of an embalming, this historic community started getting revived by Pitt's foundation. His crew pumped optimism into the Lower Ninth when it was at a rock-bottom point. At the exact spot where the Industrial Canal had breached on August 29, 2005, six eco-houses were constructed, with the promise of more on the way. All of them were aesthetically enlightened architectural gems providing above-sea-level hope in the land of below-sea-level despair.

There have been over a dozen fine Katrina books written since the deluge, arguably the worst hurricane to have ever wrought havoc on the Gulf South. The grotesque specter of shattered lives, bloated corpses, splintered schools, uprooted oaks, and heaps of moldering debris have all been dutifully recounted. I wrote one of the tracks myself. Harrowing descriptions about how the U.S. Army Corps of Engineers erected Lego levees in 1965 thereby casting a time-bomb pox over entire New Orleans neighborhoods like the Lower Ninth is now accepted fact. This, however, is a different type of book; it documents the rebound. What the Make It Right Foundation clearly understands is that behind every roofless Katrina bungalow or swallowed car lingers a loss that needs to be regained. Like in the other Katrina-related books, there are grim photographs included here of rampaging waters, taps turned off, mothers screaming, and the National Guard misaiming. There is an aura of desperate mass confusion presented here. (It's hard not to pay attention to a statistic like 1,577 dead in Louisiana, showcased in a billboard-styled advertisement.) But the core of this book is about positive change. This Pitt-inspired pioneering environmental design strategy has successfully turned tattered Lower Ninth stairways into smart-living model homes. And they're just getting started.

The burning post-Katrina question in the fall of 2005 was how to do something audacious commensurate with the scope of the man-made levee disaster in the Lower Ninth Ward. To rebuild houses like Habitat for Humanity was actively doing elsewhere in New Orleans was fantastic (their Musician's Village project, in fact, remains a towering monument to nonprofit excellence). But Pitt believed a reimagining of urban living was also called for. Couldn't a new eco-architecture arise out of the rubble? Homes that would use sustainable local materials, technologies like gray-water reuse systems, and renewable resources like harvesting rainwater and solar panels? There is an entire literature pertaining to cutting-edge sustainable design principles including permaculture, biomimicry, and carbon-neutral status. Wouldn't it be wonderful if the Lower Ninth could go off-the-grid, so to speak, and have new homes, which would be energy efficient for a hundred years? Although Pitt is a mega-star actor, he's also a committed green activist. He's known to make eyes glaze over at Hollywood and Hamptons cocktail parties by waxing forth on permaculture (i.e. designing communities by mimicking natural ecologies). That's part of the rascal's square charm.

But Pitt is also a visionary. This book is largely about his wild hopes being played out for real. Where others saw only gloom in the Lower Ninth, he looked at the broken streets with new eyes. He moved his family to New Orleans, pulled for the Saints, and plugged the Big Easy on TV every chance he got. He gave locals a lift. The sight of him bicycling around the city, with Bowery Boy cap as hatcrown, brought smiles to people's faces. Working with groups like Common Ground, ACORN, and the Lower Ninth Ward Homeowner's Association, Pitt's project took root. A little revolution, in fact, is quietly underway. A lot of credit goes to GRAFT, who helped Pitt work side-by-side with families in the Lower Ninth Ward. Reimagining an entire blasted-out neighborhood is no easy task, particularly one as historically vibrant as the Lower Ninth. Fundamentally their vision is sound (i.e. futuristic hybrid of common-sense environmentalism and new urban responsibility). The New Orleans Shotgun-house typology is embraced in these expertly reproduced architectural blueprints, right down to stoop-sitting and sun decks. Somehow these designs seem Jetson-like, fanciful Worlds of Tomorrows. Reading this lavishly conceived book makes me feel like wearing a hydrogen fuel-cell space pack and soaring forward in time travel. But the amazing change is happening now in the Lower Ninth.

There is a breathless intensity of foresight in the Pitt dream. The old maw of hyper-industrialization is being given the pointed-boot kick into the oncoming rush of the sustainability revolution. Someday, I hope, this book may be deemed a quirky souvenir of the societal switch-out from energy-draining to energy-enlightenment. It will be studied as an artifact. It will be treasured as a historical document of that eureka moment when it rained Brad Pitt pink houses in the Lower Ninth amidst the heaping piles of foul debris. Each architectural home design in these pages has integrity and star-shine. O Holy Cross! O Jazz Night! O Social Equitability! O Environmentally Sensitive City! The hot struggles of August 2005 seem distant when reading about Make It Right's ability to promote contemporary modernism while also preserving the old-fashioned New Orleans culture along the Industrial Canal. A revelation is at hand. The reader is being asked to participate. To embrace the romantic readiness of the Make It Right move-ment. Read about the attractive alliances formed between top-tier global architecture firms from Tokyo to Berlin to Houston. A collaborative freshness is inherent in this book. I've read a dozen volumes on urban planning and architecture in my lifetime, and some still stand proudly on my shelf next to the Frank Lloyd Wright books, reminding me that the "prairie school" was once considered quackery, and that visionaries like Gehry and Graves and Khan were deemed overreachers in their day. I suspect some readers will write off the Make It Right planned community as do-goodism run amok, an abstract Lower Ninth Ward freak-show curiosity destined to float away unit-by-unit with the whip and crack of the next Katrina-like gale. After all, we live in a CYA (cover-your-ass) era and everybody wants to log skepticism as a bulwark against mistake. Cynics are a dime a dozen. Reproach is as commonplace as a hacking cough. Action has been demoted by the ugly sword of personal opinion. Audacity anchored around pragmatism—the modus operandi of the Make It Right foundation—is a rare bird indeed. So at the very least get into the rooting-stands for Pitt and company. If the Lower Ninth Ward gets resuscitated then the sustainability rebuilding movement will gain further leverage worldwide. An urban planning laboratory experiment has been hatched in the Lower Ninth and I pray the swab test flashes blue in the coming decades.

I've known Brad Pitt now for fifteen years. He has a simple two-part personality. He is all heart and guts. Where others slam on brakes or are risk adverse, he is uber-hubristic with his compassion. Sometimes I worry he is crazy as a loon. But he always tries to deliver on his promises. One evening, at dusk, I went with Brad Pitt to a community meeting in the Lower Ninth. He was on a listening tour. It was held in a classroom of modest size. There were donuts and coffee. Many residents were livid at the callous-ness of the post-Katrina federal government response. Shell-shocked mothers held children's hands and prayed for their blocks of ruin. These residents had heard so many lies that nobody was beyond intense scrutiny. Brad Pitt cut through all that negativity with his heart. He made a direct appeal. Like Jimmy Stewart in *Mr. Smith Goes to Washington* he told the locals that he had a vision. That he cared. That he could help them Make It Right!! His pure empathy beamed forth and everybody smiled. This was the Missouri kid having a love affair with New Orleans, not a Hollywood sorcerer peddling tricks. After being ignored and defiled, Pitt was offering the Lower Ninth residents a sincere helping hand in the Judeo-Christian tradition. Everybody intuited he was for real.

That evening I thought about how the Lower Ninth had always lent itself to artistic personification. All those bold jazz players like Al "Carnival Time" Johnson and Joe Lastie Junior living along the levee where snapping turtles were sold by the pound. Folk artist Sister Gertrude lived in the Lower Ninth, too. Her visions of the apocalypse and redemption and mercy still hold sway. You can feel it in the way the clouds hover over-head the neighborhood like in a John Ford western. I saw a happy glint in the eyes of Malik Rahim from Common Ground as Pitt spoke about a New World Order being launched from the Old World Disorder. I heard the "uh-huhs" of Sharon Johnson as Pitt lead a discussion of helping the homeless. Sustainability was on the table. These folks had heard Pentecostal preachers say crazier things before. It was a matter of where to place faith. "We trust you," one woman said to Pitt, with a piercing directness. "We trust you more than the U.S. government."

Whew! A fifteen-minute break was in order. All the local activists needed to get their heads around the weird notion of green houses. A few cigarettes were smoked and cell phones were put to ears. A National Guard convoy went by and no one looked at it. Then the community gave Pitt a thumbs up. What a strange set of circumstances, I remember thinking, when Brad Pitt can deliver a more hopeful future than FEMA.

Brad Pitt made it clear that his interest wasn't salutary, that he was in it for the long haul. I've got a notebook full of everything that was said. Brad Pitt was both disarming and charming. Hackles evaporated under the brow of his collectivist spiel. In sum, he made a giant handshake deal with an entire community. My lingering perception of that ethereal night remains how around thirty community leaders all signed up for the eco-dwelling stratagem. Like huddled football players before kickoff, hands clasped together in a circle, they essentially shouted "Let's Go …" They would all run the extra mile to reimagine the Lower Ninth. Even if they failed, at least their children could salute their attempt.

These days after a natural disaster society is faced with a unique opportunity to rebuild communities with innovative houses that support the local economy, reduce dependency on foreign oil, and minimize impacts on Greenhouse Gas emissions. (Fact: the Make It Right houses cost less in utilities and are more disaster-resistant than pre-Katrina structures. They are healthier to live in and leave minimal ecological footprints.) While clearly Habitat for Humanity has done a numerically better job of housing Katrina victims, the Pitt plan retains a special long-range appeal. Besides all its futuristic promises, this book is a potent postcard reminder that New Orleans does things differently. Always has. Always will.

So bang the drum slowly with sticks of eco-hope. Pitt has reminded New Orleanians to not lose their sense of imagination amongst all the ghastly red tape. That alone is an important gift to the struggling city. Someday maybe trees will sprout from the Lower Ninth rooftops because we planted them there, instead of being heaved by crazed floodwaters unleashed because the U.S. Army Corps of Engineers didn't get it right when they used shoddy materials to build worthless levee walls thereby guaranteeing unnecessary carnage to unsuspecting residents. With six Make It Right homes already up and running, the Lower Ninth rebirth is real. Phase one is a success. Who knows how the other acts will play out? But you have to pull for these guys. Now, at nighttime in the Lower Ninth, instead of darkness, the new Make It Right homes glow like a dusting of lightning bugs amongst the rubble. The pipedream is over, the drama has begun, and the neighborhood drawbridges are down connecting the Lower Ninth Ward to the Bywater and French Quarter and Greater World-at-Large. Take a ride down Saint Claude Avenue to see the New Way for yourself. An incremental wonderment is underway … one house at a time.

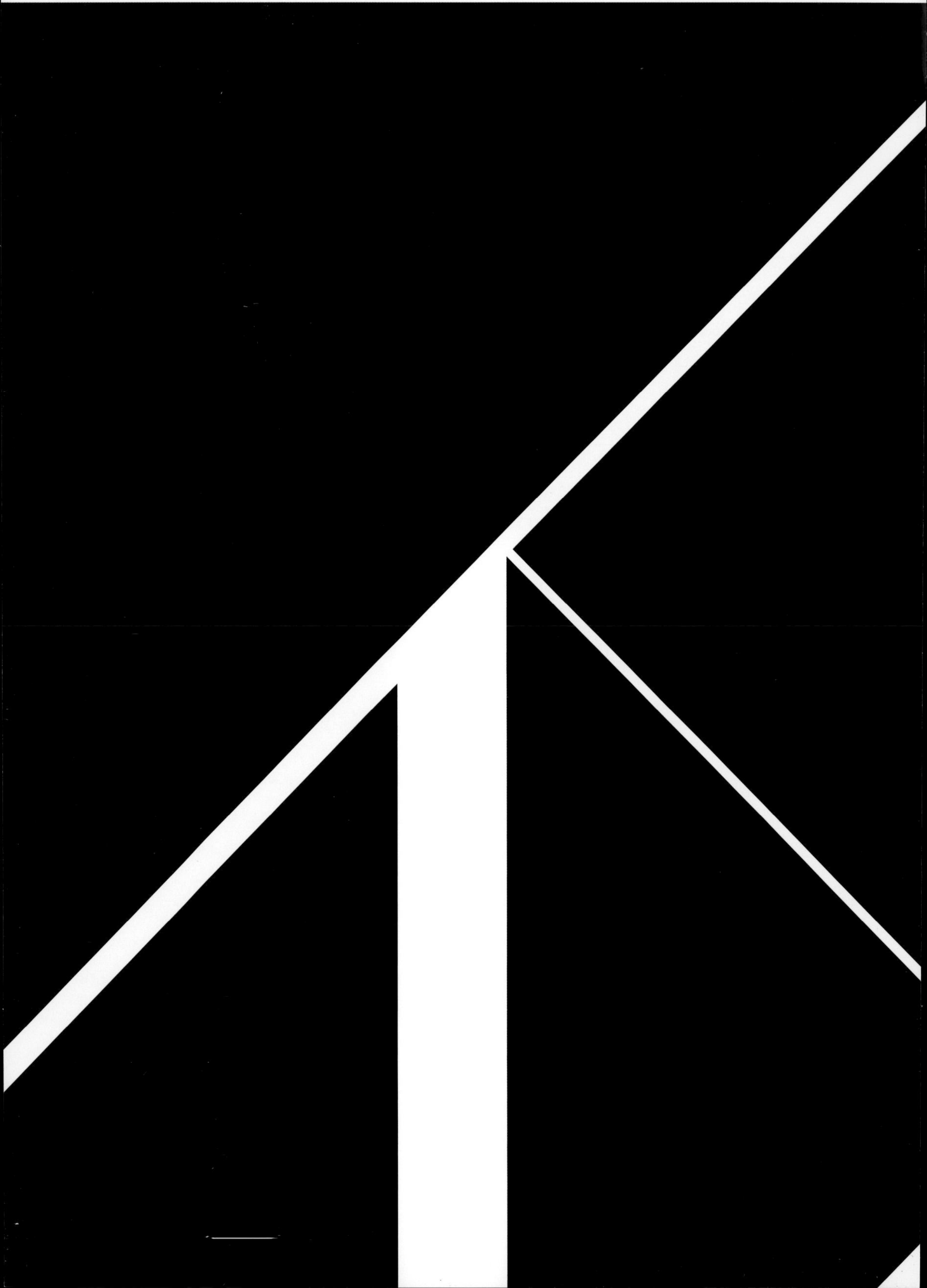

The Lower Ninth Ward and Katrina

Katrina
hit the Mississippi coastline in the early morning of August 29, 2005.

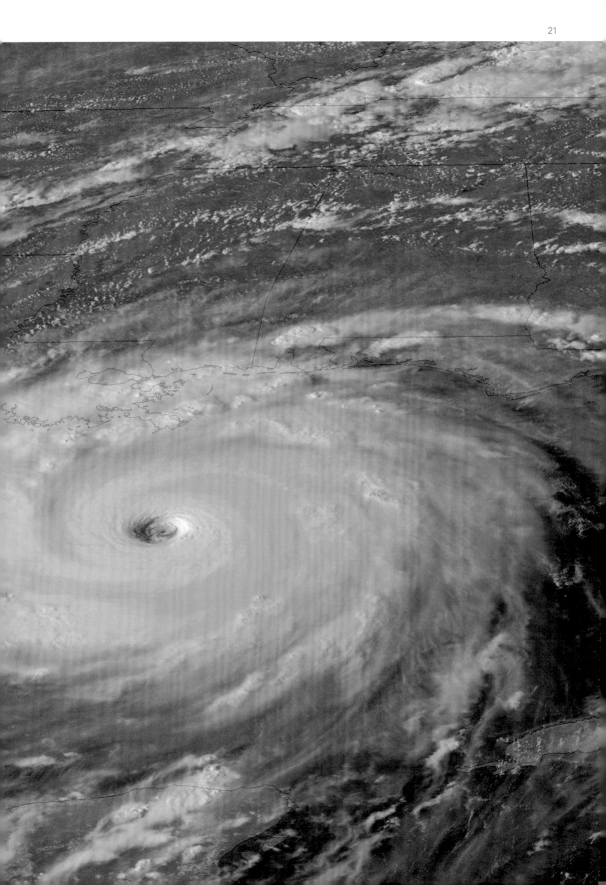

80 percent of Greater New Orleans was flooded.

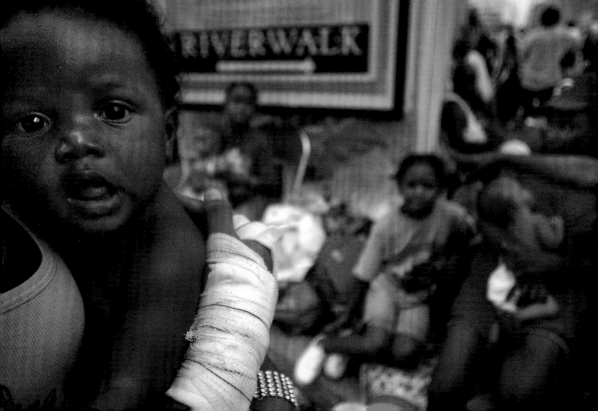

Our first responsibility in a crisis is **to help** the most vulnerable and we failed— **we failed miserably.** And to some extent we're still failing.

Brad Pitt

In Louisiana 1,577 people died in the flood water.

In the days after Katrina **people endured** temperatures in excess of more than **100 degrees Fahrenheit** and almost **100 percent humidity.**

Hurricane Katrina: Dates and Facts

Katrina hit the Mississippi coastline in the early morning of August 29, 2005. It caused fifty-three different levee breaches in greater New Orleans. This resulted in the flooding of 80 percent of the city. As of May 19, 2006, Katrina's death toll stood at 1,836, mainly from Louisiana (1,577) and Mississippi (238); 243,180 people lived in houses with over four feet of flood water. This is 50 percent of the city's population. Hurricane Katrina devastated 90,000 square miles along the Gulf Coast in August of 2005. The anguish felt during and immediately after the storm persists today in each and every survivor, whether or not they have returned to rebuild. In New Orleans, the Lower Ninth Ward was one of the most impacted neighborhoods. Its vulnerability due to levee breaches created floodwaters that tore houses off their foundations, threw houses on top of cars, erased blocks upon blocks, and left the entire community homeless. Neighbors tell stories of devastating heat, desperate attempts to save family members by hacking holes through roofs to provide air and escape from the fetid floodwaters, hours upon hours, days upon days on rooftops without drinking water in the relentless sun waiting for help. And the wait goes on more than three years later. A disproportionate number of residents of the Lower Ninth Ward owned their own homes before the storm as compared to the rest of New Orleans' residents—a testament to hard work and independence. But this was small consolation, as a disproportionate number also lost their lives to Katrina, either directly to the storm or to displacement—an inability to return to their birthplace.

Having endured temperatures in excess of 100 degrees Fahrenheit for days on end without electricity, without water, and, ultimately, without hope, the people of the Lower Ninth Ward are proving that, with passion, commitment, and collaboration, they can beat the odds.

Katrina's Path and Rainfall Diagram

Areas affected by the storm: The Bahamas, South Florida,
Cuba, Louisiana (especially Greater New Orleans), Mississippi,
Alabama, the Florida Panhandle, most of North America

- 1"
- 3"
- 5"
- 7"
- 10"
- 15"

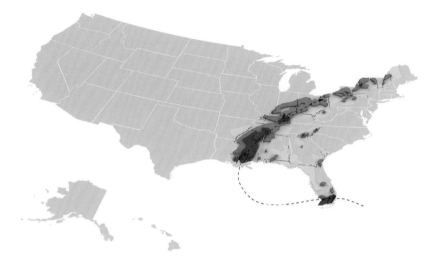

Diaspora

Victims of Hurricane Katrina have addressed themselves for
assistance to FEMA from all over the country, from every state.
The Federal Emergency Management Agency has counted
the astonishing number of 1.36 million individual filings. Some
came from faraway states like Alaska or Hawaii; others
arrived from Puerto Rico.

Number of Refugees from
Katrina spread across the U.S.

- 10,000
- 5,000
- 1,000
- 100
- 10

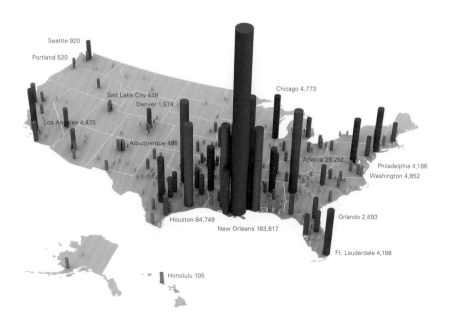

Seattle 920
Portland 520
Salt Lake City 448
Denver 1,574
Los Angeles 4,435
Albuquerque 405
Chicago 4,773
Atlanta 29,252
Philadelphia 4,186
Washington 4,852
Orlando 2,693
Houston 84,749
New Orleans 183,617
Ft. Lauderdale 4,188
Honolulu 105

Depth of Flooding

■ 0–2"
■ 2–4"
■ 4–6"
■ 6–10"
■ over 10"

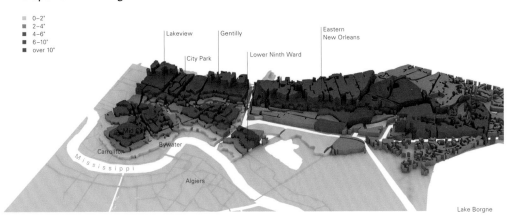

Duration of Flooding

■ 23–29 days
■ 7–22 days
■ 1–6 days

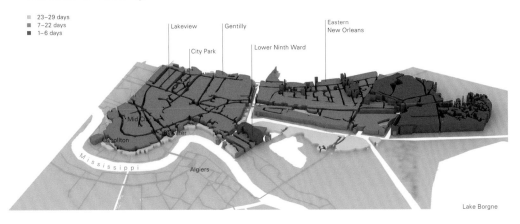

Homes with permission
to be demolished

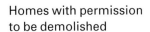

■ < 10 %
■ 10–25 %
■ 25–100 %

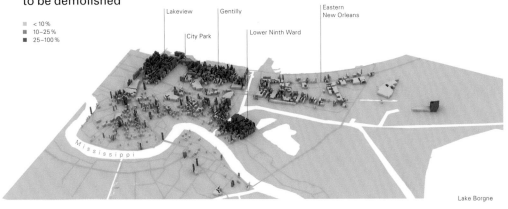

Damage done to the Lower Ninth Ward

- Pre-Katrina houses
- Post-Katrina houses

Carol McMichael Reese

From Field of Disaster to Field of Dreams: The Lower Ninth Ward

It is hoped that the four-word phrase "the Lower Ninth Ward" is, by now, firmly ensconced in the lexicon of twenty-first-century urban disaster. On the level of symbolic language, we rely upon this phrase to be a cipher, shorthand for the human agony and loss that Hurricane Katrina spawned on August 29, 2005, which we must never forget. The communicative value of this phrase is to remind us of the multiple, catastrophic failures of infrastructural and administrative systems that should have functioned to ensure protection, safety, and aid for dwellers in the urban habitat but did not. To issue "the Lower Ninth Ward" as a call to action in New Orleans is to urge that we dedicate ourselves to rebuilding a socially equitable and environmentally sustainable city, one that redresses ignorance, misjudgment, neglect, and injustice. We must "Make It Right."

What of the place that is the Lower Ninth Ward from which people and their homes were swept away? How was this particular physical locality populated and constituted over time to weave a landscape challenged by poverty and crime, but rich with community life and cultural traditions? Today the Lower Ninth Ward hangs on to life by shreds, and the Make It Right project seeks to begin to repair its rent fabric. In August 2005, the Lower Ninth Ward encapsulated many things that were, and are, right about New Orleans, as well as many that were, and continue to be, wrong. The focus of this brief history is the urbanization process by which this neighborhood and, hence, its citizens came not only to be marginalized but also to be recognized—even mythologized—as valuable contributors to New Orleans' unique urbanity. Cognizant of these historical passages, we may be able to plan and to rebuild more wisely and more humanely. Five sequences of historical change led the Lower Ninth Ward to become a field of disaster. To understand the role that the Lower Ninth Ward came to play in New Orleans' urban imaginary, we have to look at the historic development of the relatively vast Ninth Ward, which encompasses the Lower Ninth Ward. However, here we can only sketch the historical processes by which the Ninth Ward became not only a productive industrial zone and a territory of residential opportunity for blacks in legally segregated New Orleans, but also home to some of the city's most abject poverty and violent, intractable crime.

Processes of delineating political units

To refer to the "Lower Ninth Ward" is both to name a political unit—one that existed from the nineteenth century but is actually defunct—and to name a neighborhood community that is dispersed but very much alive in spirit. Confusion stems from this conflation; our subject is the neighborhood whose present-day character and extraordinary will to survive can only be understood through its historical relationship to the Ninth Ward, the larger political unit of which it is a part. New Orleans' system of political wards was established when the city was incorporated in 1805, but it has little current relevance beyond its history as a base diagram upon which voting precincts were delineated. The political unit of the Ninth Ward was established in 1852 to encompass the city's mostly unsettled eastern reaches. Today, New Orleans has a mayor-council form of municipal government, and precincts in the Ninth Ward fall under the jurisdictions of three of the city's five council members, who are elected by district (two additional council members are elected at large). The Lower Ninth Ward lies in District E, a geographically unwieldy and heterogeneous district, which is so large, as well as so economically and socially diverse, that anyone representing it in the City Council faces major challenges. Most of District E is identified with what locals refer to as New Orleans East; it includes a regional business park, a NASA space center, and a national wildlife refuge, as well as the city's most elite predominantly African-American suburb, the heart of New Orleans' politically active and vibrant Vietnamese community, and miles of suburban sprawl along Interstate 10. The desperate needs of the Lower Ninth Ward pre-Katrina found significant competition for attention within District E and little remediation. The 2000 Census reported that the average income earned in the Lower Ninth Ward was $27,499 (the U.S. average was $56,644) and that 36.4 percent of its population was living in poverty (almost three times the U.S. rate of 12.4 percent), compared with a rate of 27.9 percent in New Orleans (co-terminus with Orleans Parish).

All of the residential areas within District E suffered terribly in the flooding that Katrina spawned, and many remain largely emptied of former residents as of this writing three years later. Among them, however, only the Lower Ninth Ward was almost completely annihilated. The current council representative for District E, Cynthia Willard-Lewis, faces what would seem to be insurmountable rebuilding tasks, but remarkably community organizations have mobilized to exert political pressure at the local, state, and national levels. City-Works, a nonprofit organization that advocates for best practices in rebuilding New Orleans, has identified seven such groups that are currently active in the Lower Ninth Ward. Make It Right is needed here.

Processes of establishing neighborhood identities

Common practice in New Orleans references seventy-three neighborhoods within the parish or city limits, and these neighborhood units have played a key role in galvanizing the rebuilding of the city. It is important to our historic trajectory to reiterate that when we use the term "Lower Ninth Ward" today, we refer to a neighborhood rather than to the political unit as it was constituted in the nineteenth century and as it was understood for a large part of the twentieth century. What we might define as the "historic" political Lower Ninth Ward includes two neighborhoods that are distinct from one another, especially post-Katrina: the older neighborhood of Holy Cross that took shape in the later nineteenth century and our subject, the younger neighborhood of the Lower Ninth Ward that took shape after the mid-twentieth century.

Until roughly 1950, the only sections of the Ninth Ward with importance on the city's political and social horizons were the neighborhoods of Bywater, St. Claude, and Holy Cross. They grew downriver from the Vieux Carré (French Quarter) and back from the river's bank in a band approximately two and one-half miles long and three-quarters of a mile deep. Upriver Bywater and St. Claude belonged to what was called the Upper Ninth Ward; downriver Holy Cross belonged to the Lower Ninth Ward. In 1918, the geographic distinction between the Upper and Lower Ninth wards became truly relevant and topographically explicit, when the impressively ambitious engineering project to create a deepwater passage from Lake Pontchartrain to the Mississippi River was begun. The Inner Harbor Navigational Canal, or Industrial Canal, which opened to traffic in 1923, severed the formerly contiguous Ninth Ward from north to south along the length of its 5.3-mile route with enormous urban consequences. The Ninth Ward territory lying east of the Industrial Canal, which included the Lower Ninth Ward, seemed in many ways extraneous to the core of the city itself—distant and with access limited to bridges at discrete points; it became the city's somewhat foreign "other."

After the opening of the Industrial Canal, the image of the Lower Ninth Ward split into two urban zones defined by St. Claude Avenue, which, with its bridge, became both an east/west link and a north/south boundary. Below St. Claude lay the more thickly populated Holy Cross, with its picturesque patchwork of late-nineteenth- and early-twentieth-century architecture. Above St. Claude, the Lower Ninth Ward was more thinly settled and remained largely agricultural until industrial development further north in the Ninth Ward stimulated the sale of residential property there. Over time, the Holy Cross neighborhood seemed to belong to the city's increasingly treasured and marketed past, while the rest of the Lower Ninth Ward fell hostage to the economic, political, and social change that broadly remade New Orleans as the Jim Crow "separate-but-equal" era drew to a close. Indeed, it is telling that the Lower Ninth Ward retained a political

From Egania Street to Jourdan Road.
Aerial view of a section of the
Lower Ninth Ward, looking east, ca. 1949

Source: Images of the Month,
May 2006, New Orleans Public Library

title as its neighborhood appellation since it came to play an important role in the post-segregation culture of New Orleans. The only other neighborhood in the city that maintains its political ward identity in its name is the older Seventh Ward in the Mid-City area, home to prominent, earlier-twentieth-century Civil Rights activists. In the name "Lower Ninth Ward" are represented struggles for parity, solutions for which we must still search.

Processes of engineering topography

Gaining in population after the mid-twentieth century, the Lower Ninth Ward became a thoroughly working-class neighborhood. Residents found jobs in nearby industrial zones in the Ninth Ward, which were associated with the network of water and rail transportation that permeated the area. Relatively cheap land made possible the purchase of home lots, which contributed to the emergence of a cohesive social fabric there. But the land came cheap for a number of reasons that predicted the neighborhood would not produce a substantial yield on investment. The Industrial Canal effectively severed this section from the heart of the city, and, at the same time, promoted its image as an industrial zone with the accompanying nuisances of loud noise, noxious smell, and

congested traffic. In addition, the area was vulnerable to flooding because of the dip
in elevation between the above-sea-level heights of the natural Mississippi River's
levee to the south and Gentilly Ridge to the north. Contiguous with the cypress "back
swamp" in more central areas of New Orleans, the soggy Lower Ninth Ward became
available for dense settlement only after drainage canals were installed between
1910 and 1920 along Jourdan Road, Tupelo Street, and Florida Avenue in preparation
for the construction of the Industrial Canal. Yet, this system could not free the area
of its proclivity to flood, and the consequently devalued land found a market among
purchasers or renters of lesser economic means. Indeed, significant flooding in the
wake of Hurricane Betsy in 1965 proved the fallibility of dependence on pumping stations
and open and underground drainage canals to keep the area dry.

Processes of legislating racial geography

Even if citizens perceived the Lower Ninth Ward to be mostly secured by the city's
drainage system and were willing to invest in real estate there, the area was further
devalued by the process of increasing racial segregation that created a residentially
divided city over the course of the twentieth century. Census data from 2000, which
Richard Campanella mapped in his masterful study *Geographies of New Orleans:
Urban Fabrics before the Storm* (2006), showed western New Orleans as dominantly
white and eastern New Orleans as dominantly black. Pre-Katrina, the Ninth Ward
was the blackest in the city. Scholars have described racial residential dispersion in
colonial and antebellum New Orleans (and other cities in the U.S. South) as a "backyard" pattern, according to which slaves lived in close proximity to their owners
throughout every section of the city. Beginning with the post-Civil War Reconstruction
period, when free blacks increased in number in the city, it became more common
for blacks to cluster residentially. The so-called Jim Crow laws, which required "separate
but equal" accommodation of the races and which held sway from the 1890s until Civil
Rights legislation gathered unstoppable force in the 1960s, led to even more dramatically distinguished racial residency patterns in New Orleans. Their effect was to
consolidate black residency, not only through conventions of historic occupancy but
also through new property covenants. Under the logic of what we might term "Jim
Crow urbanism," the sparsely settled and less highly valued land in the Ninth Ward,
which was prone to flooding, as well as relatively remote and further distanced from the
historic city by the Industrial Canal, provided developable terrain for African-American
settlement. Decisions made by the municipal government in the 1940s to create two
residential sections for blacks in the Ninth Ward propelled the expansion of its non-
white image. Both these prominent black residential developments were brought to

completion under the progressive mayoralty of deLesseps S. "Chep" Morrison (1946–61), and they actually demonstrated substantial measures of "equal" in relation to "separate." They were built in concert with and tangential to developments for whites, which accommodated residents of the same socioeconomic class: low-income, in the case of the Desire and Florida housing projects, and middle-income, in the case of the Pontchartrain Park and Gentilly Woods subdivisions. However, the white developments emptied during the Civil Rights era, to be filled with black tenants and homeowners. The Desire Development, a public housing complex that opened in 1957, was the last such complex to be built in New Orleans. It lay just a few blocks north of the earlier Florida Development for whites, which was intended for war workers but was not occupied until 1946. Both Desire and Florida were sited on the western side of the Industrial Canal and across it from the Lower Ninth Ward, to which a drawbridge on Florida Avenue gave access. Pontchartrain Park, which the Morrison administration began to plan as early as 1947, marketed single-family homes to African-American buyers in a privately developed 366-acre subdivision on the western side of the Industrial Canal at the Lakefront. Its white counterpart was Gentilly Woods, separated from it by a drainage canal. Built in the 1950s by the same construction company, Pontchartrain Park and Gentilly Woods offered identical houses. Pontchartrain Park, however, was unique in the Jim Crow South for its municipally funded eighteen-hole golf course and other recreational amenities, which formed the neighborhood's centerpiece, but which also staved off threats by blacks to sue the city for access to white-only municipal courses.

With the 1954 Brown vs. the Board of Education decision by the U.S. Supreme Court and the passage of the 1964 Civil Rights and 1965 Voting Rights Acts by the U.S. Congress, New Orleans was forced to integrate public schools and housing developments, as well as parks and other public facilities. "White flight" to private schools and to new residential enclaves in Jefferson and St. Bernard parishes ensued; Florida and other public housing projects became majority and then totally black, and in Gentilly Woods homeownership shifted predominantly to blacks. The Lower Ninth Ward also became racially homogeneous.

Processes of renewal, then and now

If Chep Morrison's progressive, yet segregationist, housing policies set the stage for the intensified racial residential separation that characterized New Orleans' later twentieth-century development, his agenda to modernize the central business district also led to the compaction of poverty and racial homogeneity in sections of the city. Morrison's urban renewal programs, which leveled a large swath of the central city for a new union train station and an eleven-acre civic center, forced residents—many of whom were black and poor—from what were considered "substandard" dwellings. Sparsely settled and newly expanding sections of the Ninth Ward, namely the area near the Florida-Desire developments and the Lower Ninth Ward, offered relatively cheap alternatives to the older neighborhoods of the Tremé and the Seventh Ward, which were also identified as predominantly African American. Critically, too, for the history of the Lower Ninth Ward, it became a destination neighborhood of upward mobility, when residents of the Florida-Desire developments found themselves able to settle outside subsidized housing. Then, in the late 1990s, the U.S. Secretary of Housing and Urban Development (HUD) found the New Orleans Housing Authority (HANO) in default of its responsibilities and took control of the oversight for the future of public housing in the city, creating a long-term strategy for the renovation and extensive redevelopment of New Orleans' housing projects. Demolitions ensued, and numbers of residents who were displaced from Desire and Florida swelled the population of the Lower Ninth Ward, as did residents from housing developments such as St. Thomas further away.

The social effects of population shifts that created an increasingly racially divided New Orleans during the second half of the twentieth century were problematic in that they produced overwhelmingly low-income neighborhoods, which were plagued with crime and drug use. Nevertheless, a strong spirit of kinship also came to character-ize particularly the communities of the Ninth Ward, a spirit which was expressed in the organization of self-help "social and pleasure" clubs—an African-American tradition in New Orleans. For anyone interested in the supportive social networks that have developed in the Ninth Ward over the past fifty years, a "must read" is *Coming Out the Door for the Ninth Ward* (2006), which is a production of the Neighborhood Story Project that documents the lives and memories of members of the Nine Times Social and Pleasure Club, who participated to "let the world know the blessing that came from Desire, the third biggest housing project in the United States." It is this strength of connectedness and communal support that has fueled the remarkable resiliency of the Lower Ninth Ward residents who have mobilized to return to their decimated neighborhood.

In the predominantly black Ninth Ward of the later twentieth century, then, Pontchartrain Park and the Lower Ninth Ward represented compelling poles of urban development and experience, with remarkable convergences and divergences. Residents of both neighborhoods, the one solidly middle class and the other at risk, were almost entirely African-American; the 2000 Census recorded the percentage of blacks in Pontchartrain Park at 96.7 percent, and in the Lower Ninth Ward at 98.3 percent. Pontchartrain Park was a neighborhood of homeowners—in 2000, 92.1 percent—who held relatively stable jobs as professionals, educators, and civil servants.

In contrast, Lower Ninth Ward residents were victims of the post-industrial drawdown of New Orleans' economy and endured the significant loss of jobs, which accompanied the containerization of shipping facilities, challenges to the regional primacy of the Port of New Orleans, and the flight of oil companies and manufacturers from the city. Still, as the Lower Ninth Ward neighborhood slipped further into poverty, residents managed to retain homeownership at a significantly high level, passing down property titles from generation to generation. In the 2000 Census, 59 percent of reporting households were owner occupied, well above the 46.5 percent reported overall for Orleans Parish. Both areas are topographically challenged, low lying and flood prone. However, despite the six to eight feet of water that collected in Pontchartrain Park after the storm surge of wind-swept water and the failure of levees, homeowners there at least retained skeleton properties to rebuild, while homeowners in the Lower Ninth Ward lost everything to the power of rising flood water. Long before Katrina, citizens of both these neighborhoods became activists in the fight for Civil Rights, and post-Katrina, they became politically astute advocates for resurgence. However, the disparity in income and education is defining: in 2000, 28.8 percent of Pontchartrain Park reported attaining a bachelor's or higher degree compared with 6 percent in the Lower Ninth Ward. What can we learn from this comparison as we work to rebuild New Orleans and the Lower Ninth Ward?

First, low-lying topographies must be responsibly addressed to create safe urban habitats. This is not simply a matter of identifying historic flood stages and legislating levels at which to build new dwellings, and to which to raise existing dwellings. Instead, the expertise of civil engineers and landscape designers is required to put principles of landscape urbanism to work, making of the urban terrain an active agent in the collection, retention, circulation, and productive dispensation of the excess water that threatens New Orleans even in weather conditions that are not considered potentially catastrophic. Currently, two model projects that employ the expertise of landscape architects to address these goals include Global Green's work in the Holy Cross neighborhood and Longue Vue House and Gardens' work in Pontchartrain Park.

Second, preserving the sensibility of small-town cohesion that characterized New Orleans' neighborhoods pre-Katrina is critical to ensuring not only their short-term determination to rebuild but also their long-term prospect of social empowerment. In Pontchartrain Park and the Lower Ninth Ward, homeownership was a primary factor in the creation of attachment to place. Here, Make It Right's endeavor to design houses, which are vetted through a community-managed application process, is absolutely fundamental in re-establishing the social core and economic viability of the Lower Ninth Ward.

Third, the transportation infrastructure projects that are envisioned for the "new" New Orleans must be designed to weave these areas of the city into a network of

Leona Tate, Gail Etienne, and Ruby Bridges, three of the four
women who as young girls in 1960 desegregated the New
Orleans Public School system. They are standing in 1981 at the
entrance to McDonogh #19, where Leona and Gail, along
with Tessie Prevost, were the first black students to attend the
previously all-white school. Renamed Louis Armstrong Elementary School, the building still stands in the Lower Ninth
Ward on St. Claude between Gordon and Tupelo streets, but it
has not reopened post-Katrina.

Source: New Orleans Public Library, Louisiana Division Photograph Collection,
Keith Weldon Medley Collection

connectivity. Bounded by natural and man-made features (lakefront, canals, rail lines,
and highways) and sequestered through industrial zoning, they developed as enclaves
apart, suffering even pre-Katrina from a lack of what we might term "municipal visibility."
Inclusive transportation planning that would provide varied types of public transportation—bus and light rail, for example—could link Pontchartrain Park and the Lower
Ninth Ward more vitally to the ebb and flow of city life. Mixed-use zoning policies that
would balance existing nearby industrial sectors with new commercial and civic districts
could also strengthen their unique neighborhood identities.

Fourth, the return of urban amenities and social services to these neighborhoods is
key to their resuscitation: their parks must be revitalized; their schools, libraries, post
offices, and other community institutions must be reopened and rebuilt. Indeed, enabled
by funding from the Demonstration Cities and Metropolitan Development Act of 1966—
the so-called Model Cities program—the mayoral administrations of Victor Hugo Schiro
(1962–70) and Maurice Edwin "Moon" Landrieu (1970–78) made an exemplar of the
Lower Ninth Ward, opening a health clinic, the Martin Luther King Branch Library, and
a Head Start program there. Future mayoral administrations could celebrate the historic

notice paid to and the strides made in the Lower Ninth Ward by referencing the civic building efforts there post-Katrina to earlier regenerative efforts in what might well be considered the city's last hopeful involvement in the neighborhood's rehabilitation.

Fifth, and finally, the city should make the design and building of a memorial to those who lost their lives in the Lower Ninth Ward a priority. But another commemorative project and one that would celebrate the city's turn toward humane urbanism in the Lower Ninth Ward would be equally important—the designation of Louis D. Armstrong Elementary School on St. Claude Avenue as a historic landmark of national stature. In 1960, McDonogh #19, as it was then known, was one of the first two public schools in New Orleans to be desegregated when three African-American girls enrolled. Two thousand eight marked the 200-year anniversary of the end of the transatlantic slave trade, and it would be fitting to undertake immediately this commemorative project for the building, which still remains closed in a largely empty neighborhood, and for the Civil Rights activism that it symbolizes. Meanwhile, the Make It Right houses will rise as emblems of the hope and right of return. May they multiply and may there be children in the Lower Ninth Ward to fill the halls of Louis Armstrong School once again.

Kristin Feireiss

People and Stories of the Lower Ninth Ward

The Pink Project, initiated by Brad Pitt and GRAFT, started on December 3, 2007, with a unique event. The main idea of this large-scale public art project with 150 shapes of pink houses standing on the site was not about art, it was about people—the people of the totally destroyed Lower Ninth Ward. The goal of the globally recognized Pink Event wasn't only to win sponsors for rebuilding the houses but to get in contact with the former inhabitants of the Lower Ninth Ward. Scattered all over the United States after Hurricane Katrina, they could get to know the Make It Right initiative not only to re-establish their land, but to find a new home. On December 3, 2007, I spoke to some inhabitants of the Lower Ninth Ward.

Elder Larry and Denise Baham

The scene seems romantic. It could be a holiday shot, showing a couple at sunset. She is wearing a military outfit with a cap and golden earrings. He is dressed in jeans and a blue sweater. They stand beneath a mighty branch of an old tree with the Claiborne Bridge silhouetted by the sunset.

However, appearances can be deceiving. Dawn has broken when Denise and Elder Larry Baham arrive in New Orleans on December 4, 2007. In the morning they left Plaquemine, LA, where they have stayed since Hurricane Katrina. They were returning to New Orleans after hearing on the radio about Make It Right's program to rebuild homes in the Lower Ninth Ward.

Half an hour later, the married couple sit in their car heading to New Orleans. It is the first time after Katrina that there is hope of returning to the place where Larry Baham was born in 1958. He grew up in the house of his grandmother and moved back to the very same house in 1998 with his wife Denise.

Elder Larry Baham and his wife share the fate of many evacuees of the flood. In the chaos of escape, they lost track of each other and their family members. Denise and the children were separated from Larry for almost two months. The phone lines were destroyed, and it was impossible to reach anybody within the 504 area code. In the search for his family, Larry wanted to return to the Lower Ninth Ward, but the National Guard had blocked off the entire area without mentioning a reason.

After many months, when the phone lines finally started to work again, the joyous and liberating call arrived to reunite the family. In Plaquemine, Denise and Larry Baham tried to build up their life after Katrina, staying with relatives. Denise worked in a one dollar store, but Larry was unable to keep his job as a crane conductor after he had been diagnosed with cancer.

"If you came through this storm, there must be a reason," says Larry Baham today. His belief provided him with enough strength and power to comfort his community as a priest, to overcome his fears and all catastrophes. Furthermore, he is convinced that his cancer will be treated successfully and he will become healthy again.

When Larry and Denise Baham return to the Lower Ninth Ward on December 4, 2007, it takes a long time until they find their lot. There is no house or anything else left that could have helped them with their orientation. By a tree, one of the few that has survived the storm, they believe to recognize their lot. As Denise passionately squeezes the hand of her husband, he says quietly, "We want to go back home." And she answers determinedly, "We will."

Malik Rahim and Sharon Johnson

Gladiatorial and charismatic, with a tall and strong figure and smiling eyes and a face framed by dreadlocks, Malik Rahim is a fascinating mixture of Genghis Khan and Nelson Mandela. The sixty-year-old is an activist with heart and soul. Before he went to the Lower Ninth Ward to help after Hurricane Katrina, Malik Rahim had been a long-time housing and prison activist in Algiers, a borough of New Orleans.

Directly after Katrina hit New Orleans; he went immediately to the city government to ask if he could help. He never received an answer, but that did not prevent the big-hearted man from doing what he had done for thirty years: taking care of people who need help. His reason was as evident as unusual, "Somebody had to do it." Immediately, he went to the Lower Ninth Ward. People were still stranded, waiting to be rescued from their rooftops. More than 500 homeless were trapped on the North Claiborne Bridge. Supported by many other volunteers, Malik Rahim gathered food, drinking water, and clothes. Still no emergency aid had arrived from the city government. Why should he have done this? His answer is definite. "Through all what I had done before, I was prepared for this challenge."

One week after Katrina, Common Collective was founded by Malik Rahim, Sharon Johnson, Brandon Darby, and Scott Crow. Malik Rahim, as an experienced activist, knew that only if they are on site can they provide reasonable aid. The owner of one of the few houses left standing in the Lower Ninth Ward, who had gone to San Francisco, gave his house to Common Ground Relief in order for them to establish the organization and provide housing to volunteers. The wooden house had been built in 1947 on a concrete base. After Common Ground Relief, with the help of many volunteers, had cleaned it of debris and brought it back to usable shape, it became their headquarters. Neither the Louisiana National Guard nor an admonishment by the city government could change Malik Rahim's decision. In a short time, their grassroots organization received donations from more than 180,000 people totaling about 2.5 million dollars.

One of the first, most important, and unexpected tasks of Common Ground Relief was to keep the properties clean.

City, state, and federal governments had enacted the "Good Neighborhood Program," requiring the lot owners to keep their property clean. If property owners did not follow the guidelines—if lots were not cleaned, the grass not cut—the ownership fell to the city government. Malik Rahim knew, like the city government, that hardly anybody could follow the order. For one, the Lower Ninth Ward was blocked off for months. Additionally, residents were spread throughout the country after evacuation and they did not have the financial resources to return constantly to handle their yard work.

Common Ground Relief took care that nobody lost their lot. The first step of this aid program is preparing the ground work to stanch the catastrophe. The second step is to support the residents to return to the Lower Ninth Ward and build sustainable homes together with Make It Right. The human rights activist is convinced that the goal could only be accomplished with the help of a person like Brad Pitt, with his global reputation and profile. "His initiative brought attention. The attention we urgently needed."

When we ask Malik Rahim and his wife Sharon Johnson where they would like to be photographed, for both there is only one location: in front of the house where everything started. On a hand-painted sign it reads, "The Future Home of Anita Roddick Advocacy Center" and below, "Common Ground."

The future will soon be there.

Charles and Thirawer Duplessis

Her yellow bows are shining in the sun. Germanie Saras is dressed up since it is a special day today. Together with her grandparents, Charles and Thirawer Duplessis, she followed the invitation to the Pink installation that drew broad public attention to the Lower Ninth Ward and Make It Right's rebuilding effort. Germanie Saras came back to the place where she, at five months old, was evacuated from with her family. Today, on the day of our interview, the little girl is two years old. Together with her grandparents, we are sitting on plastic chairs on the lot where their house used to stand before the hurricane.

On Saturday, August 27, 2005, residents in the area were asked via radio and television to leave their homes. The Baptist pastor Charles Duplessis and his wife Thirawer reacted immediately. Their entire family and closest friends quickly packed their essential belongings. When the group of thirty-eight people, including eighteen children, in eleven cars left in the direction of Tuskegee, Alabama, the sun was still shining from the blue sky.

It was not the first evacuation of the Duplessises due to a tropical storm. They had already fled from Hurricane Ivan, September 2004, on the highway to the west. The lanes were packed and it took three exhausting days with insufficient provisions to get to Houston by car. To avoid traffic jams this time, they decided to head south to Tuskegee. The trip that usually takes five hours took sixteen. After Hurricane Ivan, the evacuees were able to return to their homes after three days; after Katrina, three years had to pass.

Hundreds of homeless were relocated to the University Conference Center, where they found temporary shelter. As the Duplessis family fled, one uncle chose not to join them. He was convinced the Superdome would be the better place of refuge to wait for evacuation. He never talked to anybody about the traumatic experience he had during his time at the Superdome. For

Thirawer Duplessis, it is very important to speak about those first hard days. When she is talking about her tragic experiences, she is still agitated as if it happened two weeks rather than two years ago. Furthermore, she has recorded the horrifying occurrences of that time in a six-page text with the title, "Hurricane Katrina 2005 – My Story."

Her story ends with a successful escape, but the affliction of the survivors of Katrina had not come to end. Together with her husband Charles, she wanted to return to their home in order to see what was left. When they arrived, the Lower Ninth Ward had been closed off. They were only allowed to enter the area with a bus, which they could not leave during the tour. The pastor remembers sadly, "They did not want people to get off the bus. There were no birds, no dogs, no noise, everything covered in gray mud … gray, gray, gray … It took my breath away." On the same day, Charles Duplessis and his wife returned secretly in the evening. They wanted to see the church. Only an expanse of ruins was left, but in the ruins of their totally destroyed house they found a piece of Thirawer's jewelry.

Although the government had called on the residents of the Lower Ninth Ward to settle in different places, there was no doubt for Charles and Thirawer Duplessis, "We will come back. We believe that God has called us back, that the church comes back and that the community will come back."

In summer 2008, the construction of their new home began. When moving day arrives, grand-daughter Germanie Saras will be dressed up, since it will be a very special day again.

Gertrud Leblanc

Gertrud Leblanc is sitting on the steps of her white trailer, its outlines contrasting against the blue sky, surrounded by blossoming primroses and artificial poinsettia. For forty-five years she has been living in the Lower Ninth Ward. Her stern and resolute gaze shows no doubt that nothing or nobody could expel her from here. Gertrud Leblanc is handicapped and depends on the help of others. She came back two months after Katrina to her lot, after her evacuation to Pensacola, Florida. She was one of the first to return, despite prohibitions and barriers. It is still painful for Gertrud Leblanc to recall her intense memories of those days. Her strong voice starts to tremble when she begins to recount, "My house was hanging in the trees," and she ends this sentence like many others during our interview, with a deep-drawn sigh, "Oh, honey." Even the small, used delivery truck that her grandson drove to bring cakes to her clients was totally destroyed. Thinking about it, she sighs again and adds, "I was the queen of baking wedding cakes … Oh, honey." She had started to make wedding cakes in her small house after retiring from working twenty-seven years at the post office. At the time, she had been a widow for decades after her husband's passing years before.

Due to her strong-willed demeanor, seventy-three-year-old Gertrud Leblanc was one of the first and few ones to return to the Lower Ninth Ward after Katrina. The Federal Emergency Management Agency (FEMA) provided her with a handicapped trailer equipped with a ramp. They placed it on her lot cleared of the debris of her former house. Without the support of the aid organization Common Ground Relief she would never have made it, and she adds, "With Make It Right many will be able to take the next step: rebuild their own house."

During our conversation her grandson passes by. Chris regularly looks after his grandmother. He is an outgoing young man who is used to people staring at his face, which is marked by scars and deep furrows caused by chemical burns. Hardly anybody knows the cause, and nobody would ask him. When the water rose and his grandmother left the house with the family, Chris stayed. His grandmother was the only one to understand his decision; Chris wanted to stay and help. He experienced how their home broke down and he saw people fighting to survive in the steadily rising waters. Chris rescued more than twenty people that were about to drown in the water and brought them to the bridge, where helping hands pulled the exhausted victims to safety. Shortly after, the courageous young man was airlifted by the military and taken to a hospital in Denver, Colorado.

Two weeks after Katrina hit, she did not know if Chris was alive. The phone lines were destroyed. Still, she never lost her trust in good. Not when she was unable to reach her grandson. Not when her son was a soldier fighting in Korea. She says her daily dialogue with God has given her the confidence.

It took weeks for him to recover. Later on it was revealed that the floodwaters were highly toxic. Today, like Chris, many people suffer from the lingering effects of this contamination. He does not know if the traces on his skin, reminding him everyday of the catastrophe, will ever heal. "It has not broken his courage to face life," says Gertrud Leblanc. Looking proudly to her grandson she adds, "He is like me. We are givers."

Parting, Gertrud calls, "Whenever you come back, I am right here … Oh, honey."

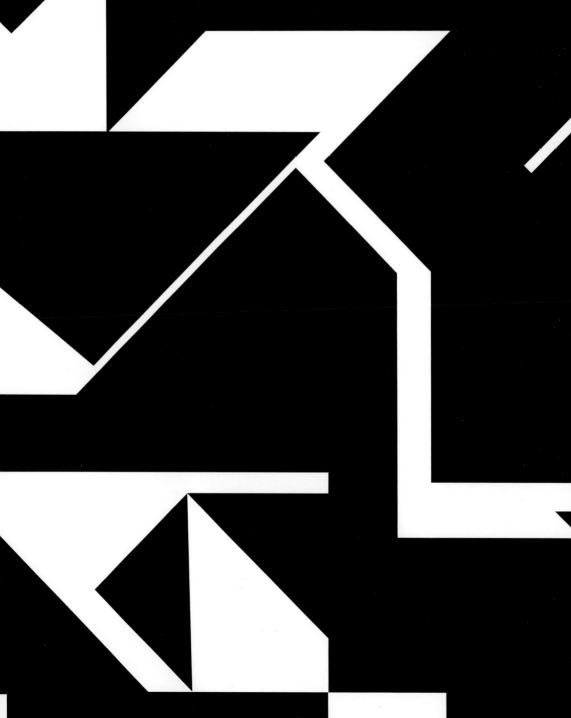

The Idea

Katrina
was the costliest
Atlantic hurricane
in history.

Total damages of Katrina: well over $100 billion

There were 53 different levee breaches in Greater New Orleans.

It is inaccurate
to call it an act of god.
Katrina was a man-made
disaster ...
and it could have
been avoided. Brad Pitt

There were
no birds,
no dogs,
no noise,
everything
covered
in gray mud.

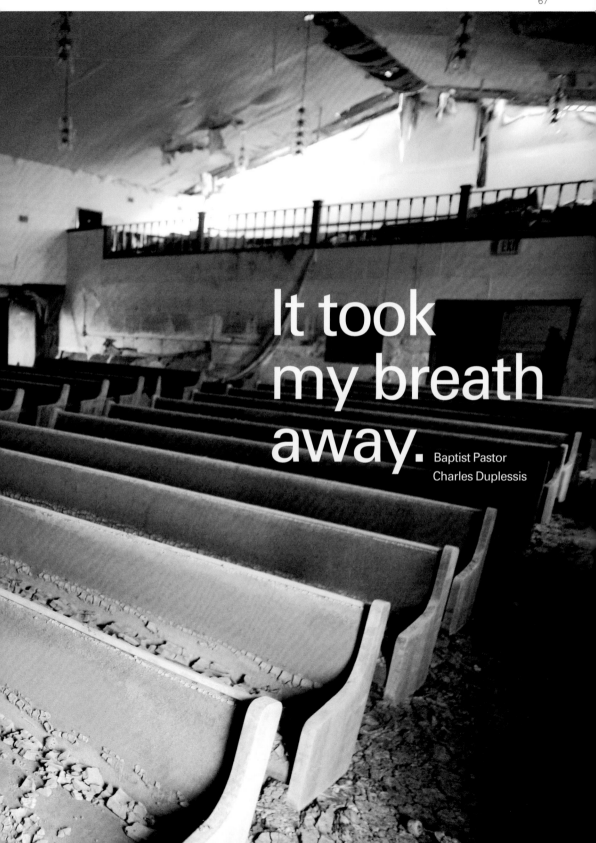

It took
my breath
away. Baptist Pastor
Charles Duplessis

Richard Campanella

Urban Transformation in the Lower Ninth Ward

The Lower Ninth Ward the world came to know after Hurricane Katrina in 2005 bore neither that name nor that form for the first two centuries of its historical development. A sequence of human interventions—some gradual, some swift—since the early 1700s transformed that natural deltaic landscape into the cityscape we know today. During the era of indigenous occupation, that landscape comprised part of a gradually sloping hydrological basin bordered on the south by the ten-foot-high natural levee of the Mississippi River, and on the west and north by the slight Esplanade and Gentilly topographic ridges, rising two to four feet above sea level. Any rainfall or high river water spilling into that basin flowed eastward out Bayou Bienvenue toward Lake Borgne and the Gulf of Mexico.

Springtime high water on the Mississippi overtopped the river's natural levees every few years. Those periodic floods did not constitute disasters; in fact, they created the entire Louisiana deltaic plain, over five to seven thousand years, by depositing layers of sand, silt, and clay at a pace faster than natural subsidence or wave action could reduce them. In this manner, the present-day Lower Ninth Ward and its deltaic environs arose from the Gulf of Mexico through periodic nourishment by sediment-laden river water. The highest lands, which lay closest to the Mississippi, declined by roughly one vertical inch for every hundred feet of distance away from the river. The lowest lands stood at or near the level of the sea, not below it. A semi-tropical climate, abundant rainfall, and rich alluvial soils allowed verdant vegetation to grow, but not all plant communities grew everywhere. Along the river arose dense bamboo-like reeds; immediately behind them grew jungle-like hardwood forests laced with vines. Farther back, at lower elevations, were palmetto-strewn cypress swamps, which petered out to grassy saline marshes where Bayou Bienvenue flowed into the sea.

"All this land is a country of reeds and brambles and very tall grass," wrote Pierre Le Moyne, sieur d'Iberville in March 1699 as the French explorer sailed up the Mississippi for the first time. About eighty miles upriver, a sharp meander challenged Iberville's expedition by positioning its ships against prevailing winds. Once past this obstacle, the Mississippi straightened out for about eight miles, then curved sharply again. Between those two meanders, on the eastern bank, lay the present-day Lower Ninth Ward, undistinguished and unnoticed by its early European visitors.

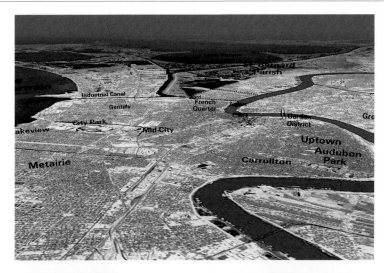

Satellite image of the New Orleans metropolitan area

Graphic by Richard Campanella, 2008

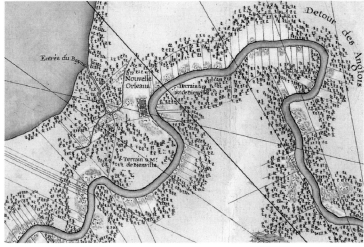

New Orleans area around 1732. The original city, now the French Quarter, appears at center left; the English Turn meander of the Mississippi River appears at upper right. The present-day Lower Ninth Ward occupies the riverside land in the upper center of this image.

Source: Library of Congress, Washington

Over the next two decades, Iberville, and later his younger brother Bienville, would establish a French colonial society throughout the region, culminating with the foundation of New Orleans in 1718. Bienville located his settlement (present-day French Quarter) on the natural levee at the cusp of that second meander, exploiting a portage route which allowed for faster and safer access to the Gulf Coast.

As New Orleans grew in the 1720s to a population of five hundred to one thousand people, fertile lands above and below the city were surveyed into French "long lot" plantations. Their elongated shape ensured that every plantation would garner a share of the most arable land, while gaining access to the Mississippi for transportation purposes. On a typical Louisiana plantation, the manor house occupied the crest of the natural levee near the river; behind it were dependencies, workshops, sheds, and slave cabins, followed by croplands and backswamp. Planters raised tobacco, indigo, rice, plus grains and vegetables, using the labor of enslaved Africans first brought to Louisiana in 1719. Maps from around 1730 indicate that such plantations had already been established around the present-day Lower Ninth Ward, their forests probably cleared by recently arrived slaves. Reported Governor Périer in 1728, "[slaves] are being employed to cut down the trees at the two ends of the town as far as Bayou St. John in order to clear this ground and to give air to the city and to the mill."

Colonial-era New Orleans struggled throughout the eighteenth century with sparse population, disease, disaster, and low prioritization under French and Spanish dominion. Then, a sequence of events around the turn of the nineteenth century reversed the city's fortunes. First, a slave insurgency in Ste. Domingue (present-day Haiti), which began in 1791 and eventually expelled the French regime, diminished Napoleon's interest in the seemingly unpromising Louisiana colony, and eventually motivated him to sell it to the United States in 1803. Concurrently, the cotton gin (1793) and the successful granulation of Louisiana sugar cane (1795) facilitated the rapid expansion of lucrative cotton and sugarcane production in the hinterland, both of which would profit New Orleans enormously. Finally, the introduction of the steamboat to Mississippi River commerce starting in 1812 allowed the new American city to exploit fully its strategic position in world shipping. Within two decades (1790s–1800s), New Orleans blossomed from an orphaned outpost of two descendent Old World powers, into a strategically sited port city of an ascendant, business-oriented, expanding New World nation. Prominent observers regularly predicted New Orleans would become the most affluent and important city in the hemisphere.

In 1805, the new American administrators incorporated New Orleans as a municipal entity, legally establishing its government, duties, privileges, and boundaries. Shortly thereafter, the city's lower limit became fixed roughly three miles downriver from the present-day French Quarter, an area within which lies the present-day Lower Ninth Ward. Designating those rural outskirts as being within New Orleans (Orleans Parish) limits would, in time, affect their use, population, and destiny. Features and phenomena that (1) people did not want to be located in the heart of the city, (2) could not be located above the city because it would pollute the water source, but (3) nevertheless had to be located within the city's limits, often ended up in the city's lowermost corner. This would become a familiar theme for the future Lower Ninth Ward: first on the list for urban nuisances, last in line for amenities.

Being the farthest-downriver corner of New Orleans also meant being the first that ships would encounter while heading upriver. For this and other reasons, the U.S. Government established New Orleans Barracks near the parish line in 1835. Now known as Jackson Barracks, home of the Louisiana National Guard, the installation served as the premier embarkation point for military operations throughout the region. It also represented the first designed development within the future Lower Ninth Ward. As New Orleans Barracks was under construction, its upriver neighbors included fifteen plantations or other land holdings principally dedicated to the cultivation and processing of sugar cane. Modern-day street names recall this now-extinct agrarian landscape: "Sister Street" once lined the convent and land holding of the Ursuline Nuns (where the Industrial Canal now lies), while nearby Deslonde, Reynes, Forstall, Caffin, and Delery streets all commemorate plantation owners from the 1830s. Flood Street was named not for the natural disaster but for another plantation owner, Dr. William Flood, who played an important role in the Battle of New Orleans in 1815.

With the rapid agricultural development of the Mississippi Valley and only one way to deliver those commodities to market effectively—by shipping down the Mississippi—New Orleans' economy boomed. So too did its population, which more than doubled between the Louisiana Purchase (1803) and 1810, and nearly doubled decennially until 1840, when New Orleans counted 102,193 residents and ranked as the third-largest city in the nation. It was also the South's largest city and its premier immigration destination, home to arguably the most ethnically, racially, linguistically, and culturally diverse population in the nation. Thousands of English-speaking, mostly Protestant Anglo-Americans had emigrated to the opportunity-rich port city after the Louisiana Purchase, where they encountered thousands of French-speaking Catholic Creoles who seemed to view nearly everything—government, law, religion, race, architecture—differently. People of African descent, both free and enslaved, as well as tens of thousands of immigrants from Ireland, Germany, France, Haiti, Cuba, Mexico, Italy, Greece, and nearly every other nation, made antebellum New Orleans like no other American city.

New Orleans' urban footprint expanded accordingly, as former "long lot" sugar plantations were subdivided as faubourgs (suburbs) and built up with new homes. Because the wealthier Anglo population tended to settle above the original city (present-day uptown), where the natural levee was wider and the river flowed free of inner-city refuse, New Orleans spread predominantly in an upriver direction, by a two-to-one ratio over downriver development. It expanded only slightly away from the river, where low-lying swamplands prevented most urban development.

The downriver expansion that did occur began in 1805 with the surveying of Faubourg Marigny, and continued into the 1810s–1840s with the subdivision of plantations comprising the present-day neighborhood of Bywater. The population that settled here tended to be markedly poorer than that of the upper city, mostly comprising Creoles, Irish and German immigrants, and representatives of smaller groups from southern

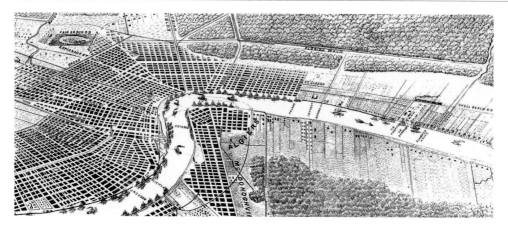

This circa-1885 bird's eye perspective shows
the semi-rural state of lower New Orleans in the
late nineteenth century. At this time, the area
formed a low-density village, only recently emerged
from an agrarian state.

Detail, "Perspective of New Orleans and Environs," 1885,
courtesy Louisiana Collection of the University of New Orleans

Europe and Latin America. Officially, the area was designated as the Third Municipality.
To some, it was nicknamed "the Creole faubourgs"; to others, it was the "old Third,"
the "dirty Third," the "poor Third," and only occasionally, and ironically, the "glorious
Third." After 1852, the lower regions of New Orleans gained a new nomenclature:
wards.

Wards as a political-geographical unit date to the 1805 chartering of the city.
Serving as voting districts, census units, and other municipal purposes, wards were
delineated and redrawn four times over the next forty-seven years. After the city's
unsuccessful sixteen-year experiment with semi-autonomous municipalities, the
reunified city government (1852) redrew ward lines for a fifth time. Because Felicity
Street had, for many years, marked New Orleans' upper boundary, the new ward
enumeration began at Felicity (First Ward) and continued consecutively downriver. To
equalize populations within wards, the high-density French Quarter was sliced into
the narrowest wards (Fourth, Fifth, and Sixth), while the lower-density "Creole faubourgs" allowed for broader units. The lowermost outskirts remained so rural that a
single mega-ward—the Ninth—enveloped the entire area. Hence the birth of the
Ninth Ward. City planners then "swung around" above Felicity Street and demarcated
upriver lands, and later Algiers on the West Bank, as wards ten through seventeen.
The modern-day map of New Orleans wards, unchanged since the 1880s, thus reflects
the city's piecemeal growth since 1852.

Urbanization first arrived to the present-day Lower Ninth Ward around 1840. While the Charles Zimpel map of 1834 indicates a solid line of plantations from the Ursulines' parcel to the U.S. Barracks, the Maurice Harrison map of 1845 shows roughly one-third of that area subdivided into vacant streets and blocks. As each planter decided he could make more money subdividing his plantation than cultivating it, more and more croplands became platted with urban grids. Names for old streets running parallel to the river (Chartres, Royal, Dauphine, etc.) were extended from the original city downriver to the U.S. Barracks, while new river-perpendicular streets often adopted the names of their anteceding plantations. Thus, the geometry of the old French long-lot surveying system drove the urban form of the emerging neighborhood.

Historical population figures for what is now the Lower Ninth Ward are difficult to ascertain because nineteenth-century censuses aggregated populations by wards, not at sub-ward levels. The vast majority of Ninth Ward residents clustered not in the present-day Lower Ninth Ward but at the upriver end of the ward, in what is now called Bywater by the river. We do know that enough residents lived in the present-day Lower Ninth to warrant the establishment of St. Maurice Catholic Church in 1857. Fourteen years later, the Brothers of the Holy Cross established an orphanage which would later become the Holy Cross Catholic High School campus. Horse-drawn street-car service arrived to the area in 1872, which brought more residents to the once-rural district. By the time the 1883 Robinson map was published, the area had been subdivided at least as far north as Urquhart Street, just one block beyond the aptly named Marais ("marsh") Street. Roughly two-thirds of those blocks (present-day Holy Cross section of the Lower Ninth Ward) were further subdivided into parcels, and of those, approximately half had homes. The neighborhood in the late nineteenth century formed a low-density dispersion of cottages and frame houses, usually with fenced gardens, arranged in a village-like setting amid open fields and an occasional West Indian-style plantation home left over from the antebellum era. Also there were railroads, a cotton press, a military hospital, warehouses, and a livestock landing and slaughterhouse— an enormous malodorous operation enabled by a controversial 1873 U.S. Supreme Court decision approving the consolidation of the city's stockyards and slaughtering facilities. It comes as no surprise that this urban nuisance got located downriver from the city proper but within city limits—that is, in the lowermost corner of the Ninth Ward. With it came railroads, soap makers, rendering plants, and related operations. They provided working-class jobs, but also drove down property values. So too did the American Sugar Refining Company, which built a fourteen-story industrial sugar-refining plant (complete with its own docking and railroad facilities) across the parish line in 1909–12. The year 1912 also saw the realignment and augmentation of the Mississippi River levee in the

The Inner Harbor Navigation Canal ("Industrial Canal," excavated 1918–1923) severed the Ninth Ward into "upper" and "lower" portions, and was later enjoined by the Intracoastal Waterway (visible at center right) and Mississippi River-Gulf Outlet Canal.

Sources: Circa-1950s photo courtesy Army Corps of Engineers, New Orleans District

area, improving flood protection for the increasing number of working-class families moving into the neighborhood.

The single most influential transformation of the Ninth Ward's environment occurred in the late 1910s. Competition among ports motivated city leaders in that era to advocate streamlining navigation routes and creating new dock space off the crowded riverfront. The vision soon evolved into the "Inner Harbor Navigation Canal." Officials in 1918 identified the corridor for the so-called Industrial Canal: a five-mile-long, six-hundred-foot-wide, mostly undeveloped right-of-way splitting the Ninth Ward in two. From the city's perspective, the proposed route made the most sense: it lay within city limits, crossed a relatively narrow land strip between river and lake, exploited a convenient position for shipping and docking activity, and was either city-owned or readily acquirable. From the Ninth Ward's perspective, the canal represented job opportunities—but also a major disruption, a barrier, and a potential threat that would have been resisted fiercely by citizens had it been proposed for the heart of the city.

Excavation took a little over a year; construction of the intricate lock system, to handle the differing water levels of the river and lake, took another three years. When the Industrial Canal opened in 1923, it succeeded in enhancing port activity in the area. It also severed the lowermost portion of the city from the urban core, inspiring the term Lower Ninth Ward. From now on, residents of this isolated neighborhood (who mostly relied on a single streetcar line for transportation into the city center) would have to

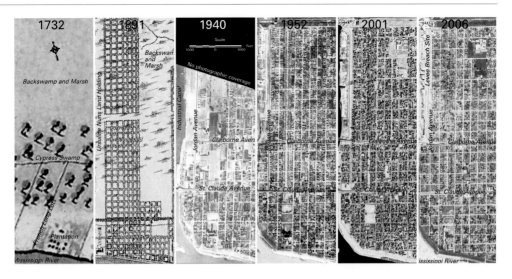

Three centuries of
urban transformation in
the Lower Ninth Ward

Map by Richard Campanella

dodge drawbridges and railroad crossings to interact with the rest of their city. More
ominously, the Industrial Canal introduced gulf water into city limits, held back only
by flimsy floodwalls and inadequate levees. Worse yet, the installation of the municipal
drainage system around the turn of the twentieth century—and a few decades later
to the Lower Ninth Ward—drained the backswamp and allowed its finely textured
sediment particles to settle and subside. Soon, former swamp and marshlands throughout the city began to subside below sea level, even as their populations increased.
Artificial levees were built along the periphery to keep water out. The topography of
New Orleans began to assume the shape of a bowl—or rather, a series of bowls, one
of which comprised the Lower Ninth Ward.

The human geography of the Lower Ninth Ward in the early twentieth century
iterated the area's topography. The 5,500 New Orleanians who resided there in 1910
(1.6 percent of the city's total population) shared certain traits: most ranked no higher
economically than the working- or lower-middle class, and nearly all were born and
raised locally. Those settling on higher ground closer to the river, in the so-called front
of town, were predominantly white, usually of Irish, German, Sicilian, French, Creole,
or Latino stock, who in previous generations lived in the "Poor Third" or in the French
Quarter. Those who settled in the "back of town" (north of St. Claude Avenue and later
Claiborne Avenue, an area that remained largely undeveloped into the 1920s–1930s)
were mostly African-American and either poor or working-class. Some were black

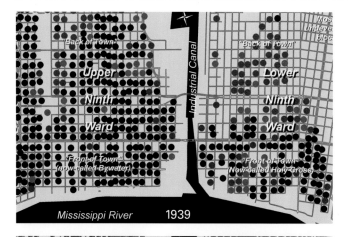

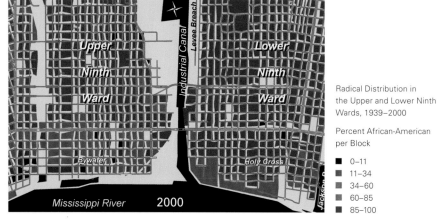

Radical Distribution in
the Upper and Lower Ninth
Wards, 1939–2000

Percent African-American
per Block

■ 0–11
■ 11–34
■ 34–60
■ 60–85
■ 85–100

This pair of maps shows the changing racial
geography of the Upper and Lower Ninth wards from
1939 to 2000. Most whites moved into neighboring
St. Bernard Parish during the 1960s–1970s.

Map by Richard Campanella based on 1941 WPA Land Use Survey
and 2000 Census

Creoles (Franco-African Americans) with generations of heritage in the city; others had
emigrated from rural areas after emancipation, or later, following the mechanization of
Southern agriculture. Immediately behind the back-of-town blocks lay the city's sewage
treatment plant—yet another municipal disamenity which had to be located downriver
from the city proper (and its water source), but had to remain within city limits. Behind
the treatment plant, another navigation canal—the Intracoastal Waterway—was
excavated in the 1930s and 1940s to facilitate east-to-west barge traffic. By World War II,
the 11,556 residents of the Lower Ninth Ward, long severed from the other 97.7 percent
of the city's population by the Industrial Canal, were now surrounded on three sides
by water bodies, even as their underlying soils subsided.

The 1960s brought more tumultuous transformations. Resistance to school integration—which was fierce within the working-class white Ninth Ward population—and other factors led to the wholesale departure of whites downriver into the neighboring suburban parish of St. Bernard. Once racially mixed with a predominantly white front-of-town and black back-of-town, the Lower Ninth Ward became increasingly African-American. At the same time, excavation commenced on a third major navigation canal: the Mississippi River-Gulf Outlet (MR-GO) Canal, designed to connect the earlier man-made waterways directly with open gulf water. Its excavation entailed the widening of the Intracoastal Waterway and the turning basin at the Industrial Canal junction. Like the earlier waterways, the MR-GO promised jobs and economic dividends; in actuality, it delivered little more than environmental degradation and urban hazard. This was demonstrated when Hurricane Betsy struck in September 1965, its surge inundating the four major hydrological sub-basins straddling each side of the man-made navigation canals. Hardest hit of all was the Lower Ninth Ward. A series of Industrial Canal levee breaches along the Southern Railroad tracks, coupled with overtopping, deluged the poor, mostly black rear section of the neighborhood by three to five feet along St. Claude Avenue, and to nine feet along the back levee. Only the streets closest to the Mississippi River—present-day Holy Cross—evaded Betsy's deluge. Severe flooding damaged or destroyed thousands of homes and hundreds of businesses throughout the Lower Ninth Ward.

The next thirty-five years saw the Lower Ninth Ward's population decline from its 1960 peak of over 33,000 (5 percent of the city's population) to under 19,500 (4 percent) by century's end. Once racially mixed, the neighborhood in 2000 was over 95 percent black. By no means was the Lower Ninth Ward the poorest or lowest-lying neighborhood of the city. It actually boasted a higher home-ownership rate than the city as a whole, and its lowest-lying areas (four feet below sea level) lay three to four feet above the lowest zones of Lakeview and Gentilly, and eight feet higher than the lowest spots in New Orleans East. Its riverside section (Holy Cross National Historic Register District) stood six to eight feet above sea level, and boasted sturdy, raised, historically significant homes mostly dating to the 1870s–1920s. Its rear section, particularly the blocks lakeside of Claiborne Avenue, possessed a humbler housing stock dating mostly from the 1920s–1970s, many of which were built on concrete slabs at grade level. Isolated from public view, dismissed by the historical and architectural community, and plagued by the same social ills found throughout inner-city America, the rear sections of the Lower Ninth Ward seemed like a world unto itself—cherished by its residents, avoided by everyone else.

At 5:00 a.m., August 29, 2005, Hurricane Katrina's low pressure and residual Category-Five storm surge penetrated the MR-GO/Intracoastal Waterway "funnel," overtopped meager levees, and introduced gulf water immediately behind the Lower Ninth Ward and St. Bernard Parish. The water stage rose dangerously in the Industrial Canal to fourteen feet above normal levels. Around 7:45 a.m., a massive section of floodwall collapsed and sent a violent torrent of brackish water eastward into Lower Ninth Ward homes. Shortly thereafter, the surge overtopped the rear levee and inundated the neighborhood from the north. More water surged westward from St. Bernard Parish. Flood levels rose by ten feet in twenty minutes. Scores of people, who either could not or would not evacuate, perished in their own homes under harrowing circumstances. Others climbed to attics or rooftops, even as their houses bobbed and drifted. Bloated gulf waters would continue to pour into the Lower Ninth Ward and every other hydrological sub-basin on the East Bank of Orleans Parish for days after the passage of Hurricane Katrina. By week's end, water levels stabilized at three to four feet deep in the highest areas of the Lower Ninth Ward, and ten to twelve feet or deeper in the lowest sections. For all the social tensions that existed between the Lower Ninth Ward and St. Bernard Parish, the two areas suffered sadly similar fates.

The federal levee failures induced by Hurricane Katrina and a century of environmental deterioration altered utterly the destiny of the Lower Ninth Ward. The neighborhood ranked unquestionably as the hardest-hit of the entire metropolis, and, not surprisingly, was the last to see utilities, municipal services, and residents return. Two years after the storm, roughly one-quarter of the Holy Cross-area population and under 10 percent of the north-of-Claiborne section had returned, the two lowest return rates in the city.

The Katrina flood also brought great notoriety to the Lower Ninth Ward, rocketing it from local obscurity to worldwide infamy as the most beleaguered urban neighborhood in the world's wealthiest nation. With the infamy came sympathy and concern, which in turn brought legions of advocates, researchers, church groups, student volunteers, documentary filmmakers, politicians, and the just-plain-curious to the once-ignored neighborhood. With its odd and ominous name, the Lower Ninth Ward seemed to bear witness and impart wisdom on a wide range of complicated and polemical topics. Poverty. Race. Social justice. Environmental deterioration. Geographical risk. Global warming. Urban and cultural sustainability. Green architecture. Decent citizens nationwide fell into two schools of thought regarding the Lower Ninth Ward's future. Some viewed the entire region as equally at-risk and dependent on levees for flood protection, and interpreted the closing-down of heavily damaged, low-lying neighborhoods as an outrageous cultural affront that should be resisted on humanistic and economic grounds. They pointed to the Netherlands as a model for how to solve this problem. Others, who could not deny the scientific realities of soil subsidence, coastal erosion, and sea level rise, encouraged the densification of higher-elevation historical districts and the relinquishing of hazardous areas to nature. This school viewed massive Netherlands-style floodwalls as dangerously deleterious to coastal wetlands, which would further increase urban risk. To the outside world taking sides in the debate, the Lower Ninth Ward became a flashpoint, a symbol, a metaphor. To the inside world of its residents, however, the Lower Ninth Ward represented very different things. Family. Friends. Schools and churches. Heritage and legacy. Home.

The Make It Right Foundation's efforts stand at the nexus of these conflicting visions. No one vision is categorically false or improper; each one represents parallel truths and values, projected upon an unknowable future. This much is certain: whatever progress the Foundation makes will influence the future transformation of the Lower Ninth Ward.

Nina Killeen

A Chance to Come Home

On a hot summer afternoon in 2006 while driving down Veterans Boulevard, my cell phone rang—it was Brad Pitt and he wanted to know if I had a minute to talk. I swerved into the Whole Foods parking lot to avoid crashing into something and said "sure." He wanted to send some architect friends of his to the city and wanted to know if I would show them around—his request, "Make them fall in love with New Orleans." Wolfram Putz and Neiel Norheim from GRAFT arrived—and they left loving New Orleans. For the next few months we did research, they did designs, and then on December 2, 2006, the first meeting was held to determine if Brad Pitt and a team could build a community of homes that would be affordable and sustainable for victims of Katrina. Over the next few months, the team grew as the project grew. Meetings were held, a site was selected, the land acquisition problem solved, architects selected, designs were drawn. My job during this time was to navigate the team through the maze that is New Orleans. Introduce the team to the right civic and governmental leaders, help establish a relationship with the neighborhood associations, identify other partners that would contribute to the objective; basically help the team form Make It Right.

When I was nineteen years old, I left home and flew to Miami to interview with National Airlines for a position as a stewardess. I made the cut up to the vice president, who told me that he would love to hire me, but that there was something about "New Orleans girls." He didn't know what it was about that city, but no girl had ever stayed in Miami for more than two years. Well, I convinced him that this wouldn't happen with me, and so he hired me. After two years, I moved back home. If you move from anywhere in the USA to anywhere else in the USA, you can pretty much find the things you left behind. But if you are from New Orleans and you have to leave … well, where else can you find Jazz funerals, Mardi Gras Indians and Creole Gumbo, French beignets, Italian muffelattas, red beans and rice in almost every restaurant on Mondays? Can you name another city that has VooDoo Queens, Mardi Gras Queens, and, well, just plain queens? Where cemeteries are tourist attractions? New Orleans is a city where the people enjoy life and one celebration just follows another: Mardi Gras by the French Quarter Fest and the Spring Fiesta by the Jazz Fest and that by the Essence Fest and the Southern Decadence and the VooDoo Fest—only to be broken by Lent—still observed as the holiest of seasons by the city's majority Catholic population.

Nina Killeen's kitchen after the flood

New Orleans is not a planned, cookie-cutter city laid out in perpendicular grids. It is a city of neighborhoods—each distinctly different from the others—that have evolved over the last 290 years. It is not homogenized with all cultures mixing together and becoming alike. It is a harmonious collection of neighborhoods, defined by the people—each one unique—each one contributing to the magic that is New Orleans. Every neighborhood is made up of people with their own culture, traditions, customs, architecture, food, celebrations, music, and sometimes even language. The neighborhoods were named according to historic people or places like the Marigny or Holy Cross; some were named after their residents like the Irish Channel, and others for their geographic location like Uptown or Bywater. The Lower Ninth Ward received its name because in 1918 a governmental bureau began dredging a canal that when completed in 1923 connected the Mississippi River to Lake Pontchartrain and isolated a portion of the Ninth Ward from the rest of the city, making it down river from or "lower."

As far back as 1914 the government had total disregard for the property or the wishes of the residents of the Ninth Ward, as they expropriated land with homes and historical buildings—demolishing them to make way for progress, progress that still today is being debated. As the canal separated the Lower Ninth Ward from the rest of the city, it also provided the inhabitants with jobs in the shipping industry. They were hard working people. Primarily African Americans, and over 60 percent owned their own homes. They were proud people. There were no housing projects in the Lower Ninth Ward. These were homes that were more than likely to have been built by family, friends, and neighbors. The homes were modest, but you can bet that each one had a porch or a stoop where people would sit on hot afternoons and watch the children play and pass the time with their neighbors. They might not even have known their names—it might have been "the flower lady" or "the preacher." They probably listened to the music of their favorite son, Fats Domino. The people of the Lower Ninth Ward didn't have much, but they had all they needed to be happy. They had their homes, their families, the food, the music, their faith. They had the properties that had been handed down for generations, choosing not to leave the neighborhood. It was home—it's where your people were—it's where you felt you belonged. Roots ran deep in the Lower Ninth Ward … until Katrina and the floodwaters of the Industrial Canal literally washed everything away. Many died in the floodwaters, because they had refused to flee from their homes. Those that had evacuated or were rescued found themselves living in places like Texas and Utah, maybe even freezing in Minnesota. The government has been slow to provide assistance to those who want to return— and the assistance they are providing is inadequate to replace the homes that were destroyed, modest as they were. It is with help from foundations like Make It Right that the people are able to afford to once again build their homes in their neighborhood.

There are no guarantees that the levees won't break again in some future 100-year storm, no guarantees that the Lower Ninth Ward and the entire city of New Orleans won't flood again. But the probabilities are that it won't. Should the Lower Ninth Ward be rebuilt? Yes, the entire city of New Orleans should be rebuilt. Every neighborhood should be rebuilt. But in the devastated areas like Lakeview, Pontchartrain Park, Gentilly, and the Lower Ninth Ward, it will never be the same—still the people of those neighbor- hoods deserve a chance to come home.

Brad Pitt

To Rebuild or Not to Rebuild, That Was the Question

It was the one question on any good journalist's mind, yet each either failed or were afraid to ask—should New Orleans be rebuilt? It was the first question we had to answer for ourselves.

In the aftermath of the destruction there was a popular belief among many academics that New Orleans should be abandoned and possibly relocated elsewhere. I was surprised how many times I ran up against this, especially when it came time to raising money.

Of course New Orleans is going to flood again, and California will continue to suffer earthquakes, and Oklahoma, Kansas, and Missouri will again be ravaged by tornadoes. These proponents of abandonment weren't considering the families whose histories resided here and who built their lives here, nor were they evaluating the cultural loss to the United States. In actuality this argument was simply a response to the price tag of fixing it—fifty billion dollars in damages, eleven billion dollars to correct the levees, the need to re-establish the wetlands.

But what is the worth of a home to the family? If this was a result of bad govern-ance on the city, state, and federal levels, isn't it their responsibility to make it right? To further exacerbate the problem of inaction, this was not a debate being held in the public forum, but one which lingered and thrived in restaurants and back rooms, accom-plishing little and further leaving residents in limbo.

Meanwhile, the people were being told, "we want you to come home, we'll help you come home, we will rebuild," and in fact were being incentivized to do so through the Road Home program. Imagine this confusing message: we want you to come home but we can't give you enough to build what you had before and certainly not enough to build safely. What are you really trying to tell the people? Furthermore, aren't you setting people up for further catastrophe? It is here that we identify an unjust gap.

Congruent with the spirit of New Orleans, it became clear to us that people were coming home no matter what obstacles were thrown in their path. So the question was not should we rebuild, but how do we rebuild.

The Federal Emergency Management Agency (FEMA) and the administration were already in the hot seat, and rightfully so. There was so much concern over the misuse of allocated money that it actually clogged the process and impaired people from coming home. Most were attuned to the assumption that the system would be mishandled.

Negative press about failing or corrupted initiatives made everybody only more hesitant to try, and sent applicants through convoluted red tape and exhaustive checks which would go on for years, testing the resolve of even the most determined.

As a matter of justice MIR made it our mandate to help people close this unjust gap. Running independent of politics we consciously decided that the need to get people in quality homes as quickly as possible superseded any risk of being taken advantage of, and even outweighed the mistakes we might make along the way. This decision has made all the difference.

GRAFT

The Concept of Make It Right

*"So why do it? Why bring not just architects here but some of the world's best?"
I'll tell you why. These people suffered a horrific event, and truthfully great injustice
in the aftermath, and they're still suffering that injustice. So what are you going
to follow that injustice with? Crap houses with toxic materials and appliances that
run up their electricity bills and may lead to a foreclosure? I mean, really. This to
me is a social-justice issue. And to create something that's equitable and fair and
has respect and provides dignity for the family within is absolutely essential to
rebuilding here.*   Brad Pitt, *Metropolis Magazine,* 2008

Make it Right is a plan for action initiated by Brad Pitt's concern for the residents of New
Orleans, his vehement refusal to accept the status quo, and his heartfelt commitment
to enact positive change. It is a private-sector initiative for disaster relief in response
to the catastrophic conditions in New Orleans post-Katrina, where efforts to rebuild this
once vibrant area had sadly fallen short. The pressure point chosen as an epicenter
for change began in the Lower Ninth Ward, a rich cultural community long known for its
high proportion of resident ownership.

When Brad Pitt first introduced us to his idea for providing aid to people in need
in New Orleans, the place and topic of the discussion couldn't have been more contrasting. It was a beautiful Southern Californian day in summer 2006 and life seemed easy.
During this meeting Brad Pitt communicated his sincere concern for the plight of New
Orleanians and what he perceived as a moral obligation to help make this right. Having
observed his engagement in the Global Green competition, an initiative in the Holy
Cross district of New Orleans, GRAFT was aware of his interest in ameliorating the
intractable circumstances facing the residents of New Orleans. Building upon the
experience gleaned from this competition, Brad Pitt proposed pursuing a larger-scale
endeavor, one which could become an inspirational role model for raising awareness,
engaging interest, and engendering rebuilding in areas which had most been affected
by the Katrina catastrophe. The starting point of the discussion originated at the
scale of a safe, affordable, sustainable prototypical single-family home with the high
design ambition of integrating a new quality of life for the families and communities.

One of the first meetings in the Lower Ninth Ward.
From left to right: Neiel Norheim (GRAFT),
Wolfram Putz (GRAFT), Brad Pitt, Tom Darden (MIR)

Many individuals desire to make this world a better place, however most local crises
are linked to larger global systems and causes. This often leads to frustrations derived
from the dilemma of being limited to act in our front yards, when the real problem
requires resolution on a more holistic level. The more we learned about the very specific
problems created in the aftermath of Hurricane Katrina, the more we discovered how
deeply these specifics were linked to problems on a national level and subsequently how
these failures were in turn part of complex global systems.

Although the idea for Make It Right was sparked by a site-specific concern, the
potency of the idea resides in its vast potential as a problem-solving model which can be
utilized globally. In the words of Pablo Picasso, "An idea is a point of departure and
no more. As soon as you elaborate it, it becomes transformed by thought." Historically,
powerful ideas generate contagiousness, lending themselves to similar applications and
multiple iterations. In this, Make It Right is no different; the framework of the project
can be extracted, providing a problem-solving model and called upon in times of need.
Local conditions inform the specific solutions appropriate to any given region, as will be
elaborated upon in subsequent chapters. Once local content has been distilled from

the project, a template remains for a system which can be utilized for disaster relief in other parts of the world suffering similar devastation.

As an opportunity to give back and to positively affect the world around them, iconic activists redirect public interest to focus on world issues greater than themselves, issues they hold dear and that are in dire need of attention. Few, however, have taken on the challenge of creating a philanthropic entity. Championing the residents of New Orleans, Brad Pitt has channeled his visibility as an iconic persona and redirected it towards Make It Right, literally bringing it into the living room of millions of global viewers as a call to arms. Since its beginning he has led the charge as the founder and visionary with unmatched efforts in fundraising and detailed interests and contributions to all aspects of this project.

The team amassed for this endeavor needed to be potent enough to address and resolve local problems, as well as act on a national level with international resonance. The final assembled group of powerful thinkers and problem solvers were collectively part of a much larger, intricate network enabling them to access vast resources in their respective fields. This core team for Make It Right was formed by actor and philanthropist Brad Pitt; GRAFT, an international award-winning architecture firm; William McDonough + Partners, a renowned pioneer in sustainable design; Cherokee Gives Back Foundation, a charitable outreach program supporting social, environmental, and economic development initiatives as a subsidiary of Cherokee, a leading private equity firm investing capital and expertise in brownfield redevelopment; and Trevor Neilson, president of the Global Philanthropy Group. With generous feedback provided by the Lower Ninth Ward Stakeholders Coalition and local Nina Killeen, the team collectively established primary targets with the aim of rebuilding 150 homes in the Lower Ninth Ward. Creative, intelligently designed architectural solutions, environmental responsibility, community outreach programs, creative financing strategies, fundraising initiatives, and construction management strategies became the primary targets to right what so many felt was wrong, and through this began to Make It Right.

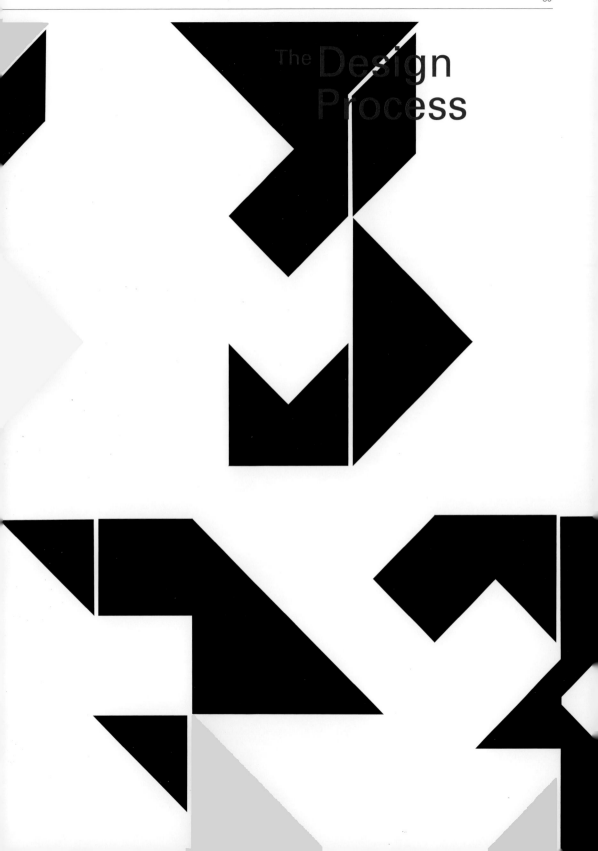

The Design
Process

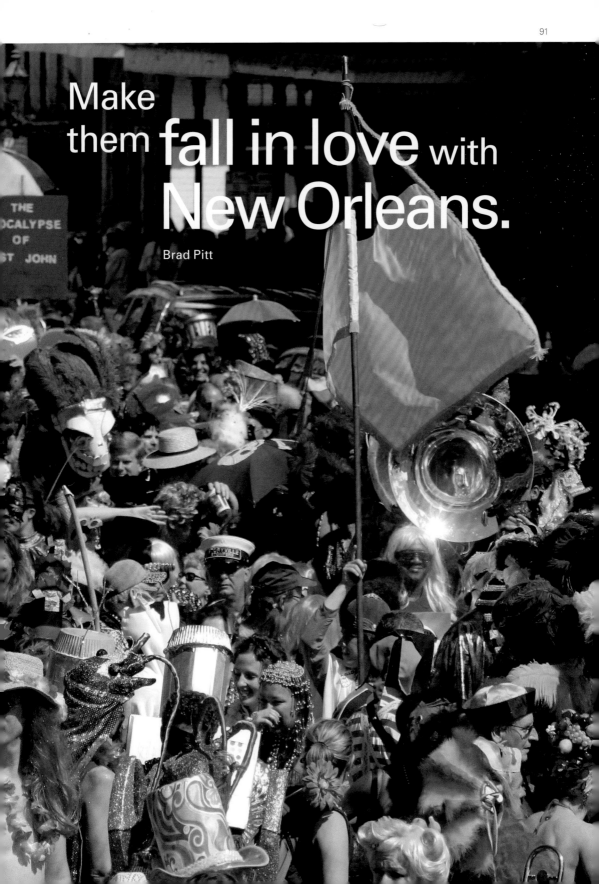

Make them fall in love with New Orleans.

Brad Pitt

Can you name another city that has Mardi Gras Queens, Voodoo Queens,

and, well,
just plain queens?

Nina Killeen

Carrie Bernhard

New Orleans Urban Structure and Housing Typology

New Orleans is unlike any other American city. Not only has it retained much of its nineteenth-century building stock, it has formed a domestic architecture that is unique to the city and its particular combination of climate, site, and history. Urban house types, such as townhouses, courtyard houses, and cottages, were imported as the building traditions of the various cultures that settled in the city. These were then adapted to local conditions of site and climate in addition to the cultural exigencies of the time. Eventually the Creole Townhouse, the Creole Cottage, and the Shotgun emerged as the ubiquitous house types of New Orleans. The simplicity of these houses, in form and organization, allowed for easy replication and the potential for multiple variations.

Today, the uniformity of these formal and organizational principles from one variation to the next maintains a legible and continuous order while the profusion of manifold variations generates the richness and complexity of New Orleans' urban landscape. The proliferation of these house types, in all their variations, is what comprises New Orleans' unique architectural identity. They stand as the datum against which variations of scale, vintage, and economies are juxtaposed. A contemporary skyscraper might stand next to a four-story nineteenth-century urban block building, a lone ranch house from the 1970s might reside among a block of Shotguns from the 1890s, or a three-block pocket of decaying buildings might flank a three-block pocket of affluence.

Despite these anomalies, or perhaps in addition to them, New Orleans has maintained a singular urban and architectural identity due to the abundance of its unique, historical housing stock. Following the events of Hurricane Katrina, however, many of these buildings suffered severe damage. While some can be saved and renovated, many are too devastated to survive, particularly in poorer neighborhoods throughout the city where high concentrations of deteriorating properties and vacant lots were serious issues even before the storm. As a consequence, the urban fabric is becoming increasingly perforated and, as large numbers of new housing begin to fill these voids, New Orleans' architectural identity is becoming increasingly diluted. It is critical now to examine and understand the city's historical domestic architecture not in order to build facsimiles, as is the tendency, but in order to achieve the efficacy of New Orleans house types. Doing so is to truly honor New Orleans' unique architectural identity and maintain its continuity in the rebuilding of the city.

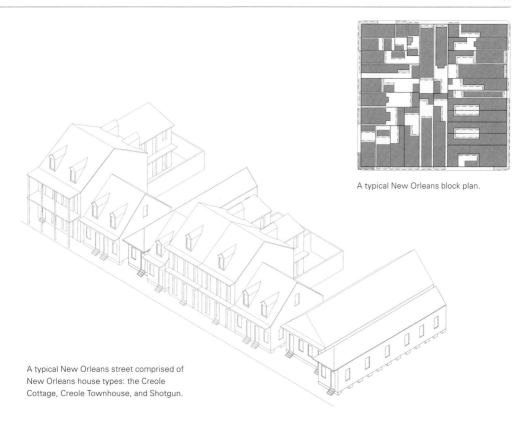

A typical New Orleans block plan.

A typical New Orleans street comprised of New Orleans house types: the Creole Cottage, Creole Townhouse, and Shotgun.

The urban structure of New Orleans formed largely as a consequence of its geography. The French first conceived its location as a strategic port location at the base of the Mississippi River. The original settlement formed on the high ground along the river's natural levee and was soon organized into a regular orthogonal street grid. Upriver from the original settlement, the land along the river was organized into individual plantations using a system whereby land was divided into long and narrow pie-shaped wedges that ran perpendicular to the river in order to provide each plantation with river frontage. As the city flourished, urban development eventually overtook these plantations. Their old dividing lines now form the major roadways that run perpendicular to the river. Parallel to the river, cross streets form radiating arcs that reflect the river's crescent-shaped curve. Together, these circumstances establish a radial street pattern that is unique to New Orleans.

The New Orleans grid is composed of blocks that are typically 300 feet square. Each block is divided into long, narrow lots that are typically 30 by 120 feet but can range from 20 to 65 feet wide by 80 to 150 feet deep. Blocks are often divided into ten 30-by-120-foot lots per opposing side and two 30-by-150-foot key lots on each of the remaining sides. The three primary house types of New Orleans, the Creole Cottage, the Creole Townhouse, and the Shotgun, formed relative to these narrow lot conditions.

Apart from their individual characteristics, New Orleans house types share many common attributes that formed in response to the same or similar exigencies. The typical New Orleans house is usually flush with the sidewalk or set back slightly. Houses range between 40 to 70 feet in depth and are followed by a rear yard or courtyard and, traditionally, a service building. Most houses are either party-walled or closely spaced at 2 to 4 feet. Adjacencies are generally closer in older neighborhoods and wider in newer neighborhoods. A typical New Orleans house is usually one or two stories tall and rarely exceeds three and a half stories. Most are raised off the ground 6 to 36 inches to permit ventilation and to separate the house from the damp ground and the occasional street flooding that occurs after heavy rains in some neighborhoods.

The interior space of a typical New Orleans house is tall, usually 11 to 14 feet, in order to allow heat to rise and escape the occupied ranges. In addition to storage, the attic of a typical New Orleans house traditionally serves as a ventilation space; windows, dormers, or vents allow heat to be drawn out from the house through stack ventilation. Openings in rooms are usually positioned across from one another in order to facilitate cross ventilation. Interior rooms are often each the same size and are commonly arranged en suite whereby circulation flows from room to room without the use of corridors. In this way, maximum living area is preserved. In the typical New Orleans house, this simplicity of spatial organization permits a wide range of flexibility such that usage can be assigned and exchanged over time.

For each New Orleans house type there are a number of variations. While type refers to a primary structuring principle of formal and organizational characteristics, variation refers to an organization of secondary formal and organizational characteristics that adapts a model to the specific conditions of a particular site and usage. The organization of secondary characteristics might describe the elongation, shrinking, doubling, stacking, or some other configuration of the primary structuring principle. The variations of New Orleans house types can be understood and described most simply and accurately by the specification of the number of bays, or openings, along the front façade, as in Two-Bay Creole Cottage or Four-Bay Shotgun.

Two-Bay Creole Cottage

 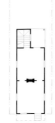 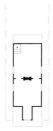 

This example of a Two-Bay Creole Cottage is of masonry construction. An external staircase provides access to the second floor.

Two-Bay Creole Cottage: first- and second-floor plans. The Two-Bay Creole Cottage is one room wide and two rooms deep followed by an enclosed service space and open gallery.

The Creole Cottage is characterized by a succession of primary spaces off the street followed by a succession of attached secondary spaces. The ridge beam spans the width of the freestanding form, resulting in a gable-sided roof that is pitched toward the front and rear.

Four-Bay Creole Cottage

 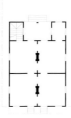 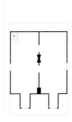 

This example of a Four-Bay Creole Cottage is of masonry construction. In place of dormers, windows and small louvered vents provide opportunities for light and ventilation.

Four-Bay Creole Cottage: first- and second-floor plans. The Four-Bay Creole Cottage is comprised of an en-suite grid of primary spaces that is two rooms wide by two rooms deep followed by an open gallery that is flanked by two enclosed service spaces.

The Four-Bay Creole Cottage is essentially two Two-Bay Creole Cottages placed side by side and is the most common variation of the Creole Cottage type.

Creole Cottage

Models of the Creole Cottage house type were built during the late 1700s until the mid-1800s. Today, surviving Creole Cottages are found all throughout the French Quarter and in older New Orleans neighborhoods.

The Creole Cottage type is characterized by a succession of primary spaces off the street followed by a succession of attached secondary spaces. The ridge beam spans the width of the freestanding form, resulting in a gable-sided roof that is pitched toward the front and rear. Creole Cottages are usually one and a half stories, range from 40 to 50 feet in depth and vary in width. Most are freestanding but some may share one or both of its sidewalls with its adjacencies. The roof shape of the Creole Cottage permits room for a half-story room or garret to be finished as an extra room or storage space. The steeply pitched gable-sided roof usually overhangs the sidewalk by 2 or 3 feet; this roof extension, called an abat-vent, protects the house and pedestrians from the rain or hot sun.

The main house is usually one or two rooms wide by one or two rooms deep. These primary rooms are generally 12 by 14 feet. Each being the same size, rooms can be interchanged and used for different purposes depending on cultural preferences. Primary rooms are followed by a series of secondary spaces; an open, covered porch-like gallery and one or two small rooms called a *cabinet*. These are multi-functional spaces where various service or leisure activities can take place. Today, the *cabinets* usually house a bathroom and kitchen. In Creole Cottages with a finished attic, the staircase is usually located in one of the *cabinets*. Beyond the main house, 70 to 80 feet of the lot is available to accommodate a rear yard or courtyard and one or more out-buildings.

Creole Cottages are usually constructed of brick-between-post or plastered brick, and raised off the ground on low brick chain walls. Less expensive Creole Cottages are comprised of wood-frame construction or the least costly "barge-board" construction. Barge-boards are flat, wide planks, usually 2 inches thick, of the kind used in the construction of river barges. Vertical boards sit directly on, or are face-nailed to, the sill. Horizontal lathe and plaster are applied to the interior surface and horizontal weatherboards are applied to the exterior surface. Barge-board and wood-frame Creole Cottages are usually raised on low brick piers.

Three-Bay Creole Townhouse

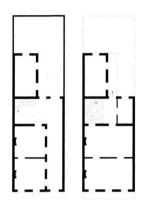

A pair of three-story Three-Bay Creole Townhouses side by side. The uppermost balcony indicates that the attic floor is a few feet below the eaves—allowing for small low windows and eliminating the need for dormers.

Three-Bay Creole Townhouse: first- and second-floor plans. The Three-Bay Creole Townhouse is essentially a Two-Bay Creole Townhouse with an added bay. The third bay is comprised of a *passage* or carriageway that leads from the street to the courtyard. The Three-Bay Creole Townhouse is one room wide and either one large room or two small rooms deep. The upper floor(s) may be one room wide and two rooms deep or subdivided into smaller units.

The Creole Townhouse is characterized by a linear succession of primary spaces and vertically oriented circulation. The ridge beam spans the width of the primary form resulting in a gable-sided roof that is pitched toward the front and rear. The Three-Bay Creole Townhouse is the most common variation of the Creole Townhouse type.

Four-Bay Creole Townhouse

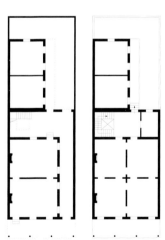

This example of a Four-Bay Creole Townhouse has a narrow carriageway that connects to the rear courtyard. A covered gallery overhangs the sidewalk, protecting both the house and passers-by from the elements.

Four-Bay Creole Townhouse: first- and second-floor plans. The Four-Bay Creole Townhouse is one room wide and either one large room or two smaller rooms deep. The upper floor(s) may be one room wide and two rooms deep or subdivided into smaller units.

The Four-Bay Creole Townhouse is essentially a Two-Bay Creole Townhouse with a wider, Four-Bay room width. The fourth bay is comprised of a *passage* or carriageway that leads from the street to the courtyard.

Creole Townhouse

Models of the Creole Townhouse house type were built throughout the 1800s. The Creole Townhouse consists of a mixture of characteristics borrowed from the Spanish Colonial type, the Creole Cottage type, and the general Townhouse type imported by Americans from the Eastern Seaboard. Today, models of the Creole Townhouse are most commonly found in the dense urban environment of the French Quarter but can also be found throughout older New Orleans neighborhoods.

The Creole Townhouse is characterized by a linear succession of primary spaces and vertically oriented circulation. The ridge beam spans the width of the primary form resulting in a gable-sided roof that is pitched toward the front and rear. The Creole Townhouse is usually two to three and a half stories tall and roughly 60 feet in depth. In a Creole Townhouse that is exclusively residential, the floor is raised 18 to 30 inches. If the Creole Townhouse has a commercial element, the floor of the commercial portion is usually raised only 4 to 6 inches to facilitate entry. While there are some freestanding examples, most Creole Townhouses share one or both sidewalls with its adjacencies. The steep pitch of the roof allows space for a half-story room, or garret, to be finished as an extra room or storage space. The gable-sided roof is pitched to allow rainwater to drain to the front and rear of the main house. The shed roof of the outbuilding is pitched toward the courtyard; traditionally, rainwater was collected and stored in courtyard cisterns.

The ground floor of the Creole Townhouse is traditionally used for commercial purposes while the second, and sometimes third, floor is residential. The residential quarters on the upper floors are usually accessed by an open *passage* or carriageway that leads from the street to a staircase in a loggia off the rear courtyard. The second floor may be followed by another full story of bedrooms or the half-story of the attic. The organization is en suite. Service or secondary rooms are located in a two-story service building that is usually attached to the main house and accessed on the second floor by a balcony that overlooks the rear courtyard. The outbuilding is one room wide and either a simple rectangle or L-shaped. Balconies and galleries usually extend from the front and rear façades of the main house in addition to the service building. Creole Townhouses are typically constructed of masonry or may be wood frame, covered with plaster or weatherboards and raised off the ground on low brick chain walls.

Two-Bay Shotgun

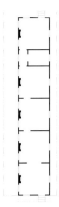

A pair of Two-Bay Shotguns side by side. Some singles are as narrow as 10 feet, and others as wide as 15 feet.

Two-Bay Shotgun: first-floor plan. The Two-Bay Shotgun or "Shotgun Single" is one room wide and three or more rooms deep. The organization is en suite. A half bay, usually located near the rear of the sequence, is used for service functions— most commonly a bathroom.

The Shotgun is characterized by a linear progression of spaces aligned perpendicularly with the street. The ridge beam spans the length of the freestanding form resulting in a gabled roof that pitches toward the sides.

Four-Bay Shotgun

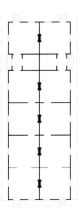

This particular example of a Four-Bay Shotgun is located on a corner lot. A secondary entry is accessible from the side street.

Four-Bay Shotgun: first-floor plan. The façade of the Four-Bay Shotgun typically consists of a door and window on each side. Circulation is en suite. Commonly, a door at the side of the house provides a secondary entry.

The Four-Bay Shotgun or "Shotgun Double" is essentially two "singles" placed side by side, divided by a shared wall, and intended as two separate residences. It is the most prolific variation of the Shotgun and the most common house type in New Orleans. Today, they are sometimes converted to function as single-family residences.

Shotgun

Models of the Shotgun house type were built in New Orleans from the late 1800s through the early 1900s. Like the Creole Cottage, the simplicity and variability of the type promoted its profuse replication; individual houses could be adapted to accommodate occupants of various means, culture, and usage requirements. Shotguns are the most abundant traditional house type in New Orleans and can be found all throughout the city except for areas near the lake that developed later in the twentieth century. Locally, a Two-Bay Shotgun is commonly referred to as a "single" and a Four-Bay Shotgun as a "double."

The Shotgun type is characterized by a linear progression of spaces aligned perpendicularly with the street. The ridge beam spans the length of the freestanding form resulting in a gabled roof that pitches toward the sides. Shotguns are one or two stories and range from 40 to 70 feet in length. The floor is usually raised 18 to 36 inches. Most Shotguns sit on a typical lot size of 30 by 120 feet and are situated roughly 2 to 4 feet from the side property lines. Shotguns are situated either flush with the sidewalk or set back slightly. The house is followed by a rear yard and, traditionally, a detached service building located at the rear property line.

The rooms of a Shotgun are arrayed one after the next. Circulation either flows from room to room or along a hallway or exterior gallery. In Two-Bay and Three-Bay variations of the Shotgun, openings are located along its length and situated across from one another to facilitate cross ventilation. In double-wide variations with a central wall, if openings are more or less aligned along its length, cross ventilation can occur in the long direction.

In series, shotguns are spaced slightly wider apart than Creole Cottages; rainwater runs off to the sides of the gabled roof rather than the front and rear. The front of the roof may be hipped to meet the street and may include a dormer or small window for light and ventilation. The small attics of Two-Bay and Three-Bay Shotguns usually serve as storage space. The larger attics of Four-Bay Shotguns are sometimes converted as spare rooms. Shotguns may have front and rear porches or balconies or galleries on one or more façades. Shotguns are comprised of either wood-frame or barge-board construction and are usually raised on low brick piers.

William McDonough

Cradle to Cradle: Making It Right

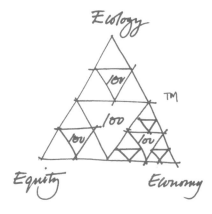

Fig. 1: Fractal triangle

Source: William McDonough + Partners

Before we began I ran across a statistic that stated a staggering 40 percent of all our pollution comes from the construction and operation of our buildings. The current paradigm, stemming from the industrial revolution, took pride in the fact that we could force ourselves on our environment ... even manipulate our environment to our pleasure ... or so we thought. But there seems to be a price for this arrogance: wars over oil, climbing prices of gas, climate change, growing disease rates ... do we think we can keep consuming ourselves into extinction? But what if a city could actually produce more energy than it consumed, what if it could actually filter the air instead of pollute the air. What if we could insert ourselves into the ecosystem and, as in nature, eliminate our concept of waste? One of the most defining partnerships I would form would be the author of this new paradigm Bill McDonough. Brad Pitt

Our goal, as designers and as humans, is a delightfully diverse, safe, healthy, and just world—with clean air, water, soil, and power—economically, equitably, ecologically, and elegantly enjoyed.

Design is the first signal of human intention. Many of the intentions underlying the Industrial Revolution were good ones, such as raising standards of living and giving people more opportunities. But it was an incomplete agenda that did not include perpetuating the vitality and diversity of the oceans, rivers, forests, air, soil, and animal

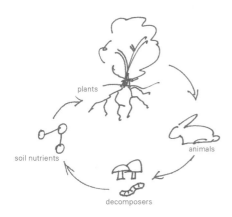

Fig. 2: Biological nutrients

Source: William McDonough + Partners

Fig. 3: Technical nutrients

Source: William McDonough + Partners

populations. The result is a massive human artifice of dangerous materials that require regulations and vigilance; today, we measure prosperity by activity instead of legacy. What if we intended something more positive? Albert Einstein wrote, "The world will not evolve past its current state of crisis by using the same thinking that created the situation." It is time for designs that are creative, abundant, prosperous, and intelligent from the start.

Cradle to Cradle design is an opportunity to create value throughout the wide spectrum of human concerns anchored by economy, ecology, and equity. A fractal triangle (fig. 1) illustrates the trio of concerns and serves as a conceptual tool for analyzing and understanding opportunities to grow value. The triangle shows how each design decision has an impact through the spectrum. The goal is not simply to recognize and address economy, ecology, and social equity considerations, but to optimize and maximize value in all areas. Some of the questions that we ask in the process include: Does this design contribute to the economic health of the community? Is it achieved while providing fair benefits and wage practices? Is it improving the quality of life of all stakeholders? Is it enhancing stakeholders' health and safety? Is the design safe for local and global communities and ecosystems? Is it creating healthy habitat? Is it making effective use of resources? Any point in the fractal triangle could yield many alternative questions, each of which presents an opportunity for creating value.

Cradle to Cradle Material Assessment Tool

7th Generation

4th Generation

1st Generation
(present day)

The Materials Target shows the relative "greenness" of construction materials and systems for each house. Using the Cradle to Cradle protocol, materials and systems are analyzed for effects on human and environmental health, durability and performance appropriate to the Lower Ninth Ward community in New Orleans, Louisiana.

The Target uses the following categories:

Conventional
Used in current acceptable building practice; any "green" attributes are either unknown or unavailable to the public.

Improved
Marketed as "green," however claims are not currently third-party certified.

Optimized
Performance certified by an approved third party; use typically contributes to eligibility for green-home certification programs.

Cradle to Cradle Inspired
Components are safe and can be separated and returned to a biological cycle (safely composted back to earth) or a technical cycle (remanufactured at equal or greater value without down-cycling), OR it has been Cradle to CradleSM Certified.

Our goal is to identify safe, healthy materials available for homes today (1st Generation), while encouraging continued improvement in the building industry. We are working toward a future where the public has ready access to an array of affordable products optimized in true Cradle to Cradle cycles, a gift to our 7th Generation and beyond.

Source: William McDonough + Partners

MIR Strategies Matrix
Be native to place – Lower Ninth Ward, New Orleans, Louisiana

Cradle to Cradle Philosophy

Create safe objects of long-term value	Rely on the sun	Use nature as model	Support the local community
Climate specific			
Specify materials which resist moisture and pests using most benign methods possible	Prioritize passive design techniques: solar, ventilation, high ceilings, shading devices	Incorporate active cooling, heating, and energy-recovery ventilation systems working in synergy with local climate	Respect local architectural precedent with forms influenced by climate-driven solutions
Design construction systems for disassembly and reuse			
Incorporate details that meet or exceed best practices for hurricane-resistant construction and floodwater mitigation			
Location specific			
Exceed FEMA elevation requirement	Incorporate south-facing roofs (anticipatory design for active solar installations)	Provide rainwater collection, capture stormwater flows on site (rain gardens, street-side bioswales)	Provide diversity of design solutions driven by owner choice
Test site soils and implement necessary mitigation	Consider off-grid power and/ or battery alternatives for use in grid power outages	Prefer regionally sourced materials with design and manufacture that protects native environmental health	Support efforts to create a neighborhood evacuation plan and designated location for obtaining emergency supplies
Design a place of refuge into each house			
Sustainable model			
Prioritize use of readily available interior materials and finishes which support human health	Fund solar hot water and solar electric installations using group purchasing power	Fund gray-water reuse installations using group purchasing power	Use design to support Lower Ninth Ward community's goal to become a model for the rest of the nation
Prefer materials in closed loop biological or technical cycles	Specify appliances and fixtures at highest level of Energy Star certification	Specify fixtures and fittings with lowest water use profiles	Design houses to meet or exceed LEED for Homes, NAHB, Earthcraft, and Energy Star certification standards
Eliminate jobsite and life cycle waste to the greatest extent possible			
Homeowner driven			
Specify materials and systems which require minimal maintenance	Design building systems (MPE, solar) that are easy to operate and can be maintained by local technicians	Create site design using locally sourced native and bio-adaptive plants	Design homes to be adaptable to changing owner needs (extended family, live/work, ADA)
Design to accommodate changing uses and improvements in technology over time		Allocate space for household recycling, composting	Support neighborhood efforts to establish community centers (parks, commerce, transit links, building supply/ reuse store)

Source: William McDonough + Partners

Together, they signal the possibility of acting with positive intentions across a wide spectrum of concerns.

Michael Braungart and I describe our Cradle to Cradle design approach in our book, *Cradle to Cradle: Remaking the Way We Make Things* (North Point Press, 2002). Cradle to Cradle design seeks to maximize economic, ecological, and social value by following principles inspired by nature:

– **Waste equals food** Design materials and systems that will be cycled repeatedly in biological and/or technical metabolisms; in natural systems, waste equals food.

– **Rely on renewable energy** The quality of energy matters; use renewable energy sources that protect human and environmental health.

– **Celebrate diversity** Natural systems thrive on complexity; technical systems thrive on coherency. Make design decisions that support economy, ecology, and equity.

– **Anticipate design evolution** A fourth principle that supports the other three. This idea acknowledges that we are working toward positive states, and we must adapt over time. With this in mind, we design to accommodate changing uses over time, adaptation to improved technologies, and safe disassembly and reuse of components.

Nutrient Cycles

Materials that flow optimally through the biological metabolism are called biological nutrients (fig. 2). As defined for Cradle to Cradle products, biological nutrients are biodegradable (or otherwise naturally degradable) materials posing no immediate or eventual hazard to living systems that can be used for human purposes and safely return to the environment to feed ecological processes. Products conceived as biological nutrients are called products of consumption. They are designed for safe and complete return to the environment to become nutrients for healthy living systems.

A technical nutrient (fig. 3) is a material, frequently synthetic or mineral, that remains safely in a closed-loop system of manufacture, recovery, and reuse (the technical metabolism), maintaining its highest value through many product life cycles. Technical nutrients are used in products of service, which are durable goods that render a service to customers. The product is used by the customer but owned by the manufacturer, either formally or in effect. The product of service strategy is mutually beneficial to the manufacturer and the customer. The manufacturer maintains a relationship with valuable material assets for continual reuse while customers receive the service of the product without assuming its material liability. The manufacturer or commercial representative of the product also fosters long-term relationships with returning customers through many product life cycles.

Water Analysis

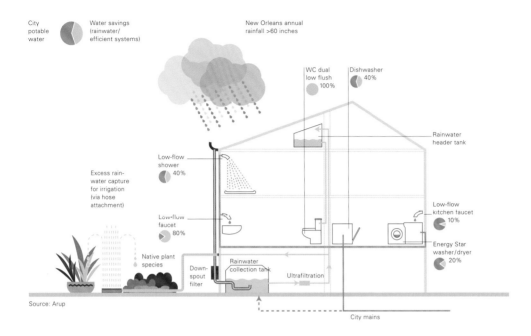

City potable water

Water savings (rainwater/ efficient systems)

New Orleans annual rainfall >60 inches

WC dual low flush
100%

Dishwasher
40%

Rainwater header tank

Low-flow shower
40%

Excess rain-water capture for irrigation (via hose attachment)

Low-flow kitchen faucet
10%

Low-flow faucet
80%

Energy Star washer/dryer
20%

Native plant species

Down-spout filter

Rainwater collection tank

Ultrafiltration

City mains

Source: Arup

Energy Analysis

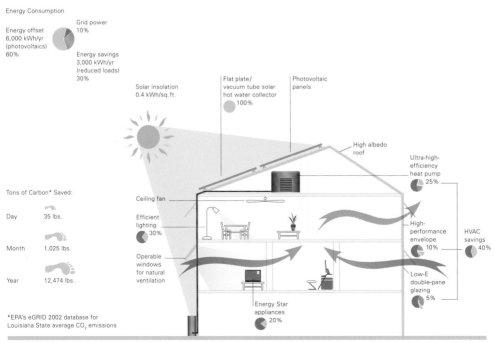

Energy Consumption

Energy offset 6,000 kWh/yr (photovoltaics)
60%

Grid power
10%

Energy savings 3,000 kWh/yr (reduced loads)
30%

Solar insolation 0.4 kWh/sq.ft.

Flat plate/ vacuum tube solar hot water collector
100%

Photovoltaic panels

High albedo roof

Ultra-high-efficiency heat pump
25%

Tons of Carbon* Saved:

Day   35 lbs.

Month   1,025 lbs.

Year   12,474 lbs.

Ceiling fan

Efficient lighting
30%

Operable windows for natural ventilation

High-performance envelope
10%

HVAC savings
40%

Low-E double-pane glazing
5%

Energy Star appliances
20%

*EPA's eGRID 2002 database for Louisiana State average CO_2 emissions

Source: Arup

McDonough Braungart Design Chemistry (MBDC) has refined the Cradle to Cradle principles into specific assessment criteria to help orient product design toward 100 percent ecological intelligence over time. Products can be evaluated for their relative achievement of these criteria and receive Cradle to Cradle^{SM} Certification at one of four levels. We see certification as a critical market transformation tool. The real value is that consumers, designers, and product manufacturers are becoming more aware of the true characteristics of products—ingredient safety, material chemicals, the embodied energy of processes, and other aspects and impacts of their making, transport, and use. For too long, most of us have lived with very little information about the true nature of the vast array of human artifice that touches our lives.

Cradle to Cradle Certification is a recognition that requires achievement in multiple areas—use of materials that are safe for human health and the environment across their life cycles; products and systems designed for material reutilization, such as recycling or composting; use of renewable energy; efficient use of water, and maximum water quality associated with production; and company strategies for social responsibility and employee well-being. Overall, data are collected and assessed for thirty-nine criteria of ecologically intelligent design. Measures include items such as carcinogenicity, endocrine disruption, mutagenicity, reproductive toxicity, acute and chronic toxicity, aquatic toxicity, persistence/biodegradation, and bioaccumulation. Assessments on individual ingredients down to 0.01 percent of a formulation, entire materials, and products are completed using peer-reviewed data and hazard cut-off values established by MBDC. Such detailed analysis identifies existing positive attributes and areas for ongoing improvement. Cradle to Cradle Certification is recognized by the U.S. Green Building Council as an innovative metric of sustainable design, and recognized by the U.S. EPA as a label that meets its Environmentally Preferable Purchasing guidelines.

Some of the benefits and opportunities presented by designing products as biological and technical nutrients include: a new perspective, fostering design innovation; strong, lasting customer relationships; valuable materials perpetually put to valuable use; additional means for understanding and measuring progress; natural resources replenished through safe, productive commerce; chemicals, materials, and processes designed for health and perpetual recyclability; customers receiving valuable services without material or toxic liability; and risks are effectively managed by designing them out of products and systems.

William McDonough + Partners seek to bring Cradle to Cradle thinking to the scale of the building, the community, and even regions. Our philosophy is rooted in Cradle to Cradle thinking. We see sustainability as an integrated part of any intelligent design.

In fact, we believe that the natural principles inspired by Cradle to Cradle thinking can be applied to all scales of design—molecular, regional, and even global.

Applying the four interdependent principles to the complex systems of buildings and communities requires rigorous attention to the optimization of ecologically, economically, and socially intelligent strategies. For Make It Right, these principles are the underpinnings of a framework through which we and the design teams have explored a broad range of strategies. For example, waste equals food encourages the exploration of prefabrication; we see modularity in nature. Relying on renewable energies encourages us to celebrate passive strategies, employ smart systems design for performance optimization, and look into all manner of resourceful harvesting—solar, wind, and rain. Celebrating diversity has been an important principle for this project since the outset—this idea is inherent in the mission of the project to celebrate the unique culture of this community. That played out in the design process in a number of ways, including how vernacular features were interpreted by some teams. It was also a reminder that each home and the neighborhood as a whole represent an opportunity to showcase diverse solutions that together will make the Lower Ninth Ward as safe and healthy as possible. Anticipating design evolution, the fourth principle, picks up on the first three; we asked all the teams to think about adaptability so that the houses, landscapes, and the community as a whole will get better over time, as new systems and technologies become available and affordable, and as the needs of the families evolve.

Our goal, as designers and as humans, is a delightfully diverse, safe, healthy, and just world—with clean air, water, soil, and power—economically, equitably, ecologically, and elegantly enjoyed. Make It Right seeks to get people into homes as quickly as possible. We also want to show how to bring affordable, replicable, design innovation to the Lower Ninth Ward while working towards next-generation Cradle to Cradle benchmarks. We are working to make this neighborhood a milestone on the path toward a future where all human design is a signal of positive intention—a Cradle to Cradle world.

GRAFT

Design in Times of Need

The humanitarian challenges we currently face as a global community are vast in quantity, geographic scope, and in regard to their respective complexities. Pollution and global warming; the spread of diseases such as malaria, tuberculosis, and HIV/AIDS; the lack of potable water, adequate nutritional supplies, proper sanitation, and shelter in many parts of the world compose the most readably noticeable issues. There are also the matters of armed conflict and the lack of education, both of which often exacerbate existing problems. The daunting task of determining which issues to focus upon and how to provide solutions leaves many nonplussed. Ultimately, neglecting any of these issues will compromise the stability of human life on this planet. It is up to each one of us to contribute to the eradication of the great dangers that are present within so many people's lives and to come to the aid of those in harm's way when catastrophe occurs.

The Make It Right project sought to identify a center of attention and action, a pressure point within the urban fabric of New Orleans, which will trigger the redevelopment of larger areas within the city, and potentially identify techniques for providing shelter to those in need around the globe. The Lower Ninth Ward was chosen as the epicenter for this change. The most devastated neighborhood in New Orleans, the Lower Ninth Ward is predominantly occupied by low-income families, whose available monetary means for rebuilding are limited, if not nonexistent. However, this neighborhood composes one of the richest cultural communities in the country and was, until Hurricane Katrina in August 2005, a comprehensive vibrant crossroad of families, music, and social interaction in New Orleans.

With any given challenge, developing a robust solution requires proper identification of all of the factors in play, all the needs that could be met. The more comprehensive and specifically those factors are defined and the more accurately they are evaluated insofar as to how one factor relates to another, the more likely an ideal solution becomes. Within the discipline of architecture, the base necessities that a building must service have historically been too thin. Due to the knowledge accumulated over the hundreds of years of design and the increasingly effective and powerful technologies, buildings can now do more for less. Providing built solutions that account solely for proper sanitation and shelter from adverse environmental conditions stands as merely adequate.

We must acknowledge the immense value of retaining cultural capital and preserving the world's ethnosphere[1] as well as the biosphere. We must remember that built architecture ideally serves entities other than itself, that buildings are to be used as tools for not only survival but also for harnessing the vast imaginative and creative energies so unique to our species.

As Albert Einstein so astutely stated, "Everything that can be counted does not necessarily count; everything that counts cannot necessarily be counted." And so it is that all of which was lost to the Lower Ninth Ward's residents cannot be summed up through the enumeration of physical requirements. Many of the complex needs left in the wake of Katrina are difficult to define in a positivist manner, yet these needs are so powerful that they become tangible. The majority of the homes were passed down through the decades, therefore holding the memories of many generations, as well as providing families with grounding and identity. These homes formed a cornerstone of the once intensely vibrant New Orleans community.

Cultural considerations for rebuilding this community are every bit as crucial as finding proper resolution for the functional, safety, and sustainability needs. As a culture rich in history, music, as well as community interaction, the uniqueness of the Lower Ninth Ward can be reinvigorated, cherished, understood, and physically expressed as such. The psychological resonance the building has with its occupant, the sense of well-being it provides, and the ability to create a platform from which the residents can meaningfully and creatively interact with the world around themselves is fundamentally the heart of design.

When faced with the vast undertaking of rebuilding the Lower Ninth Ward, the sense of urgency becomes almost overwhelming, calling for an immediate solution: shelter for those who have lost their homes, provided without hesitation as efficiently and affordably as possible. However, it is at this moment when, as architects and planners, it is most critical to comprehend the distinction between providing shelter and providing a home.

Although globalization has led to new and sweeping opportunities, it has also brought about the endangerment of diversity, "the erosion of humanity's cultural and intellectual legacy."[2] Public housing projects, while rapidly providing affordable shelter solutions, imperil diversity, suppress the human spirit, and obfuscate the means to establishing dynamic communities. Projects have never existed within the Lower Ninth Ward, which is not hard to believe upon realizing that the area has an exceptionally high percentage of owner-occupied housing. The suburban project, although markedly

1   Wade Davis, "Cultures at the Far Edge of the World,"
TED Conference, June 24, 2008.
2   Ibid.

more generous of an environment than public housing, typically provides little variation and often neglects to incorporate local cultural conditions.

Ideally, architecture reinforces the capabilities, drives, and ambitions of each individual, as well as the local, regional, and global communities within which each individual belongs. The more positive reinforcement architecture provides, the more a house becomes a home, subsequently espousing uniqueness, the empowerment of individuals, families, and communities. As architects and planners we must foment the opportunities for maintaining or potentially even increasing positive diversity as a core pursuit.

In order to understand and contextualize the spirit of the problems needing resolution in New Orleans more intimately, MIR collaborates with a large group of local associations throughout the rebuilding initiative. The Lower Ninth Ward Stakeholders Coalition is an active part of the Make it Right Project, working on site to develop the housing initiative in cooperation with the residents of the Lower Ninth Ward from the onset of the process.

The residents have been generous with their time, participating in lengthy and candid discussions regarding their lifestyles, fears, the values they hold dear, the beautiful and profound meaning of community specific to the Lower Ninth Ward, the optimism and belief in the revitalization of New Orleans, and the heartfelt hope to finally come home. Landownership is a fundamental core belief that forms part of the American Dream; it is the belief in this dream, the belief in their family and extended family of community that fuels what could best be described as a grassroots movement, MIR. These dialogues have provided remarkable insights to a dignified people whose perseverance is exemplary.

Helplessness echoes vehemently as an underlying sentiment of the victims of Katrina: initiated during the storm, carried into the subsequent diaspora, and reinforced by ineffectual government assistance. Community residents had no other choice than to abandon their homes, their lives, and seek shelter across the country. One of the strongest countermeasures that can be provided to the individual is the power of choice. The process of selecting their house design provides an outlet for control to be returned to the landowner; it offers the expression of individuality, pride, and difference. Empowerment of the individual provides a platform for personal and family growth, from which a powerful sense of community can emerge.

Despite recent efforts to provide affordable modular housing to an ever-depleting middle class, the outcomes ultimately fail to hit a middle-income target audience. Architecture over the last fifty years has increasingly become a discipline, which services the upper and upper-middle class, generating the perception that it is an elitist pursuit. Ideally, however, architecture can and should provide solutions for all social strata. The ultimate goal for architecture is to better the quality of life for mankind. Design is a necessary tool to change surroundings, to create a sense of well-being. A product and vehicle for progress, design is capable of improving living conditions at all scales of civilization. Architecture lays a groundwork onto which community can be created.

Primarily a product of technological advancement and experience gained from our collective history, humankind's ability to communicate is progressively becoming more intricate in range, specificity, and means. As communication directly folds into community formation and evolution, we have found ourselves as members of communities that are wider in geographic scope, more robust in content, and inter-twined through more infrastructural systems. Additionally, as inter-community communication has grown so have interdependence and the formation of the world as an ever-tightening, increasingly detailed web of information and influence. Identified as a pressure point within present-day civilization, the community of the Lower Ninth Ward, through its rebuilding and the sharing of the rebuilding process, is capable of positively affecting the condition of the communities of designers, donors, New Orleans, the United States, and the remainder of the world. It is about the positive growth of our species and consequently cannot be exclusive to certain social classes. We are a single community, a community that must take the time to rebuild trust and to bolster the growth of one another.

GRAFT

Design Guidelines and Selection of Architects
A Call for Participation

From the onset, Make It Right's goal was to join the history of the Lower Ninth Ward with creative new architectural design solutions mindful of environmental and personal safety concerns in order to encourage both the evolution of aesthetic distinctiveness and the conscientious awareness of natural surroundings.

With its aim and the desire to achieve a community of vitality and diversity the MIR team decided to open up the discussion and creative discourse to the international community of architects. Social consciousness in many ways is an unspoken but ever present principle for an architect. MIR aims at raising awareness for the global relevance of this project and to encourage a growing participation of architects.

The urge to incorporate local, national, and international architectural knowledge effectively into the process of rebuilding the Lower Ninth Ward made it mandatory to carefully analyze needs of the local community and build up a direct dialogue with the people who lost their homes. It became evident that a clear set of design guidelines were paramount in order to coordinate a process of such complexity and ambition with a number of architects from around the world.

Guidelines

Once having identified the resurrection of a once vibrant community as the ultimate objective, it became the driving force behind the formation of MIR guidelines. The Lower Ninth Ward was a predominantly low-income and overlooked community, in some cases lacking the resources to afford typical amenities, much less high design with its associated high price point. The architectural parameters became high design at a low cost, which was a very challenging and exciting endeavor. New Orleans vernacular as a point of departure ensured contextual relevance and bolstered the intention to advance the New Orleans' already vivacious and renowned cultural foundation. Prominent design influences were New Orleans' long-standing architectural typologies like the Shotgun, Camelback, or Double, coupled with the appreciation of the traditional lifestyle ignited by these icons. Suburban paradigms of seclusion and independence were avoided in favor of openness and utilizing the house as a social channel to the community. The face of the house, particularly its conduit to the street, the porch, took the primary position espousing community connection. By increasing the connectivity between neighbors, we aimed to embolden the sense of community and re-enacted an old tradition of New Orleans architecture.

Within the field of disaster relief activities time is of the essence. Critical voices had been raised after Katrina about the hubris of rebuilding on lower ground or using a given lot size proportion that many feel stems from historical urban zoning concepts that have architectural limitations for the modern user.

We chose to work within the existing urban fabric of lot sizes to be able to partner with the disaster-ridden community immediately. If you have lost your home and live in a FEMA trailer sitting on the only thing left to you—your piece of land—these priorities are self-evident. In the future and whenever there is room for learning and adopting MIR will look into improving these pre-conditions.

GRAFT's research of New Orleans' vernacular architecture and cultural context was compiled into a thorough handbook that was distributed to all designers involved. It was up to the individual architecture firm to take the provided information into con- sideration while designing their respective proposal. The information contained within the research was utilized by most architects, integrating elements of the same into their housing proposals in an interpretive and metaphorical fashion.

Brad Pitt and the MIR team had grave concerns regarding flood damage. In order to mitigate the possibilities of water damage a number of strict criteria for the homes' passive survivability were established:

1. Houses needed to be raised up 5' to 8' above grade level.
    (Most of the homes are 8' above grade.)
2. The homes needed to be structurally engineered to withstand
    hurricane weather, including flood surges.
3. The materials and construction were required to resist
    water damage and molding.
4. In addition to the structure, hurricane-resistant roofing, siding,
    and window systems should be utilized.
5. Rooftops needed to provide raised patios that could operate
    as safe havens during floods.

William McDonough + Partners played the key role in ensuring design strategies and material selection for the MIR project were guided by Cradle to Cradle thinking to evidence regenerative design principles that promote human and environmental health. William McDonough + Partners developed a Cradle to Cradle framework specific to the Lower Ninth Ward community, forming a guide for the design and construction

Selection of Lots for Existing Parcel Map

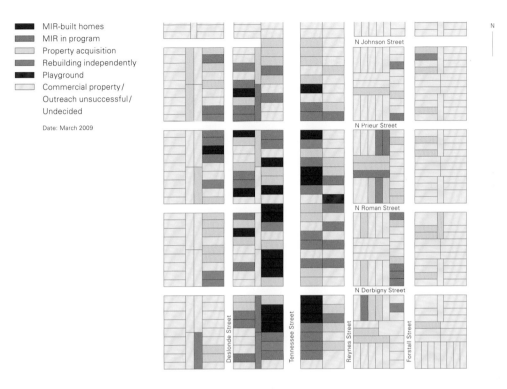

- ■ MIR-built homes
- ▨ MIR in program
- ▢ Property acquisition
- ▨ Rebuilding independently
- ▨ Playground
- ▢ Commercial property/
  Outreach unsuccessful/
  Undecided

Date: March 2009

process. Those design guidelines incorporate climate-specific strategies, location-specific (Lower Ninth Ward) information, environmentally intelligent design, and healthy construction/building system strategies. The guidelines emphasize that MIR homes are to be replicable models of sustainability. Having started with providing the relevant parameters, William McDonough + Partners are working with all architecture teams, each of which is charged to design a house.

In order to achieve the goal of affordable housing, the budget requirement for base construction costs were identified at $200 per square foot for the first prototype and $130 per square foot for all replicable models thereafter. Base construction costs include structure, foundation, finishes, millwork, MPE systems, appliances, as well as plumbing and lighting fixture packages. Site preparation costs and atypical building systems (solar systems or gray-water recapture) were not included within the base construction cost and were developed separately by the MIR core team.

Being socially conscious and environmentally responsible are inextricably tied together; therefore, implementing sustainable design was an obvious additional imperative. It is important for architects and designers to build smarter, as opposed to bigger and faster. Vernacular design came into play again; using existing understandings of

Parameter for House Sizes on Existing Lots

House sizes due to building code

- Lot
- Actual house
- Porch

40' × 105' lot; max. house size 2,080 sq. ft.

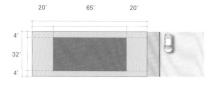

House centered on the lot,
setbacks due to building code

French Quarter style: House closer to
public road, creating a larger backyard

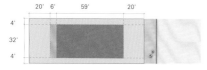

1 covered porch

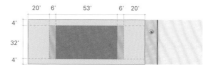

2 covered porches

30' × 110' lot; max. house size 1,680 sq. ft.

House centered on the lot,
setbacks due to building code

French Quarter style: House closer to
public road, creating a larger backyard

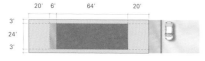

1 covered porch

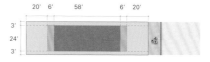

2 covered porches

ventilation, shape, and shading served as passive means to create climatic efficiency. MIR infused these ideas with the use of contemporary systems and materials like geo-thermal heat pumps, water catchment systems, green sandwich construction, and re-cycled non-off-gassing materials. With this as a foundation, MIR could act smarter when building, utilizing important principles like the Cradle to Cradle philosophy for direction.

A Cooperative Process

Local cultural influences gave rise to the pre-Katrina architecture emblematic of the area. Within this project MIR's overarching priority became to work in close cooperation with former residents of the Lower Ninth Ward, aspiring to help recreate and nurture the unique culture and spirit of the neighborhood. MIR's approach to new home design relies heavily on a trustful dialogue with community representatives and the homeowners themselves. As such, the first set of reconciled guidelines for architectural design in the target area was initially developed and continuously updated with community mem-bers, representatives, and individuals regarding homeowner-defined needs.

To further anchor all design efforts of MIR in the vibrant and rich tradition of the local community, the design process was started as an ongoing dialogue between the archi-tects, the MIR team, and the local community in order to create the spirit of a collaborative effort. Furthermore, homeowners always have the final say in which designs would be built.

GRAFT set up an in-house team to interface with all architects around the globe, to coordinate and communicate feedback from the community, and to update on guide-lines and schedules in close collaboration with Brad Pitt, William McDonough + Partners, the local MIR team, and John C. Williams Architects as executive architect.

Each architect prepared and submitted a prototype design, which was then value engineered to arrive at the same construction cost in a collaborative process with input from the MIR core team of architects, system engineers, solar consultants, cost estimators, and representatives of the Lower Ninth Ward neighborhood coalition. All design presentations were open to community groups and the homeowners and addi-tional feedback meetings had been arranged frequently to make sure that nothing rested unspoken or ignored in this complex procedure.

The set of design guidelines including general requirements, budget requirements, construction requirements (through an affordable planning guide and a material selection guide), as well as submission requirements were continuously updated. Community feed-back, structural feedback (typical foundation and framing schemes), and budget spread-sheets were provided by MIR, ensuring that all designs would fulfill the requirements to become part of the MIR design catalogue for the Lower Ninth Ward.

Frontage Options

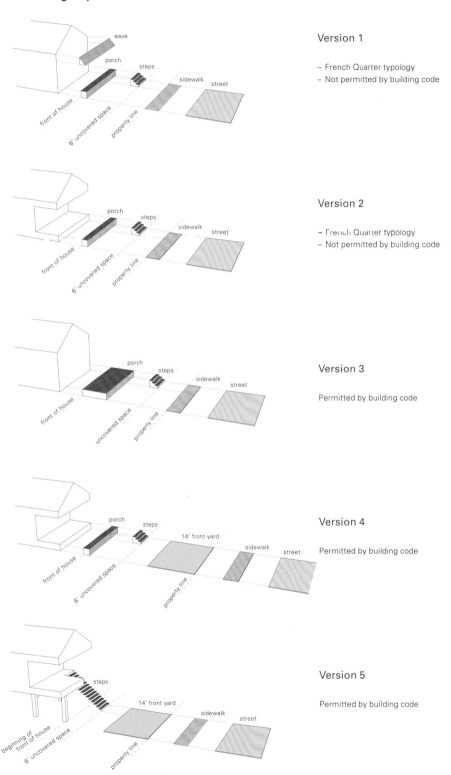

Version 1

– French Quarter typology
– Not permitted by building code

Version 2

– French Quarter typology
– Not permitted by building code

Version 3

Permitted by building code

Version 4

Permitted by building code

Version 5

Permitted by building code

Selection of Architects

When assembling the MIR architectural panel, GRAFT and William McDonough + Partners solicited the guidance of MIR Founder Brad Pitt; Reed Kroloff, at the time Dean of Architecture at Tulane University in New Orleans; and a coalition of Lower Ninth Ward community groups along with specific residents. Leading voices of the international community of architects were asked to recommend architectural firms in order to bring a wide range of expertise to one table. The process began with over fifty architects who were selected based upon their exceptional reputations and a carefully considered list of criteria which were specifically defined as the following:

- Prior interest or involvement in New Orleans,
  preferably post-Katrina, and/or experience with disaster relief
- Familiarity and interest in sustainability
- Experience with residential and multi-family housing
- Proven to be skilled innovators on low-budget projects
- Experience dealing with structures that have to successfully
  address water-based or low-lying environments

There was also attention to include some younger and smaller firms and to ensure that there would be a good mix of local and globally active firms. Architecture firms were assembled into three groupings:

- Local (from the New Orleans area)
- National (from all over the United States)
- International (from all over the world)

Local

Billes Architecture – New Orleans, LA
Eskew+Dumez+Ripple – New Orleans, LA
concordia – New Orleans, LA
Trahan Architects – Baton Rouge, LA
John C. Williams Architects – New Orleans, LA

National

BNIM – Houston, TX
KieranTimberlake – Philadelphia, PA
Morphosis – Santa Monica, CA
Pugh + Scarpa – Santa Monica, CA

Customization

Interior features

The interior of the houses offer the possibility to feature service walls, built-in furniture, and other amenities.

Porch

Open and closed porches will add to the living quality of the houses.

Efficiency

Floor plan options will include the possibility of having efficiency units or assisted-living facilities.

Decorative connotation

Houses can feature an interpretation of typical New Orleans porch decoration.

Floor plan

A variety of different floor plans will cover different concepts from closed to open floor plans.

ADA

The house design will take ADA guidelines into account.

Egress

Safe haven

The rooftops will consist of raised patios that can double as safe places during floods.

Waterproof materials

Materials that can grade floor and below should be constructed of waterproof materials in order to resist temporary flooding.

Emergency storage

Within the safe haven there should be emergency equipment storage to access during a major flood.

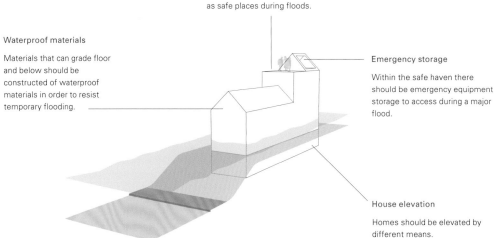

House elevation

Homes should be elevated by different means.

International

Adjaye Associates – London, England

GRAFT – Los Angeles, CA; Berlin, Germany; Beijing, China

MVRDV – Rotterdam, Holland

Shigeru Ban Architects – Tokyo, Japan

The opportunity to work for a cause intended to aid those in need was received almost unanimously by all designers MIR reached out to. All of them responded immediately and were willing to fly to New Orleans on short notice to participate. Their work and designs are a donation to the residents of the Lower Ninth Ward and society as a whole, which ultimately is the most important and stimulating aspect of architecture.

Ongoing Process

Once eligible, homeowners review all designs and select the project they prefer. Once the resident decides upon a design, their house will be fully developed on their lot within the appropriate budget. There are two different tracks for the designers according to their designation: the local architects head into design development and then construction documents to finalize their house designs. The national and international architects will hand over their schematic designs to the appointed executive architect John C. Williams Architects, a local New Orleans firm, to be taken through design development, construction documents, and finally construction administration. Although John C. Williams Architects will follow through on the design development, it is to be developed with the express consent of the original designers, who are encouraged to communicate with the executive architect as much as possible. The list of project materials is extensive, and will constantly evolve as the project is developed, designs are refined, and as new materials and systems become available and affordable or as they are donated to the cause. MIR and William McDonough + Partners will continue to assess materials throughout the project; as such, there is no definitive set of approved methods, since this would be contrary to the project's goal to encourage and support adaptation in the marketplace.

They are some of the brightest architects in the world and all we had to offer them was a coach ticket and a box lunch.

Brad Pitt

Adjaye Associates

David Adjaye

Billes Architecture

Gerald W. Billes

Richard S. Kraver

BNIM

Bob Berkebile

Mark Shapiro

concordia

Steven Bingler

Bobbie Hill

Construct LLC

Joe Osae-Addo

Eskew + Dumez + Ripple

Steve Dumez

Allen Eskew

Chuck Rine

Tracy Lea

GRAFT

Mark Ripple

Gregor Hoheisel

Lars Krückeberg

Alejandra Lillo

Wolfram Putz

Thomas Willemeit

KieranTimberlake

Stephan Kieran

James Timberlake

Morphosis

Thom Mayne

MVRDV

Nathalie De Vries

Winy Maas

Jacob van Rijs

Pugh + Scarpa Architects

Lawrence Scarpa

Trahan Architects

Trey Trahan

Shigeru Ban Architects

Shigeru Ban

Page 140

Adjaye Associates

London, Great Britain

A graduate of the Royal College of Art, David Adjaye started a small practice in 1994. In June 2000 he re-formed his studio as Adjaye Associates with eight employees and the firm has since expanded to thirty in London with offices in Berlin and New York. In June 2001, Adjaye Associates won the Idea Store competition to design two new-build libraries in the London Borough of Tower Hamlets, part of a program based on a new type of information and learning provision. The Idea Store, along with the residential project Dirty House, was included in the São Paulo Bienal, Brazil, 2003, the Venice Biennale of Architecture in 2004, and won the national accessibility award from RIBA in 2005. The practice recently completed a new market hall in Wakefield, Yorkshire, and is currently working on a 300-unit housing development in Birmingham, the design of the Moscow School of Management, Skolkovo, new libraries for Washington, DC, as well as further projects in the United States, Southeast Asia, the Middle East, and Africa.

Pages 148/266

Billes Architecture

New Orleans, LA

Billes Architecture is committed to the continuum of the history of New Orleans and to its communities. The firm seeks to construct interventions that elevate the built environment and inspire the residents of the city. They approach each project not with a formula, but a design process that assesses economic feasibility, site, program, and the opportunity for sustainable solutions. Green design is a responsibility of the industry and is the foundation of the firm's process. For over thirty years, Gerald W. Billes has been part of many of New Orleans' most progressive, high-profile architectural projects, from the City of New Orleans' first Comprehensive Housing and Neighborhood Preservation Study (1973), to the Repair and Renovation of the New Orleans Superdome (2006). Mr. Billes is the recipient of numerous AIA awards, honors, and recognitions for preservation. Billes Architecture's work has appeared in a variety of national and international publications including *1000 x Architecture of the Americas, Architectural Record, Metropolis,* and *Urban Land.* In addition to the MIR project, the firm is currently engaged in various redevelopment projects in the New Orleans area.

Presentation of Designs I

Pages 156/274	Page 164

BNIM
Houston, TX

concordia
New Orleans, LA

For BNIM, sustainability is a way of life; design is an act of optimism and hope for the future. With these philosophies in mind, BNIM continues to build on almost forty years of history, design innovation, and environmental stewardship. BNIM is a pioneer in the design of healthy buildings and communities, having helped to develop the USGBC LEED® rating system and Living Building standards for restorative design. The firm is committed to an inclusive design process, one that values close collaboration with all stake-holders, from end users, to local agencies, to neighborhood groups. With a holistic approach to issues of place, function, context, and com-munity, BNIM creates architecture that not only performs technologically but also stirs the imagination of its users while reconnecting them experientially to the living world. BNIM's projects have won over 200 design awards including national AIA/COTE Top Ten Green Project Awards and recognition from such organizations as the AIA, the General Services Administration, the American Planning Association, and the Urban Land Institute.

Concordia was formed in 1983 to pursue partici-patory processes and integrative design practices. For more than twenty-five years the concordia team has worked to develop a corporate social entrepreneurship dedicated to the principles of public planning and architectural design. Their projects span a wide range of building types, from the Jackson Brewery Festival Marketplace, the Contemporary Arts Center, and the Aquarium of the Americas in New Orleans, to the nationally acclaimed Henry Ford Learning Academy in Detroit, Michigan. Concordia's award-winning work has appeared in a wide range of national publica-tions, including *Architectural Digest, Progressive Architecture,* and *Newsweek*. Research alliances have included the MIT Media Lab, Harvard University's Project Zero, the University of New Mexico, National Aeronautics and Space Admin-istration (NASA), and the West Ed Research Lab.

Pages 172/290

Constructs LLC
Accra, Ghana

Joe Osae-Addo was born in Ghana, West Africa, and trained at the Architectural Association in London. He set up his practice in Los Angeles in 1991. His work has been influenced by genius loci, and how architecture can/should respond to this in creating pieces which are both site-specific and meet the needs of people who will interact with it. Joe Osae-Addo moved back to his native country Ghana in 2004 and is currently the CEO of Constructs LLC, an "inno-native" design firm based in Accra and Tamale in Ghana, West Africa. Constructs LLC is currently working on several projects as both developer and architect, with a primary focus on developing manufacturing, using and promoting indigenous materials and technology for construction in a contemporary way. The firm has expanded its mandate to become a think tank of sorts, to engage in the discourse of economic development in Ghana and Africa as a whole.

Page 180

Eskew+Dumez+Ripple
New Orleans, LA

Eskew+Dumez+Ripple is a design-driven studio producing diverse projects in architecture and planning by blending a signature collaborative process with creative thinking and emerging technologies. The work of the firm encompasses a broad range of types and scales, from intimate chapels and residential projects to significant civic and institutional buildings and large-scale urban planning projects. Consistent throughout their work is a commitment to enhance and protect both the cultural and natural environment of their community—evident in the beauty and technical craftsmanship of their designs and in the long-term sustainability of their projects. Based in New Orleans, the firm draws from the rich cultural and architectural heritage of the city to develop a practice of national range and recognition. As a result, the firm has received over 100 awards over the past 20 years, including over a dozen national awards for design excellence.

Pages 188/314

GRAFT
Los Angeles, Berlin, Beijing

GRAFT is a full-service design firm located in Los Angeles, California; Berlin, Germany; and Beijing, China. With the collective professional experience that encompasses a wide array of building types including fine arts, educational, institutional, commercial, and residential facilities, the firm has won numerous awards in Europe, the U.S., and Asia. In January 1998 the label GRAFT was created by German architects Lars Krückeberg, Wolfram Putz, and Thomas Willemeit in Los Angeles. GRAFT opened an office in Berlin, Germany in 2001, and in 2005 Gregor Hoheisel became a Partner in GRAFT Beijing, which was founded the same year. In 2007 Alejandra Lillo became a partner of GRAFT LA. GRAFT was conceived as a label for architecture, urban planning, exhibition design, music, and the "Pursuit of Happiness." With the core of the firm's enterprises gravitating around the field of architecture and the built environment, GRAFT has always maintained an interest in crossing the boundaries between disciplines and "grafting" the creative potentials and method-ologies of different realities.

Page 196

KieranTimberlake
Philadelphia, PA

KieranTimberlake Associates LLP has focused on solving complex design issues innovatively for over twenty years. Their process is holistic, in-volving many layers of information and participants at one time. Their art is the discovery of external and internal logics derived from this exploration. An award-winning and internationally recognized architecture firm, KieranTimberlake Associates is noted for its research, innovation, and inventive design. Founded in Philadelphia in 1984 by Stephen Kieran, FAIA, and James Timberlake, FAIA, the firm is comprised of fifty-four professionals. Recent projects include Loblolly House in Taylors Island, Maryland, the new Sculpture Building at Yale University, Sidwell Friends School in Washington, DC, and the West Campus Residen-tial Initiative at Cornell University.

Page 204

Morphosis
Santa Monica, CA

Pages 212/322

MVRDV
Rotterdam, Netherlands

Morphosis was founded in 1972 in Los Angeles as an interdisciplinary and collective practice involved in rigorous design and research. Today, with offices in Los Angeles and New York City, the firm consists of a group of more than fifty professionals. Named after the Greek term *morphosis*, meaning to form or be in formation, Morphosis is a dynamic and evolving practice that responds to the shifting and advancing social, cultural, political, and technological conditions of modern life. A critical practice where creative output engages contemporary society and culture through architectural design and education, Morphosis is a process-driven firm that seeks new and different design challenges and has resisted becoming specialized in any particular building type. With projects worldwide, the firm's work ranges in scale from residential, institutional, and civic buildings to large urban-planning projects. With founder Thom Mayne, the 2005 Pritzker Architecture Prize laureate, Morphosis works closely with its clients to help them define the ethical and functional goals of the project, then translates those goals into a design that satisfies the unique requirements and aesthetic opportunities of the program, site, and context. The ultimate goal is to produce an architecture that surprises and inspires—a critical architecture that contributes to the conversation about how we live today. Over the past thirty years, Morphosis has received twenty-five Progressive Architecture awards, seventy American Institute of Architects (AIA) awards, and numerous other honors.

MVRDV was set up in Rotterdam, the Netherlands in 1991 by Winy Maas, Jacob van Rijs, and Nathalie de Vries. MVRDV produces designs and studies in the fields of architecture, urbanism, and landscape design. The firm pursues a fascination of radical methodical research on density and on public realms. Clients, users, and specialists are intensively involved at an early stage of the design process. Reactions to the first designs can be processed quickly, creating a high degree of support for the design and encouraging the sort of new insights that can lead to specific innovative solutions. The products of this approach can vary therefore completely. They range from buildings of all types and sizes, to urban designs, publications, and installations, as well as the development of software programs.

Pages 220/330

Pugh+Scarpa Architects
Santa Monica, CA

Lawrence Scarpa, AIA, and Angela Brooks, AIA, are recognized leaders in design innovation: formal, social, and sustainable. Under their direction as lead designers at Pugh+Scarpa, the firm has received thirty-six major design awards, notably eleven National AIA Awards, including 2006 and 2003 AIA Committee on the Environment Top Ten Green Projects awards, 2005 Record Houses, 2003 Record Interiors, and the 2003 Rudy Bruner Prize. In 2004, the Architectural League of New York selected Lawrence Scarpa as an "Emerging Voice" in architecture. They have taught and lectured at the university level at numerous schools including UCLA, University of Florida, Mississippi State University, and SCI-arc. Mr. Scarpa and Ms. Brooks are also co-founders of Livable Places, a nonprofit development and policy organization dedicated to promoting healthy communities and improving quality of life through policy reform and responsible mixed-use housing developments.

Page 228

Shigeru Ban Architects
Tokyo, Japan

Shigeru Ban Architects (SBA) was established in 1985 in Tokyo and has three offices—Tokyo, Paris, and New York—with a total of thirty to thirty-five professional staff. Dean Maltz of Dean Maltz Architect became an established partner of Shigeru Ban Architects and manages the New York office. SBA's design experience stems from working in a wide range of project types from private residences, collective housing, hotels, museums, and libraries. SBA continually seeks to develop innovative structural systems and construction methods in the pursuit of individually iconic projects while founded on a basis of structural rationality, environmental awareness, and spatial simplicity. SBA's projects include the new satellite Pompidou Centre in Metz, France; the Seikei University Library in Tokyo, Japan; and the Metal Shutter House in New York City, U.S. SBA has unique experience in volunteering for disaster relief causes such as providing shelters for victims of earthquakes in Japan (1995), Turkey (1999), and India (2001), as well as working with the United Nations High Commissioner for Refugees (UNHCR) to develop appropriate shelters in the refugee camps of Rwanda.

Page 236

Trahan Architects

Baton Rouge, LA

The recipient of three national AIA honor awards in five years and numerous national and regional awards, Trahan Architects was one of three U.S. firms honored with *The Architectural Review* Emerging Architecture Award. Through the unique use of natural materials and light, Trahan designs provide an experience that enhances a building's true purpose and grows richer with time. Most notable among Trahan designs are two internationally honored church designs and a university learning center. Trahan Architects also designed master plans that were awarded first prize in international design competitions in Beijing, China, for a Pharmaceutical and Bioengineering Industry Base and a Medical Research facility.

Executive Architects

John C. Williams Architects LLC

New Orleans, LA

John C. Williams Architects LLC is a dynamic firm composed of twenty professionals based in New Orleans, Louisiana, providing architectural, planning, and interior design services. The firm's success is founded on its ability to create exceptional designs within strong programmatic elements (design, site, financial, time, criteria). Their clients include the cities of New Orleans and Mobile; institutions such as Tulane University, LSU, Spring Hill College; and businesses such as the Whitney National Bank and the Ritz Hotels. Their work varies in scale from a gate in the French Quarter to an elementary school in Violet, LA, to multi-acre sites along the Mississippi River. Whether a job is new construction or renovation/restoration, Williams is a leader in using sustainable design—taking it to a new level in the Gulf Coast region.

Adjaye Associates

London, Great Britain

The ideas that help inform this design for a family home in the Lower Ninth Ward were based on five environmental/cultural imperatives:

– Reinforcing the typical foundation of the Shotgun house to withstand the additional forces of hurricane winds and flooding.

– Transforming the ornamental filigree patterns found in New Orleans balconies to become a new storm screen that protects windows and outdoor spaces.

– Inverting the typical pitched roof to become a solar and water collector, and offering the roof as a shaded terrace.

– Acknowledging the New Orleans Shotgun and shutter house typologies as the basis for a contemporary New Orleans house.

– Responsible design for long-term environmental benefit.

Plan   Working within the prescribed setbacks, the house occupies a building footprint of 24' × 44' (1,056 gross sq. ft.), with the main living level is elevated + 5'0" for flood safety reasons. Living, dining, and kitchen functions exist in a single continuous space that opens to the front and rear yards. Bedrooms and bathrooms are stacked alongside the main living space. Plumbing and mechanical equipment are consolidated to minimize pipe runs and associated costs.

Stairs   Two 12'0"-wide cast-in-place concrete stairs are located at the east and west ends of the house, allowing for fluid circulation from the front to rear yard through the main living space. The stairs have two tread/riser dimensions similar to stadium seating so that they can function as informal seating areas where people can congregate. In situations where handicap accessibility is required, an exterior chair lift can be mounted to the concrete guardrail.

Structure   The foundation system consists of cast-in-place concrete grade beams with concrete piles, on top of which an elevated concrete frame supports the main level. Above the concrete, conventional balloon-frame construction and manufactured wood floor joists are used. A lightweight aluminum frame supports the stretched fabric canopy.

Exterior Finishes   The exterior cladding of the house is composed of cement board panels of three dimensions (4'0" × 5'0", 4'0" × 7'0", and 4'0" × 8'6"), with an applied silkscreened pattern. Exterior doors are overclad with the panels to match. At the terrace level, red cedar planks are used for decking over a TPO membrane, as well as parapet walls and exterior stairs.

Glazing   The design calls for 3'0" × 3'0" casement windows with hurricane-resistant impact glass. Each space in the house has a lower and upper casement for cross ventilation and stack ventilation.

David Adjaye, Joe Franchina, and Brandon Padron

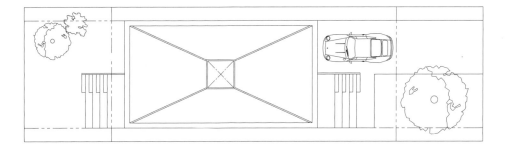

Roof plan

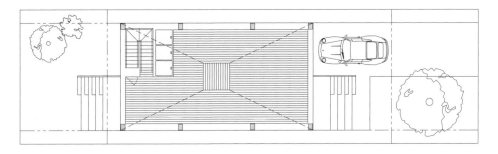

Second floor

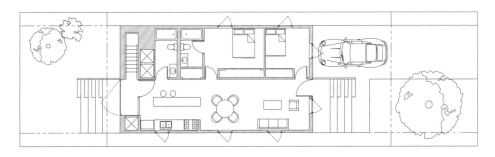

First floor

0 2 5 10 N

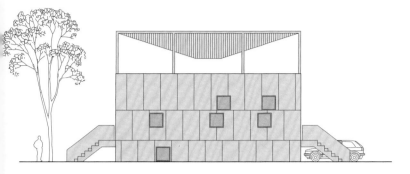

Southern elevation

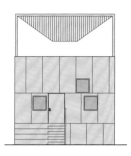

Eastern elevation

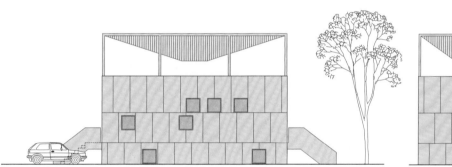

Northern elevation

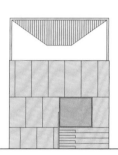

Western elevation

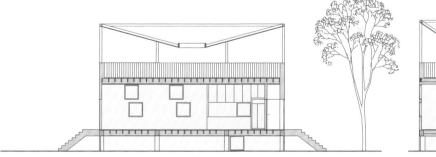

Longitudinal section

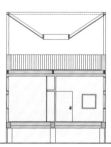

Cross section

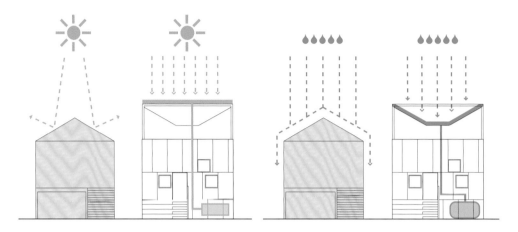

Solar collection   Water collection

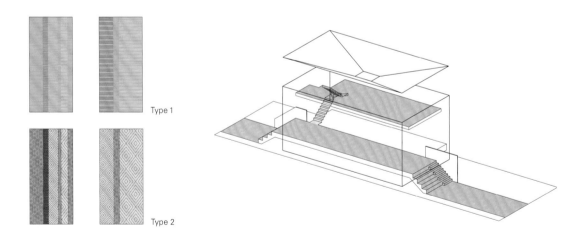

Type 1

Type 2

The exterior cladding of the house is composed of cement board panels of three dimensions (4'0" × 5'0", 4'0" × 7'0", and 4'0" × 8'6"), with an applied silk-screened pattern. The rear door is a 7'0" × 8'0" metal or wood screen door with a custom cut filigree pattern to match the cement board panels. The design calls for 3'0" × 3'0" casement windows with hurricane-resistant impact glass.

Two 12'0"-wide cast-in-place concrete stairs are located at the east and west ends of the house, allowing for fluid circulation from the front to rear yard through the main living space. The stairs have two tread / riser dimensions similar to stadium seating so that they can function as informal seating areas where people can congregate. In situations where handicap accessibility is required, an exterior chair lift can be mounted to the concrete guardrail. A third exterior stair connects the main living level to the terrace above. This is intended to be a wood stair where the treads, risers, and walls have a red cedar finish to match the terrace deck.

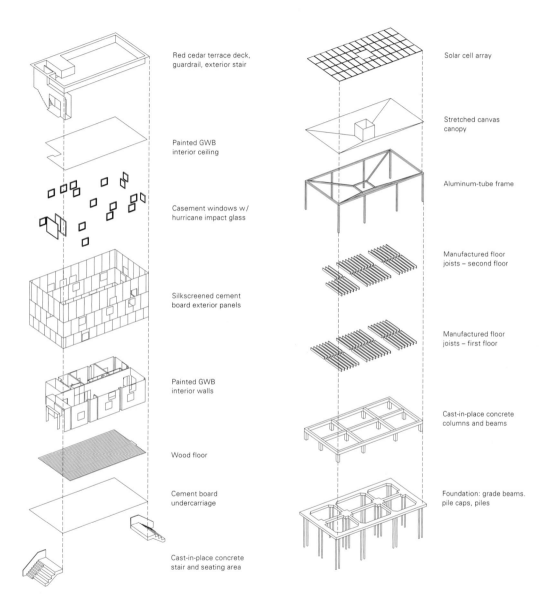

Red cedar terrace deck, guardrail, exterior stair

Painted GWB interior ceiling

Casement windows w/ hurricane impact glass

Silkscreened cement board exterior panels

Painted GWB interior walls

Wood floor

Cement board undercarriage

Cast-in-place concrete stair and seating area

Solar cell array

Stretched canvas canopy

Aluminum-tube frame

Manufactured floor joists – second floor

Manufactured floor joists – first floor

Cast-in-place concrete columns and beams

Foundation: grade beams. pile caps, piles

Building systems

Billes Architecture
New Orleans, LA

The form of the building is a response to the New Orleans area climate while respecting local culture and architectural traditions. The design utilizes natural ventilation, controlled daylighting, high ceilings with fans, shading devices, and thermal mass in the same manner as traditional New Orleans architecture. These building concepts work together to provide a comfortable environment for the homeowners while reducing reliance on mechanical air conditioning and energy consumption. The floor plan is based on a modified Shotgun with a linear transition of spaces from outdoor to indoor and public to private while being adapted to modern living with a hallway. A generous front stoop and porch is a key element in the re-establishment of the vitality of the community.

The design promotes long-lasting value to the homeowner by incorporating materials and systems that are durable, low maintenance, and contribute to lowering utility bills. The design also features common construction techniques making it affordable and allowing it to be built with local resources. The structure includes provisions to handle local weather events by being raised five feet above the ground, the incorporation of impact-resistant windows, and the design of an attic for storage and emergency refuge with an elevated means of escape.

The building seeks to be a model for sustainable living by incorporating solar panels, plumbing and air conditioning systems that reduce water and power usage, a cistern that collects rainwater from the roof for non-drinking water use, and permeable paving to reduce stormwater runoff. Building materials will be specified with regard to local sourcing, durability, non-toxicity, recycled content, and manufacturing processes that are environmentally responsible. In the spirit of Cradle to Cradle, preference will be given to "natural" products that can safely decompose or "technical" products that can be reused or recycled.

Gerald W. Billes, CEO/Principal; Richard S. Kravet, Principal; Erin E. Porter, Designer; Lauren E. Hickman, Designer

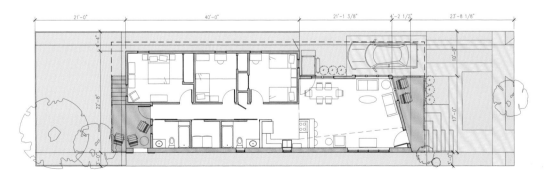

First floor

Roof plan

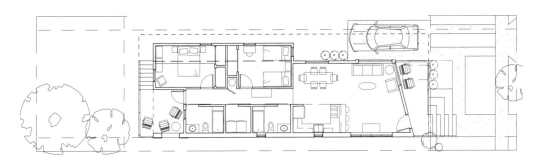

First floor

Sections

0 2   5   10   N

■ Private
■ Public

Modified Shotgun

Linear progression of spaces adapted
to modern living with hallway

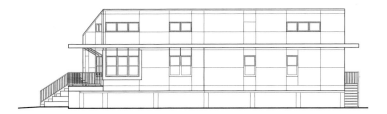

Northern elevation

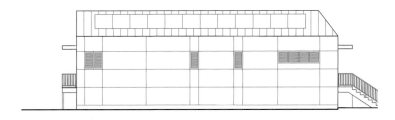

Southern elevation

Western elevation

Eastern elevation

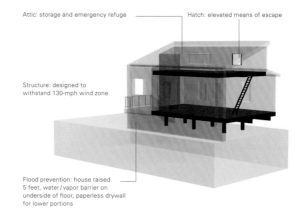

Attic: storage and emergency refuge

Hatch: elevated means of escape

Structure: designed to
withstand 130-mph wind zone

Flood prevention: house raised
5 feet, water/vapor barrier on
underside of floor, paperless drywall
for lower portions

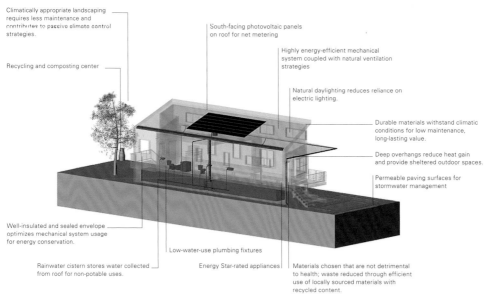

Climatically appropriate landscaping
requires less maintenance and
contributes to passive climate control
strategies.

South-facing photovoltaic panels
on roof for net metering

Highly energy-efficient mechanical
system coupled with natural ventilation
strategies

Recycling and composting center

Natural daylighting reduces reliance on
electric lighting.

Durable materials withstand climatic
conditions for low maintenance,
long-lasting value.

Deep overhangs reduce heat gain
and provide sheltered outdoor spaces.

Permeable paving surfaces for
stormwater management

Well-insulated and sealed envelope
optimizes mechanical system usage
for energy conservation.

Low-water-use plumbing fixtures

Rainwater cistern stores water collected
from roof for non-potable uses.

Energy Star-rated appliances

Materials chosen that are not detrimental
to health; waste reduced through efficient
use of locally sourced materials with
recycled content.

Sustainable elements

Sun
– Avoiding excessive solar heat gain
by controlling apertures through the use
of louvered shutters on limited south-
facing openings and deep overhangs on
west and east exposures
– Providing a well-insulated envelope
that utilizes thermal mass on the south-
facing surfaces
– South-facing portion of roof can also
easily accommodate solar panels

Light
Maximizing the admittance of natural,
indirect light on the north façade

Wind
Controlling air movement through the
placement of operable openings, ceiling
fans, and high ceilings to promote stack
ventilation and cross ventilation

Water
– Use of pitched roofs to shed water
expeditiously and collect rainwater in
cistern for non-potable use
– Permeable paving for stormwater
management on site
– Control of moisture migration through
the building envelope through selection
and detailing of materials

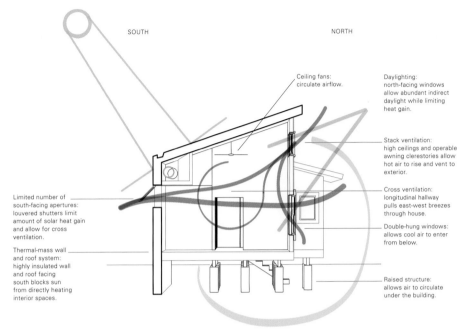

SOUTH

NORTH

Ceiling fans:
circulate airflow.

Daylighting:
north-facing windows
allow abundant indirect
daylight while limiting
heat gain.

Stack ventilation:
high ceilings and operable
awning clerestories allow
hot air to rise and vent to
exterior.

Limited number of
south-facing apertures:
louvered shutters limit
amount of solar heat gain
and allow for cross
ventilation.

Cross ventilation:
longitudinal hallway
pulls east-west breezes
through house.

Double-hung windows:
allows cool air to enter
from below.

Thermal-mass wall
and roof system:
highly insulated wall
and roof facing
south blocks sun
from directly heating
interior spaces.

Raised structure:
allows air to circulate
under the building.

Summer

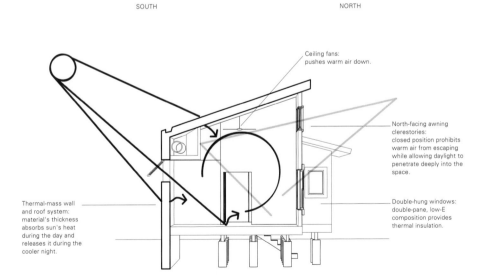

SOUTH

NORTH

Ceiling fans:
pushes warm air down.

North-facing awning
clerestories:
closed position prohibits
warm air from escaping
while allowing daylight to
penetrate deeply into the
space.

Thermal-mass wall
and roof system:
material's thickness
absorbs sun's heat
during the day and
releases it during the
cooler night.

Double-hung windows:
double-pane, low-E
composition provides
thermal insulation.

Winter

BNIM

Houston, Texas

BNIM's design rethinks the classic Shotgun vernacular with innovative environmental design strategies. The result is a 940-square-foot energy-efficient home that respects the unique aesthetic of New Orleans architecture. The home is easy to construct, considers flood safety, provides for durability over time, and offers a comfortable and efficient indoor environment. Ample outdoor spaces create areas for residents to gather both as a family and as part of a thriving public community.

In order to perform with highest efficiency, the new Shotgun home is in tune with local climate conditions including sun, heat, and water. To mitigate sun and heat absorption, generous overhangs shade the east, west, and south façades. The east and west façades, which directly face the most aggressive sun, are minimized in size. Operable windows are glazed for UV protection and increased energy efficiency, and they are positioned to maximize cross ventilation and passive cooling. The roof, which is a lightweight, reflective metal, is ready to receive south-facing solar panels—an addition which would contribute to the goal of a zero-energy home.

In addition to addressing sun and heat, the home is designed to use the region's large volumes of rainwater to the advantage of the family. The roof and gutters are designed to capture and direct water into a storage tank located beneath the house. This water is then redirected and used to flush toilets and irrigate climate-appropriate landscaping. With this rainwater harvesting system in place, the overall consumption of municipal water sources is decreased when compared to the traditional Shotgun home.

A primary consideration for the design of this home was the residents' safety in the event of a future hurricane. To prevent elevated water levels from entering the home, the structure is raised. The walls, which consist of structural insulated panels, have been tested for impact resistance. The home provides a refuge area and includes a portable solar energy pack to provide renewable energy in a time of need.

Ensuring the safety and well-being of the residents, BNIM designed a lasting, efficient building with the spirit and determination of the people of

the Lower Ninth Ward at heart. With a New Orleans style that really feels like home, this dwelling is a comfortable, healthy, and safe place for residents to return and rejuvenate.

BNIM Architects, Houston, TX
Principal in Charge: Kimberly Hickson, AIA
Principal Advisors: Bob Berkebile, FAIA;
Steve McDowell, FAIA; Mark Shapiro, AIA
Project Manager: Filo Castore, AIA
Project Designer: James Anderson, Jr.
Architectural Engineers Collaborative, Austin, TX:
Charles Naeve, P.E.; Rik Haden, P.E.
Sustainable Building Solutions, Inc./VerdeCapital
Dewees Island, SC/Houston, TX:
John Porretto

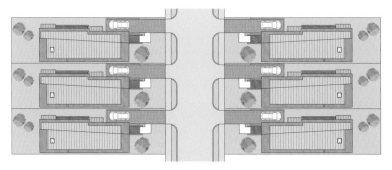

Situation

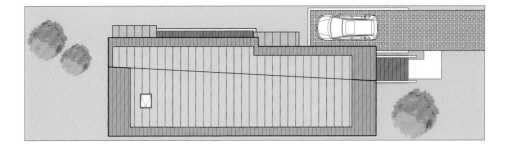

Roof plan

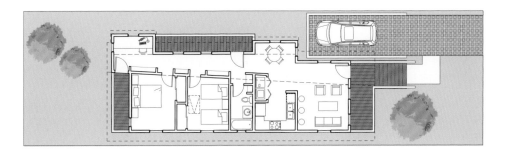

First floor

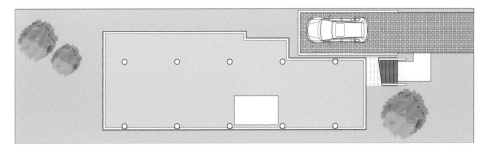

Ground floor

0 2   5   10   N

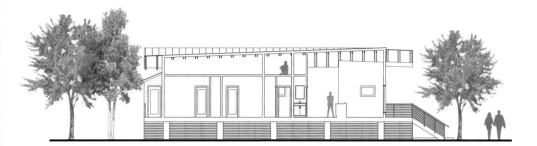

Longitudinal section

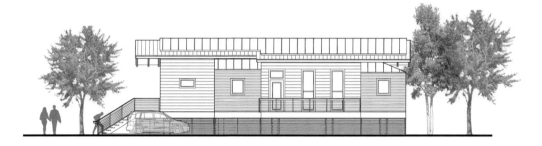

Southern elevation

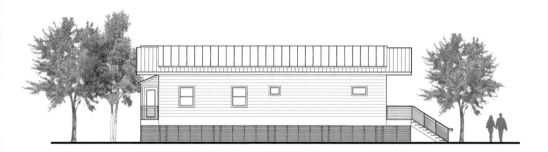

Northern elevation

Western elevation

Eastern elevation

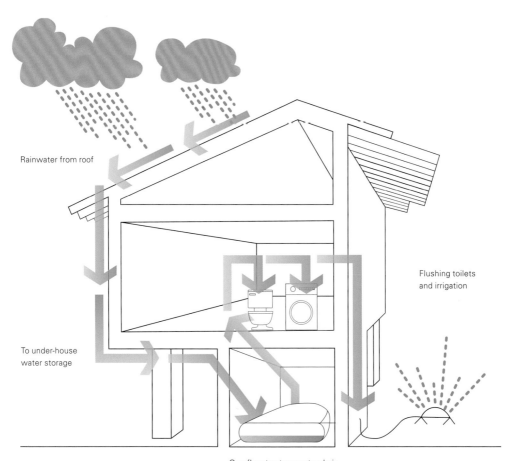

Rainwater from roof

Flushing toilets
and irrigation

To under-house
water storage

Overflow to stormwater drain

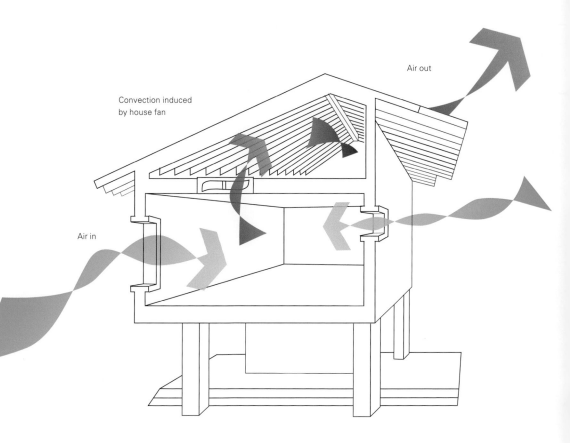

Air out

Convection induced
by house fan

Air in

concordia

New Orleans, LA

In the Lower Ninth Ward neighborhood, as in most of New Orleans, much of the community interaction takes place on one's front porch— "stoop-sitting," as it is commonly known. For the architects, providing a comfortable place that facilitates casual encounters when the main level is a story above street level was a design challenge. The Lagniappe House designers met this challenge in several ways. The house has a shaded driveway and wide, inviting steps creating a stoop with plenty of places to sit and relax. The stairs lead to an elevated front porch. The design also comes with the option of an attached or detached porch. The detached porch option creates space for a courtyard which provides additional landscaping and cross ventilation. Another design option is either a flat or sloped front porch roof. Under the porch is a fenced-in space where chairs and tables can be stored for front-yard parties like crawfish boils. An optional double sink for storing ice and a counter for food preparation can be installed in this space.

Raising the house also provided an opportunity to enhance outside living by creating a shaded verandah located below the rear of the house. On the second floor, a more private family deck on the south side of the house fosters more private communication opportunities with the next-door neighbors. This deck can also serve as an area of rescue in the case of emergencies.

The Lagniappe House, by virtue of its long, narrow shape, will accommodate many different living activities at once. Secured access to the more private zones of the house is provided by the fence and optional garage door at the carport. A third-story bedroom addition can be easily converted to an efficiency apartment by means of a separate entrance from the south-side deck. The lower level of the Lagniappe House is designed to allow moving water to flow around the pier and is devoid of structural walls that could be pushed over in a flood event. The main level is elevated 8'8" above grade, more than 3' above the FEMA elevation requirement. The recommended exterior material, stucco over Aerated Autoclaved Concrete (AAC) has submersion-resistant qualities in addition to its fire-resistive, sound-mitigating, insulating, and insect-proof benefits.

The main roof slope of the Lagniappe House is oriented to the south to maximize the collection area for photovoltaic panels. The north-facing slope will feature either manually or thermally operated windows that admit gentle daylight into the rooms and release built-up heat. Passive ventilation is augmented by low south-side windows for capturing the prevailing summer winds, high ceilings, and ceiling fans. Shaded decks on the south side are designed to reduce solar heat gain in the summer while inviting the warming winter sun. Even in a region that sometimes suffers from too much water, the community can benefit from rainwater collection for non-potable uses by reducing the energy needed to deliver municipal water and by providing families a source of drinking water in an emergency. Gray-water recycling systems can be used to further minimize dependence on the city's utility infrastructure.

concordia, Lagniappe House Project team: Steven Bingler, Gina Andre, Ximena San Vicente, Joel Ross, Ritchie Katko

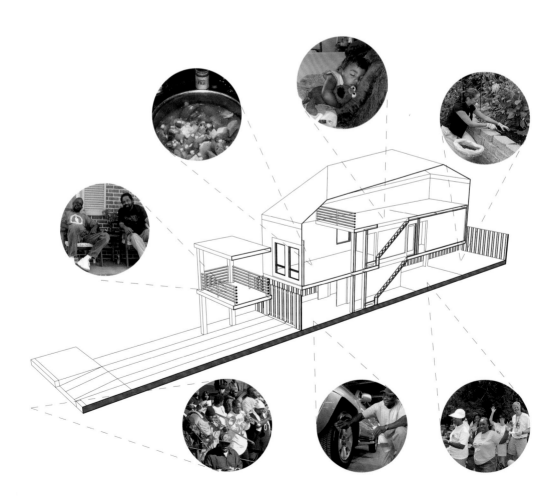

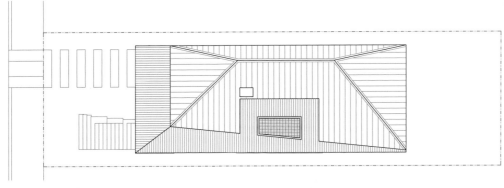

Roof plan

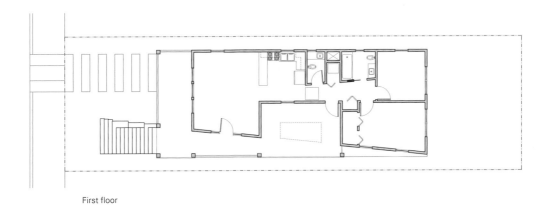

First floor

Ground floor

0 2   5   10   N

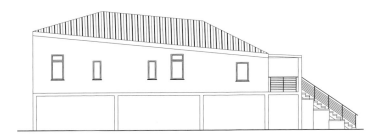

Northern elevation

Eastern elevation

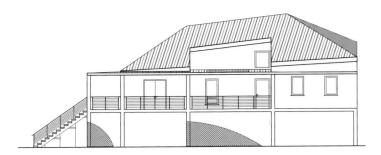

Southern elevation

Western elevation

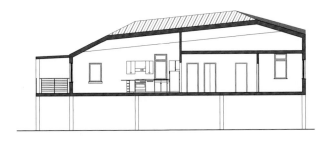

Longitudinal section

Cross section

Solar and passive ventilation diagram

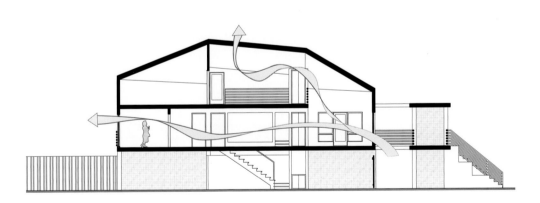

Passive ventilation diagram

Constructs LLC

Accra, Ghana

The design concept is a reinterpretation of the classic Shotgun house traditional to New Orleans. The origin of this has been traced to the Yorubas of West Africa. The approach is to introduce an "animated" corridor or "street" to connect the rooms. This evokes the dynamism that New Orleans street-life represents. To that end the scheme consists of a "linguist wall" of adobe or alluvial earth from the "floods," which will be both a functional service wall and an arts wall created by the family, as done by the Ndebele of South Africa and the Sirigu women of Northern Ghana. These connections are important to emphasize because sustainability is not only about high-tech and sophisticated manufactured interventions; e.g. solar and recyclable materials, but also nature and how ordinary people can harness it "inno-natively"™ to better their lives.

From the street the home is set back twenty feet and elevated six feet off the ground. A wide, welcoming entry stair brings people gracefully up to the front porch, along a "linguist" or art wall, to be designed by the homeowners. This entry stairway is an experience in itself with clear corrugated panels atop a timber-framed roof, bringing in light but keeping out the rain, and supported on one end by steel rods, producing a floating effect. The entry door opens into a foyer with high ceilings, so that the transition from outdoors to indoors is seamless. The living and dining rooms have a dramatic, raised roof, which supports the solar panels at the appropriate angle for optimum efficiency, and opens up to the front terrace and links to the rear kitchen, separated by a low "linguist wall." This space is designed to be about light and ventilation, a connection to the street, but also privacy. The internal animated "street" or corridor connects to two bedrooms and a rear deck area evoking the dynamism that New Orleans street-life represents. The proposed future third bedroom will be in this deck area. The use of "soft" materials which are environmentally friendly yet meet the aesthetic and functional needs of the families is the primary aim—a home that speaks of culture, history, and innovation, and is about the people who will live in and around it, integrated into the community as a whole. It is not about edifice but "healing" people and society.

Disasters such as that which has occurred in New Orleans offers great opportunities to dig deep and reach out to Africa in particular for inspiration and guidance, as it pertains to re-building the human "spirit." What can this office contribute that is uniquely New Orleans and certainly African? They have a unique opportunity and position not to come up with interventions but rather be design socio-economists. These new homes are not just houses to be lived in but "spiritual cathedrals" where memories and forgotten cultures are rediscovered and celebrat-ed through an "inno-native"™ response to site and place, through architecture. This contribution is not about edifice but environment. We need to engender that communal spirit by encouraging ownership of "real estate" beyond the physical boundaries of ownership. Residents will take over their sidewalks as canvases for outdoor art and street signs will bear imprints of their culture and

traditions. The interstitial spaces and outdoor spaces will take on added significance and will be all about flora and light. These will need to perme-ate the indoor spaces, seamlessly. This may be a wonderful opportunity to introduce other trees and plants from the African Diaspora into the local mix which not only soothe the senses of sight but the palettes of taste—the edible landscape, plants that can provide sustenance, and have homeopathic attributes. In this approach, certainly the architecture matters; but more importantly, will it and its environs nourish the soul? Construct LLC is certain it will; the spirit of New Orleans, that extraordinary blend of African and other, will ensure that.

Design Principal: Joe Osae-Addo
Project Coordinator: Josephine Dadzie
Project Administrator: Nii Armah Armar
Project Design Team: Hans Sachs, Sophie Morley, Gabriel Appo, Phanuel Okrah, Sefako Gbomita, Kofi Akakpo, Kathleen Carthy

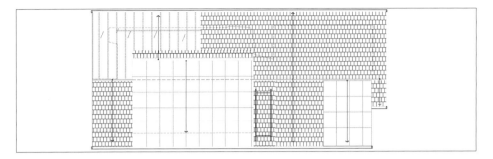

Roof plan

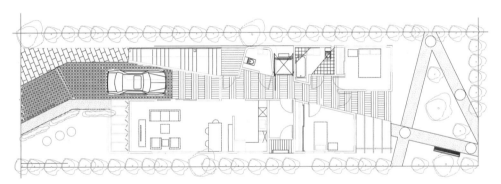

First floor

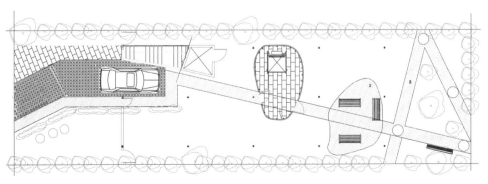

Ground floor

0 2   5   10   N

Northern elevation

Western elevation

Southern elevation

Eastern elevation

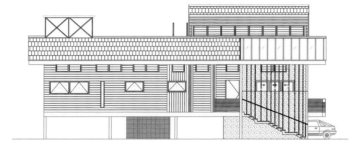

Northern elevation

Western elevation

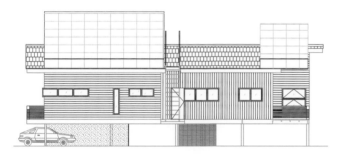

Southern elevation

Eastern elevation

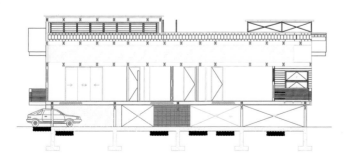

Longitudinal section

Cross section

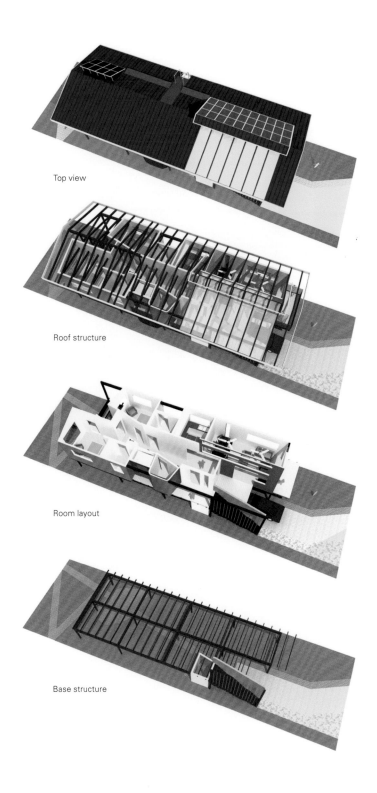

Top view

Roof structure

Room layout

Base structure

Eskew+Dumez+Ripple
New Orleans, LA

The design of the house developed out of transforming local housing traditions to accommodate changes in modern living standards. While the design has two parallel bars, an idea similar to the New Orleans typology of the Double-Shotgun house, the layout alleviates the problems of the enfilade circulation typical of Shotgun homes. The marriage wall between the bars divides the space and program into the living spaces on one side and the more private sleeping spaces on the other. This arrangement maximizes the efficiency of the space because the house has no defined circulation corridor, thus maintaining a similarity to the efficiency of the Shotgun typology. This also allows for fluid movement between the bedrooms and living spaces creating a more openly accessible layout. While the interior layout repositions the typical New Orleans home, the use of the porch remains as an essential element in the design—placing an importance on how the house interacts socially to its community. Between the front porch and the living space are large windows which create a reading of the porch as an extension of the interior space while addressing the communal aspect of New Orleans neighborhoods. The design also has a bench, sunshade, and garden at grade which help establish a lower communal level of the porch similar to a stoop. At the rear of the house the interior spaces extend outside to include more raised porches allowing air circulation to occur throughout the entirety of the house. At the rear of the ground level is a screened porch, allowing for outdoor shaded spaces able to keep cool in the hot and humid climate. The design focuses as much attention on its interior spaces as it does the function of its exterior spaces.

The design merges differing architectural traditions while maintaining a commitment to enhance the cultural and natural environments of the community. The project generally follows modernist traditions of efficiency by looking to manufacturing and production techniques that would allow for mass production and also maintains a direct connection between formal design strategies and functional concerns. Breaking from the modernist paradigm of undecorated simplicity, the design

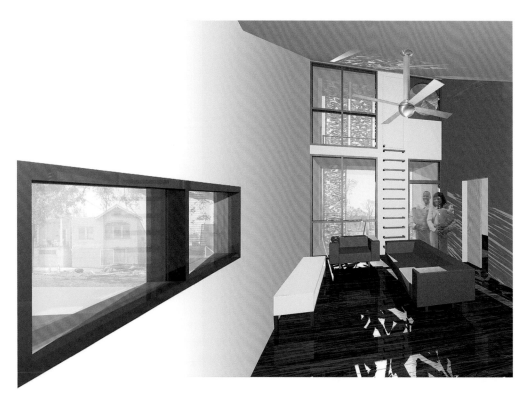

embraces traditional ornament as a means of creating local responsiveness to the historic nature of New Orleans architecture. From the interior the shutters allow for diffuse light to enter the house creating vivid light patterns and a diaphanous interior condition enabling occupants to experience spatially the effects of the specific pattern selected. The movable shutters at the front and rear of the house, while decoratively patterned, also serve the function of protecting the windows during hurricanes.

The simple overall form of the design allows for a reduction of cost by being materially efficient and easy to construct. While initially it is assumed that the first generation of the house may be constructed on site, the design allows for the potential of off-site fabrication creating two modular units that could be connected at the marriage wall which runs through the house. The off-site

fabrication potential allows for less material waste and on-site labor, while increasing quality and affordability. The material selection continues to follow Cradle to Cradle practices. The use of impervious materials such as gravel, gardens, grass, and stone pavers, rather than large areas of concrete, prevent localized flooding around the site. All stormwater is retained on the site reducing demand on city infrastructure. Gardens on the site produce native vegetables creating increased self-sustainability and cost savings. There is the potential for a vertical garden at the rear of the house which allows for healthier vegetable production that decreases problems such as soil rot, crawling insects, and increases exposure to the sun. It also has the opportunity to shade and filter the low, early eastern sunlight reducing heat gain in the morning.

Steve Dumez, Thaddeus Zarse

Roof plan

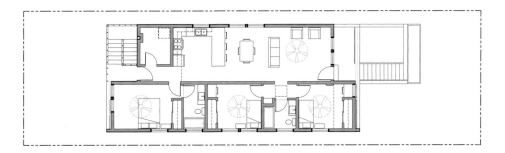

First floor

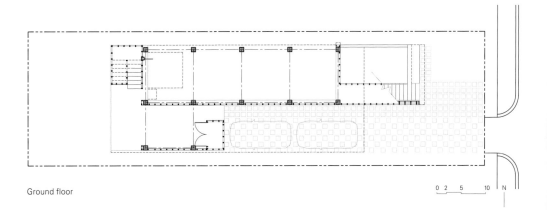

Ground floor

0 2   5   10   N

Fats Domino image

Dot pixelization

Panelization

Part of the office's concept for Make It Right is "Making It Yours" through personal customization. In addition to offering several plan configurations each homeowner is also able to make choices concerning the exterior appearance of the design. The design also offers opportunities to personalize what type of shutter system is placed on the front and rear of the house. In the example shown, an image of local musician Fats Domino is transformed into perforations then cut into metal panels. Other options include natural patterns such as leaves, ivy, or flowers similar to the iron ornamental detailing found in many New Orleans buildings or also more typical wood shutters found on homes across the city.

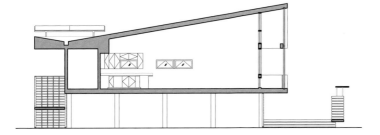

Longitudinal section

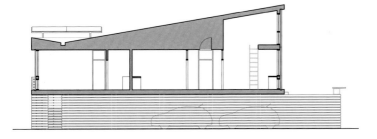

Longitudinal section

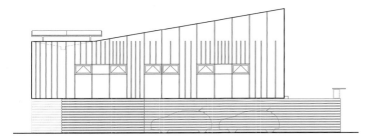

Northern elevation

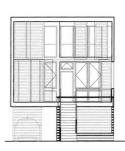

Eastern elevation

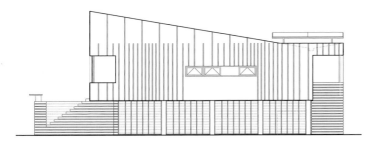

Southern elevation

Western elevation

Exploded axonometric

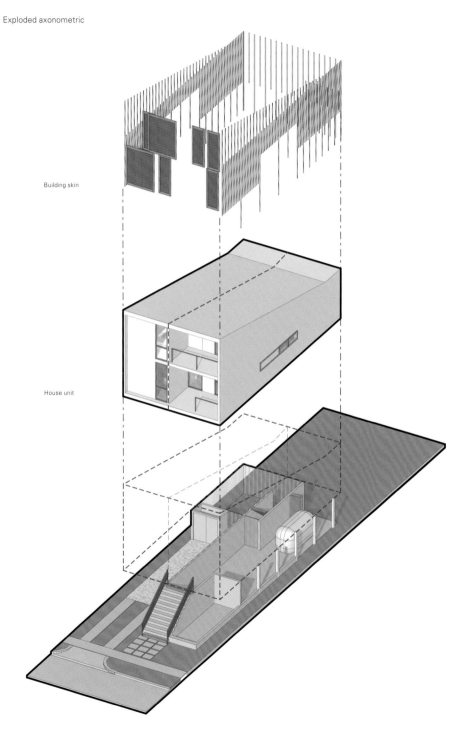

Building skin

House unit

Site preparation

One of the design's priorities was to deal with maximizing the potential of the site's natural flows. The slope of the roof is designed to direct rainwater to the rear of the house where a vertical channel collects it in a cistern located at grade below the house. By utilizing gray water for the toilets and landscape irrigation, the house reduces its operating costs and reliance on city infrastructure. Future improvements to the system could address on-site water purification—reducing municipal water needs to zero. The slope of the roof works in reverse for the ventilation of air through the interior. The "attic fan," located at the top of the wall at the front of the house, pulls warm air out of the house. The rear stair, which connects to a shaded screened porch located below the house, assists this ventilation by providing cool air to circulate into the house. Both flows are intensified by giving visual importance to the sloped roof, both on the interior and exterior, the downspout, and the fan, thus allowing a stronger understanding of the processes at work. Solar power is collected and harnessed on the roof to reduce power costs and heat water. In case of a flood emergency the house has an exterior covered and shaded upper-level balcony that also has an area for emergency supplies.

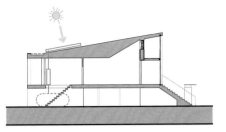

Solar water heating

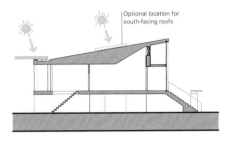

Solar power collection

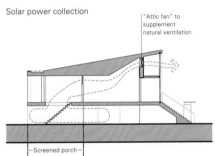

Natural ventilation

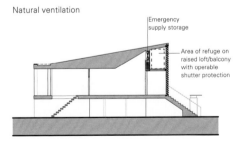

Passive survivability

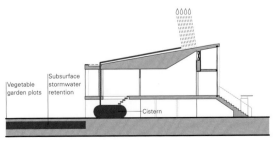

Stormwater management / Rainwater harvesting

GRAFT

Los Angeles, Berlin, Beijing

GRAFT's proposal for housing in the Lower Ninth merges metaphorical abstractions of traditional and modern architecture, driven with the purpose of capitalizing on the more successful components within each as a means with which to generate a more robust whole.

The proposal positions itself from the starting point of a traditional New Orleans housing typology, the Shotgun house, which is abstractly represented through an expressive, almost exaggerated gable roof and generous front porch. The fluidity of the relationship between home and community, the provision of areas designated to interaction with neighbors and friends, is truly one of the things that makes the Lower Ninth Ward so incredibly special. GRAFT felt it important to pay homage to this. Through progression of the project, the house is coupled with modern affordable sustainable amenities. The transition of the short section of the house reflects the progressive transformation, until finally arriving at a representation of contemporary modernism, expressed at the rear of the home in an iconic collage of cubic volumes and flat roofs, commonly associated with the apex of modernism.

This resulting flat roof space offers the opportunity to program a safe haven, a space designed to aid in life safety by providing a strategy for passive survivability.

Sustainable features include: solar panels, water catchment system, geothermal system with heat pump, tankless water heater, high ceilings for stack ventilation, operable windows which aid in stack ventilation and cross ventilation, highly insulated hurricane-resistant windows, high-R-value insulation, non-off-gassing paint and finish materials, permeable pavement, Energy Star appliances, ceiling fans, and low flow toilets.

Alejandra Lillo, Asami Tachikawa, Atsushi Sugiuchi, Carsten Gauert, Casey Rehm, Christoph Rauhut, Eddie Herman, Francesca (Celi) Freeman, Gregor Hoheisel, Ian Ream, Juyen Lee, Lars Krückeberg, Lorena Yamamoto, Marcus Friesl, Mark Grohne, Michael Haas, Michael Zach, Mick Van Gemert, Naoko Miyano, Neiel Norheim, Nora Gordon, Seyavash Zoohori, Shelly Shelly, Susanne Woitke, Thomas Willemeit, Tin-Shun But, Verena Schreppel, Wolfram Putz

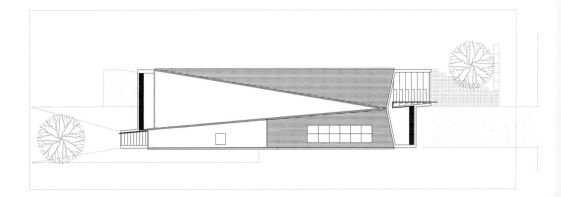

Roof plan

First floor

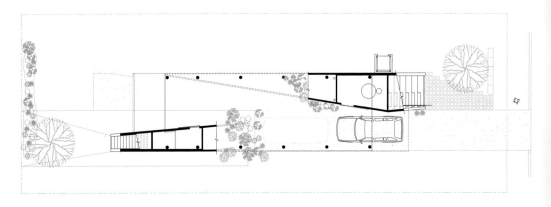

Ground floor

0 2   5   10   N

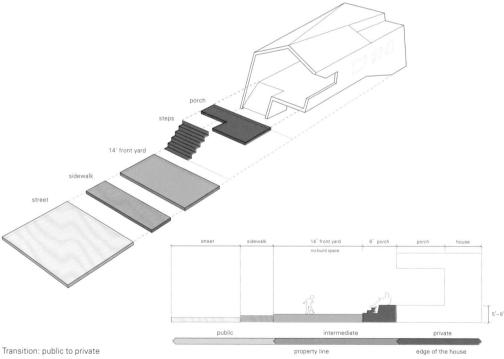

Transition: public to private

Northern elevation

Eastern elevation

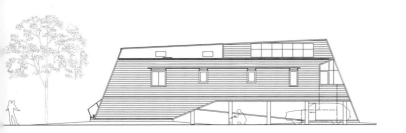

Southern elevation

Western elevation

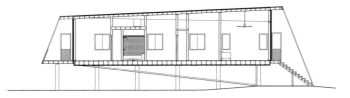

Longitudinal section

Cross section

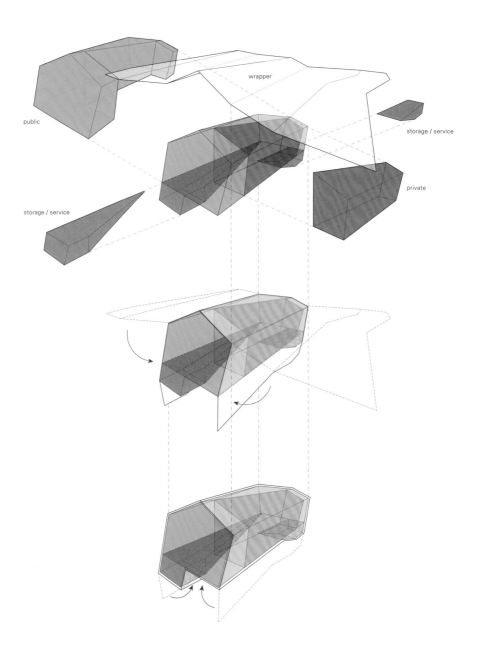

Shell as continuous wrapped surface

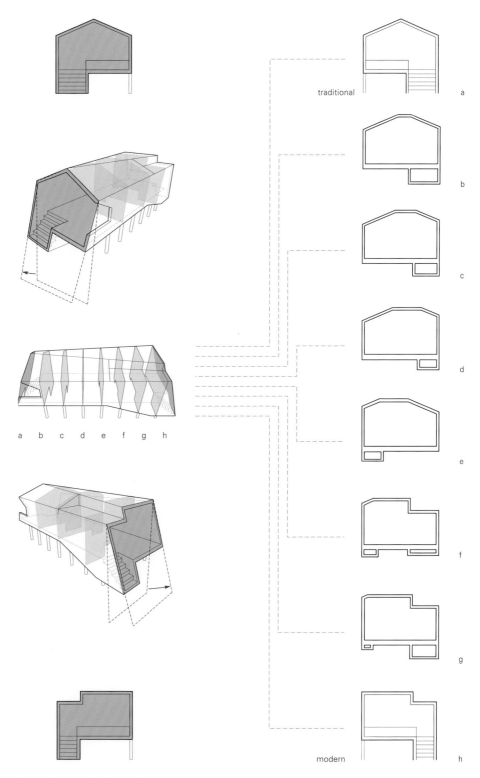

traditional — a

b

c

d

e

f

g

modern — h

a b c d e f g h

Morph of cross section iconography

KieranTimberlake
Philadelphia, PA

The proposed design is a flexible, integrated system developed to accommodate a range of customizable options from interior program to environmental systems to aesthetics. The design anticipates a transition from stick-built construction in the first generation to local off-site fabricated subassemblies in later generations. The basic structure and organization of the house is comparable to the chassis of an automobile fitted with optional components and assemblies that vary the specifics of its function and its appearance. Through selection of options the house is readily customized to satisfy a range of conditions and desires. Homeowners are encouraged to deploy this array of variables as they see fit. The architects see this approach as essential toward rebuilding a neighborhood and not simply providing shelter.

Two options are depicted, but it is important to note that many sub-options for materials, systems, and aesthetics are available. The Garden prototype includes a roof deck, sunscreens, and mesh trellis. The Gable prototype includes sunscreens, slatted trellis, and an area of refuge. The chassis is the same for both. The floor plans consolidate "dry" and "wet" spaces into zones to maximize efficiency and allow for options. Plumbing systems are consolidated into a linear cluster of "wet" rooms that facilitate choice in the quantity and arrangement of these spaces. A small study or a screened side porch can be substituted for an extra bathroom. These spaces are treated as modules that can be selected, grouped, and ultimately fabricated as individual assemblies that make up a whole. Similarly the quantities and types of "dry" living spaces can be grouped linearly in arrangements that are limited mainly by the length of the site. Variations to the exterior fit-out, including photovoltaic panels, sunscreens, grade level storage, and an expandable rainwater collection system, allow the house to accommodate the varying needs and budgets of a range of homeowners.

Economies of Scale As the process of construction moves toward a component-based approach in the second generation of implementation, each house becomes simpler to assemble, customize,

and ultimately disassemble. As a construction system, this process offers substantial improvements over conventional stick-built practices, not only in terms of reducing on-site labor and increasing quality, but also in terms of reducing waste and streamlining fabrication processes.

Rebuilding the Local Economy   In the spirit of Cradle to Cradle protocol, the technology and materials associated with this house will continue to be optimized with time. This extends beyond selection of materials to include jobsite construction practices that promote safe and healthy working conditions and minimize waste. As the prototype transitions from stick-built construction to off-site fabrication, KieranTimberlake advocates establishing a local facility for fabrication of building components and assemblies. An existing

warehouse space can be adapted for this purpose. Utilizing Lower Ninth Ward labor, this model aspires to create a self-sustaining local industry of component fabrication that can be maintained after the Lower Ninth Ward and surrounding areas are rebuilt. Recognizing the great need for low-cost, customizable, and sustainable housing in New Orleans and beyond, this effort will facilitate high quality standards for rebuilding and capitalize on a burgeoning market demand. Ultimately an economically revitalized and physically renewed Lower Ninth Ward could be the phoenix that arises from the great tragedy of Katrina.

Team: Stephen Kieran, FAIA; James Timberlake, FAIA; Richard Maimon, AIA; Jules Dingle, AIA; Mark Davis; Andrew Evans; Aaron Knorr; Jeremy Leman; Sarah Savage

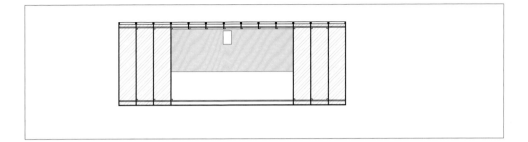

Roof plan

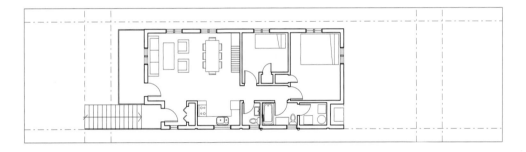

First floor

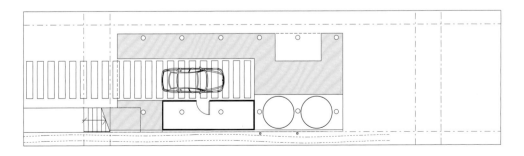

Ground floor

0 2   5   10   N

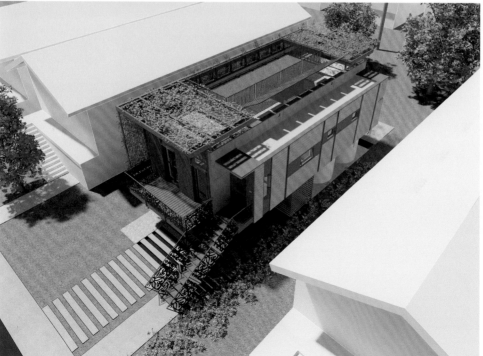

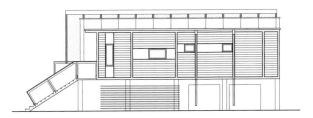

Northern elevation

Eastern elevation

Southern elevation

Western elevation

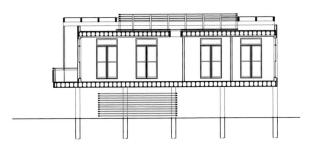

Longitudinal section

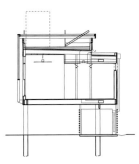

Cross section

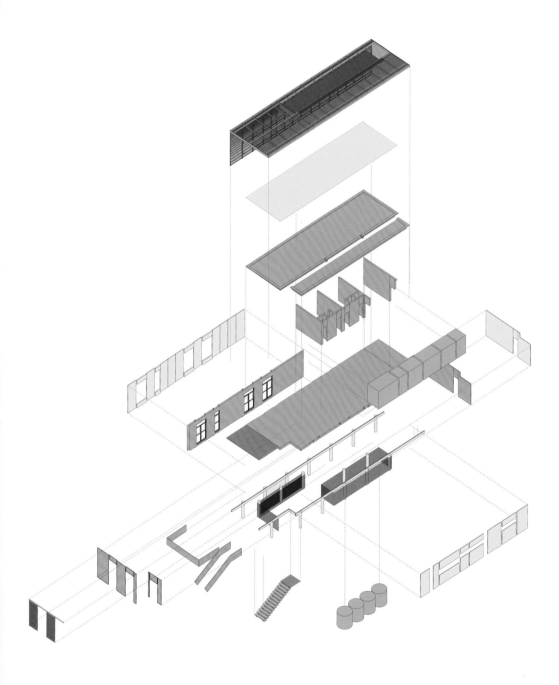

Third-generation fabrication strategies

On-site, stick-built construction
Off-site panelized assembly
Off-site modular fabrication

Common Components

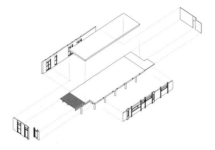

Platform structure, exterior shell system

Personal Choices

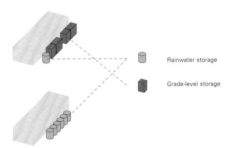

Rainwater storage

Grade-level storage

Roof system

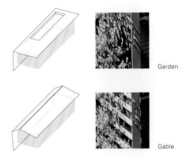

Garden

Gable

Ground-level usage

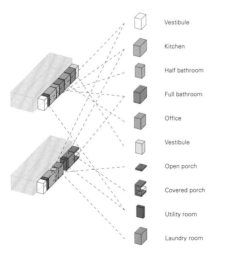

Vestibule

Kitchen

Half bathroom

Full bathroom

Office

Vestibule

Open porch

Covered porch

Utility room

Laundry room

Wet-core component layout

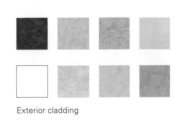

Exterior cladding

Laser-cut cement board,
metal, or marine-grade plywood

Local artist fabrication

Filigree pattern

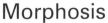

Morphosis
Santa Monica, CA

New Orleans will not endure without a broad, macro-scale vision that addresses and synthesizes the region's unique social, cultural, economic, and ecological conditions. Morphosis has responded to the Make It Right Foundation's initiative "to be a catalyst for redevelopment of the Lower Ninth Ward, by building a neighborhood comprised of safe and healthy homes that are inspired by Cradle to Cradle thinking, with an emphasis on high quality design, while preserving the spirit of the community's culture," with what can be considered a micro-scale solution to the region's problems— a prototype for a single-family dwelling that addresses the immediate and critical need for safe and healthy housing in the Lower Ninth Ward. The design for this prototype proposes a self-sustaining structure designed to function independent of civic infrastructure and services and to survive the inevitable environmental dangers of the area without catastrophic damage and loss of life.

As designers, the office has chosen to exploit its strengths as outsiders—removed from local politics and conflicts of interest—while addressing the potential weakness of their "naiveté" by engaging local advisors in the process. This process involved ongoing dialogues with pillars of the local architectural, political, and academic communities; compilation and analysis of both pre- and post-Katrina press, reports, proposals, and data; precedent studies of historical disasters and comparable world cities; and finally, the proposal of their own solution as a way to analyze and define the problem, and move the important dialogue about this city's future forward.

Floating House   The Shotgun house, predominant throughout New Orleans, can be broken down into two primary components: the house itself, where the residents live; and the foundation, on which the house sits. To enable the residents of the Lower Ninth Ward to once again craft their culture, Morphosis has reinvented the foundation upon which they can build.

The concept is twofold:

1. To design a foundation that enables the house to function independently of the basic infrastructure and public services that have yet to be adequately repaired in the Lower Ninth Ward and which are likely to fail again.

2. To create a new house that rests upon that foundation but is wholly integrated with the natural environment, respectful of New Orleans vernacular, and enriched with sustainable technologies.

To accomplish this, the foundation of the house must be simultaneously specific and forgiving, like the chassis of a car. The chassis hosts all of the essential mechanical and technological equipment to provide the house with power, water, and fresh air. Additionally, the foundation should protect the house from future water and weather threats. To accomplish this, the foundation was engineered out of expanded polystyrene foam, which is encased in glass fiber-reinforced concrete. This composite results in a strong, resilient foundation that will float with rising flood water.

The chassis of the house is the primary element around which the rest of the house is organized and assembled. Consisting of a thickened raft slab, a service core, and a large rooftop rain collector, it is designed to take maximum advantage of shop labor rates and quality control available through off-site fabrication. Constructed of polystyrene foam and glass fiber-reinforced concrete, the prefabricated unit is shipped as a whole to the site with all required wall anchors, rough-ins, electrical and mechanical routing pre-installed. Sized for transportation on a standard flatbed trailer, all required system storage and internal infrastructure are installed in the shop. The unit is placed on site atop four stabilizing concrete pads located between two rear steel masts which act as the anchors for the house when in flood mode. The concrete pads and their associated grade beam are constructed on site using local labor and conventional construction techniques. Finally, the modular wall framing, interior finish elements, prefabricated roofing, and remaining system components arrive on site for assembly in the field. The specific design and resultant form of the chassis allows for easy maintenance of all systems. Rainwater collection tanks are accessed from outside the house, while filters, batteries, and mechanical components are accessed from within.

Principal Designer: Thom Mayne
Project Manager: Brandon Welling
Project Designer: Andrea Manning
Project Team: Andrew Batay-Csorba, Anne Marie Burke,
Natalia Traverso Caruana, Tim Christ, Hugo Martinez,
Greg Neudorf, Martin Summers, Aleksander Tamm-Seitz
With: Sustainable Consulting: Ted Bardeke, Global Green
Structural Engineer: Bruce Gibbons, Thornton Tomasetti
Local Urban Consultant: Allen Eskew, Eskew + Dumez + Ripple

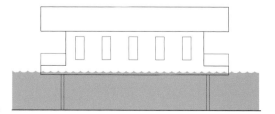

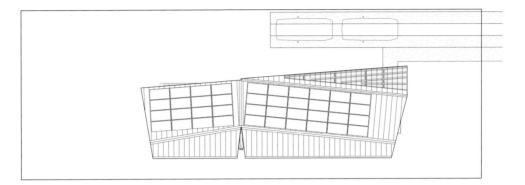

Roof plan

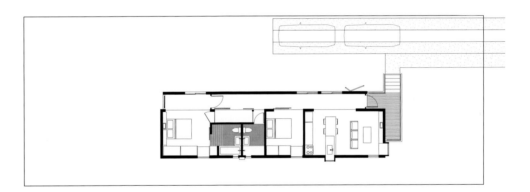

Floor plan

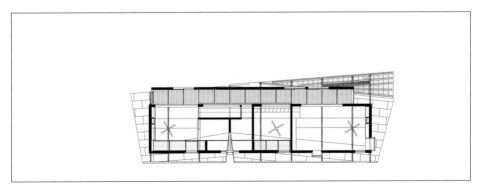

Reflected ceiling plan

0 2   5   10   N

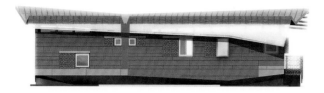

Southern elevation

Eastern elevation

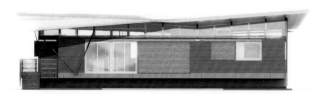

Northern elevation

Western elevation

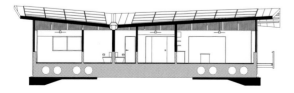

Longitudinal section

Transverse section

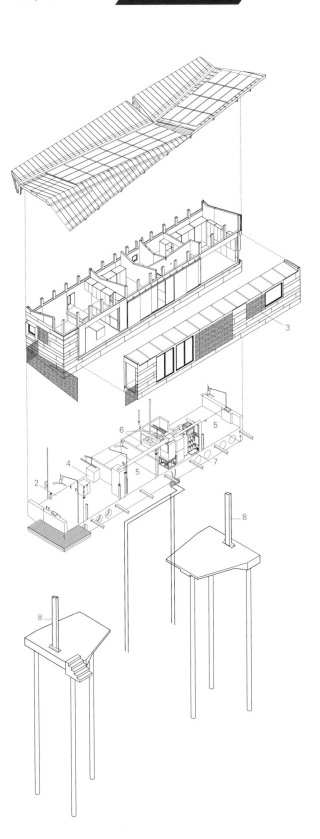

1 Front porch
2 Living room
3 Gallery
4 Kitchen
5 Bedroom
6 Bath
7 Mechanical
8 Guide posts

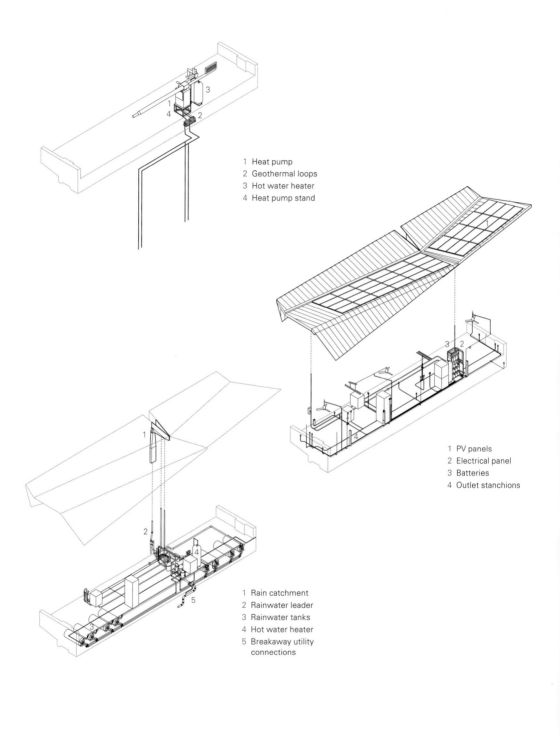

1 Heat pump
2 Geothermal loops
3 Hot water heater
4 Heat pump stand

1 PV panels
2 Electrical panel
3 Batteries
4 Outlet stanchions

1 Rain catchment
2 Rainwater leader
3 Rainwater tanks
4 Hot water heater
5 Breakaway utility
  connections

MVRDV

Rotterdam, Netherlands

The Lower Ninth Ward contradiction: the attempt to rebuild the Lower Ninth Ward in New Orleans, just where the levees broke, is one of a highly courageous level. Since the height and quality of the levees as the connection with surrounding levees is not sufficient to reduce the risk of flooding, living there means living in danger. The primary task is to repair the levees in such a way that they guarantee for this safety. But how long can the population wait for that? Wouldn't they lose even more, namely the ground value, due to that? So: why not starting? With that message every building activity becomes political. Why not stressing that? Why not showing this contradiction explicitly?

By accepting the traditional Shotgun house, with its stretched volume, its painted wood, its porches, the former neighborhood can be restored. It adds to the specialty and the recognition of New Orleans. By adapting this house to the potential risk of flooding, it gives this special typology a way to survive even the hardest storms or floods. By making this the underlying design concept, the houses will show this transition to a wider audience. It becomes a message!

A series of prototypes has been developed. They can create a neighborhood that combines a collective language with a diversified interpretation. It enlarges the diversity and it strengthens the collectivity …

The results are in five Escape Houses which are lifted in a different way. In each lifting act a shady place is created underneath the house. This area can be used as a shadow garden and a carport. It functions as a cooling buffer and facilitates natural ventilation of the house.

MVRDV, Rotterdam, Netherlands
Escape Houses
Design team: Winy Maas, Jacob van Rijs, Nathalie de Vries, Stefan de Koning, Stefan Witteman, Robert Grimm

The Floating House (The Boat)

This house is inspired by recent Dutch housing developments. By positioning the Shotgun house on top of a concrete barge, the house can float in case of floods. It gives the house a distinct concrete socket and the house can be entered at ground level. In the concrete barge the buffer basins for water can be created. It has pockets for the natural ventilation. The house is attached to piles that keep the house in its position when rising with the water level. The front porch can function as a garage so that the car will float with the house.

The House on the Lift

This house is one of the milestones of the operation. By positioning the Shotgun house as high as possible on top of a lift with a stair, the whole house is above potential water level and it becomes a house with a view! By lifting the house to this height the entire lot can be used as a garden.

The Tilted House

By tilting the Shotgun house on one end, the house slopes from the back to the street, reaching its escape position. This creates for the interior a theater-like setting of platforms with rooms, combining intimacy with overview. One enters the house from the back. There is a rear porch close to ground level to enter the garden from the living room. The front porch is at its highest point, creating a great view at street side.

The House on the Ramp

By positioning the Shotgun house on top of a wall with a ramp that is equipped for handicapped access on top, the whole house is above potential water level. It provides a beautiful delicate balancing impression. There is a big shadow space below the house. The ramp structure is enclosed to create garden storage.

The Bent House

By bending the Shotgun house in two directions, a carport at the front and a shadow garden at the rear side is created. For the interior this bending act means that an escape to both the front porch and the rear porch is created. Both the bedrooms and the living room are above water level. It creates an internal collective valley of platforms with rooms that reveals itself while entering. The lower part collects the excess water.

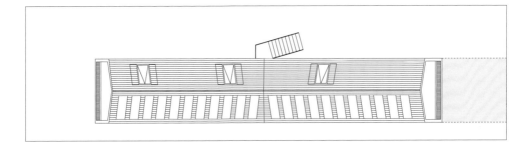

Roof plan

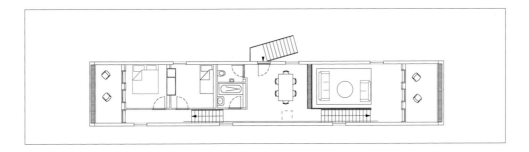

First floor

0 2 5 10 N

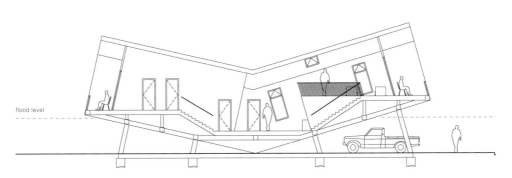

flood level

Longitudinal section

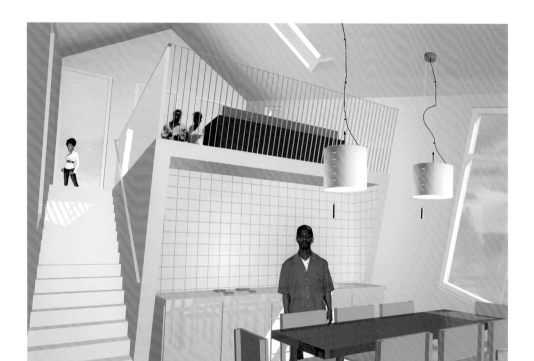

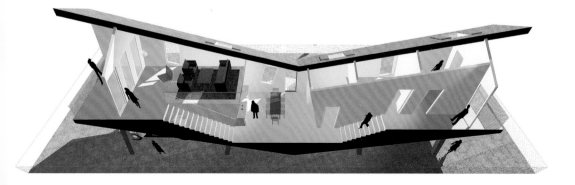

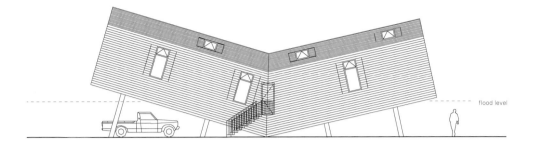

flood level

Northern elevation

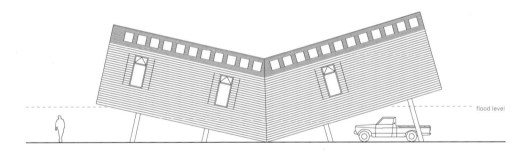

flood level

Southern elevation

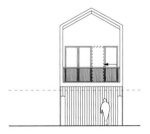

flood level

Eastern elevation

Western elevation

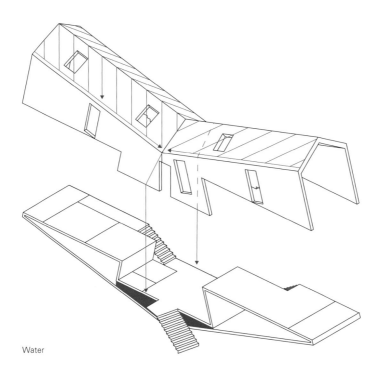

Water

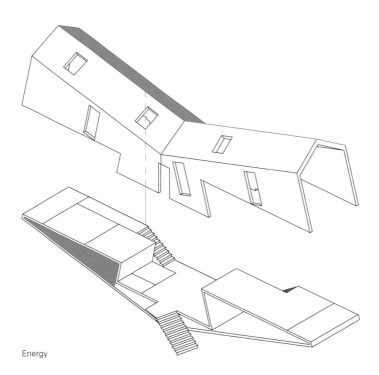

Energy

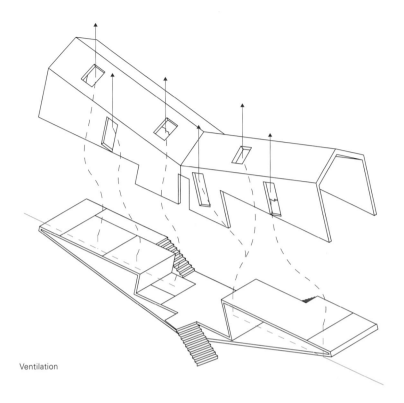

Ventilation

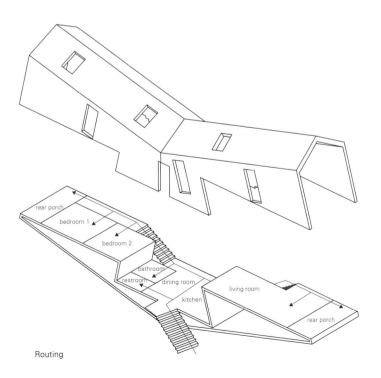

rear porch

bedroom 1

bedroom 2

bathroom

restroom   dining room

kitchen

living room

rear porch

Routing

Pugh+Scarpa Architects
Santa Monica, CA

Pugh+Scarpa's Make it Right (MIR) home seeks to redefine the concept of a home into a flexible, multifunctional, and adaptable space addressing the needs of today's modern family on a limited budget. Offering shelter and comfort, the MIR home breaks the prescriptive mold of the traditional home by creating public and private zones in which private space is de-emphasized, in favor of large public living areas. The organization of the space is intended to transform the way people live—away from a reclusive, isolating layout toward a family-oriented, interactive space. The inspiration for the home came from American patchwork quilting traditions, exemplified by the Gee's Bend Quilters Collective abstract geometric style, which is itself influenced by newspaper and magazine collages used for insulation on the inside walls of homes in the early rural American South. Recycled wooden pallets are repositioned here as a patch-worked shade screen wrapping the building, an innovative alternative to expensive façade materials that lends its own unique character and texture.

The visually expressive pallets impart an imperfect, rough-hewn individuality that Pugh+Scarpa find particularly appealing. The office is working with local manufacturers to ensure the viability of this cost-effective and sustainable off-the-shelf product, easily obtainable and readily replaceable. The pallet wrapping is joined by decoratively perforated cement board on the east and west façades, providing both shade and privacy while allowing views out and dappled, indirect daylight and breezes to enter. All the exterior elements will combine and interweave, emerging as a distinctive pattern-making aesthetic.

Pugh+Scarpa's approach to Cradle to Cradle sustainability begins with passive solar design strategies, such as locating and orienting the building to control solar cooling and heat loads; shaping and orienting the building for exposure to prevailing winds; shaping the building to induce buoyancy for natural ventilation; and shaping and planning the interior to enhance daylight and natural airflow distribution. The building responds to the specific conditions of the New Orleans climate in several ways:

On the south side, a generous exterior porch with deep overhangs and a shade screen provides passive solar protection for the building's interior. Similarly, openings on the east and west sides are protected with deeper overhangs, vertical screens, and porches. The north side is allowed to be flat and exposed, which affords natural daylighting with a minimum of solar heat gain. The roof is sloped to induce airflow. The non-structural exterior skin—made from recycled wood pallets and cement board—offers shading and a thermal break to the building structure, providing relief from direct solar heat gain. High ceilings and abundant cross ventilation allow heat to escape the building's interior. Cooling airflow inside the home is enhanced by ceiling fans, a direct-drive exhaust fan, and operable windows, which create abundant cross ventilation. All materials selected are commercially available, cost-effective, and eco-friendly. All appliances are Energy Star rated. The interior organization separates living and sleeping areas into two zones, permitting them to be independently conditioned. This compartmentalized strategy means that more efficient systems can be used, increasing sustainability and cost savings to the homeowner. The home's high ceilings promote an airy, spacious ambiance, and will be less reliant on artificial lighting.

Pugh + Scarpa Architects, Santa Monica, CA
High House
Project Team: Larry Scarpa, Angie Brooks, Niki Randall, Brad Buter, Jordon Gearhart, Matthew Majack

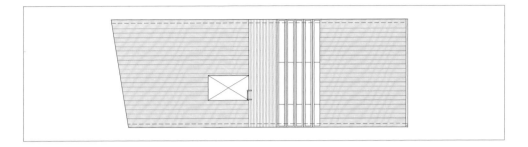

Roof plan

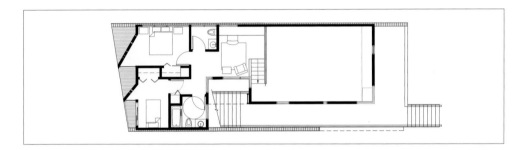

First floor

Ground floor

0 2 5 10 N

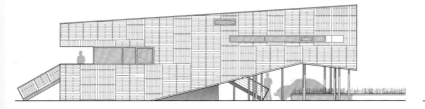

Northern elevation

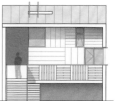

Western elevation

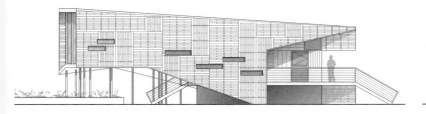

Southern elevation

Eastern elevation

Longitudinal section

Cross section

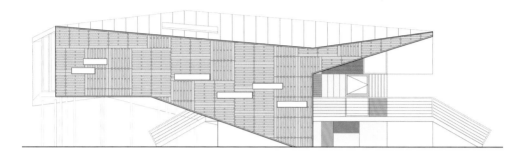

South façade material patterning

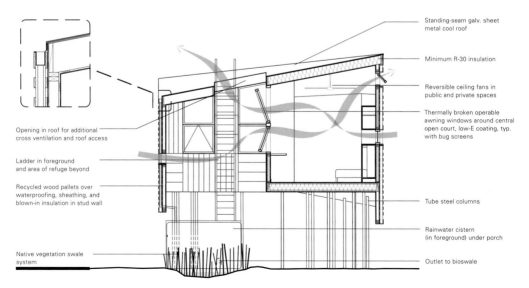

Standing-seam galv. sheet
metal cool roof

Minimum R-30 insulation

Reversible ceiling fans in
public and private spaces

Thermally broken operable
awning windows around central
open court, low-E coating, typ.
with bug screens

Opening in roof for additional
cross ventilation and roof access

Ladder in foreground
and area of refuge beyond

Recycled wood pallets over
waterproofing, sheathing, and
blown-in insulation in stud wall

Tube steel columns

Rainwater cistern
(in foreground) under porch

Native vegetation swale
system

Outlet to bioswale

Sustainable systems diagram

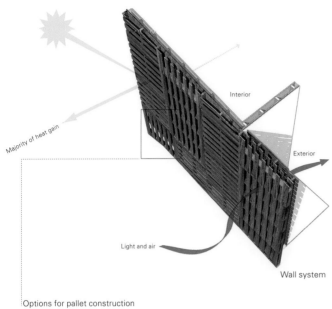

Interior

Exterior

Majority of heat gain

Light and air

Wall system

Options for pallet construction

Pallet Option 1
Typical wood pallet

Pallet Option 2
Trex wood pallet

Pallet Option 3
Cement board pallet

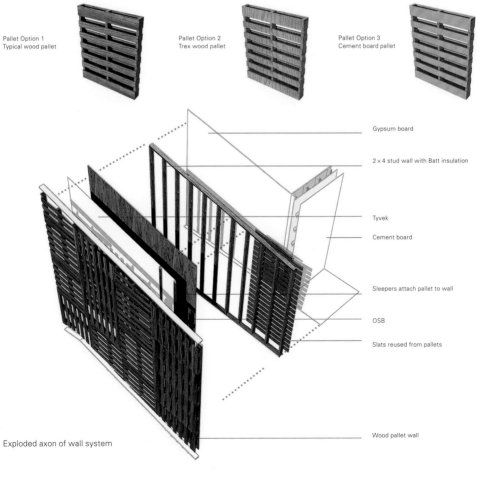

Gypsum board

2 × 4 stud wall with Batt insulation

Tyvek

Cement board

Sleepers attach pallet to wall

OSB

Slats reused from pallets

Wood pallet wall

Exploded axon of wall system

Shigeru Ban Architects
Tokyo, Japan

The structural furniture unit (SFU) is the foundation of Shigeru Ban's approach to the housing proposal for the Lower Ninth Ward. In this integrated structural component, storage, insulation, and materiality are already defined and provided. The most significant advantages of incorporating the SFUs are lower costs and increased safety. Constructed off-site, the prefabricated SFUs ensure high quality while driving down costs. The SFUs are able to withstand hurricane winds while providing structural bracing to support the roof allowing for an open floor plan and walls of glass that open to the outside. The repetition of these elements will enable affected residents to have a pre-established place to house clothes and personal objects alike.

The structural furniture units are constructed in a factory environment which allows for greater precision than field construction techniques. The modular nature of the structural system provides a method to rapidly erect the structure while greatly diminishing construction costs, and because the units are easily moved and installed by a single individual, the construction process relies less on highly skilled labor. Vertical framing is eliminated and the sideboards are constructed with backboards to create a wooden structure in the shape of a C-channel. Due to its shape, the structure can bear the lateral forces parallel to the backboard, and although its efficiency decreases, it is also able to bear lateral forces in the perpendicular orthogonal direction.

The house itself takes on a form similar to the Shotgun style of New Orleans typology and keeps intact the important connection to the outside and surrounding community via both front porch and terrace. At the terrace, located at the center of the house, resides a Bald Cypress tree—native to and state tree of Louisiana—to provide not only a natural shading/cooling device for the residence, but to restore a part of the New Orleans landscape that was once taken away. Additional components include a standing-seam metal roof defining an attic space that provides a safe haven in the event of future floods and as an area for future expansion of the house. Passive environmental strategies have been incorporated through floor-to-ceiling

operable walls and windows allowing cross ventilation, reduced sun exposure, and sustainable material selection.

The house is oriented on a typical east-west lot with the terrace facing south. This orientation is important in order for the tree to provide shade in the summer while allowing warm sun to penetrate the house in the winter. Additional native plants and trees would be added at both front and back yards to produce the same effects. The driveway consists of grass/concrete pavers in order to avoid impervious surfaces being placed on site. The house would be mirrored along the east-west axis to be sited at other east-west lots with east entries to the lot to preserve the original orientation of the house and south-facing terrace.

Shigeru Ban Architects, Tokyo
In association with Dean Maltz Architects, New York
Furniture House 6
Shigeru Ban, Dean Maltz, Grady Gillies, Chad Kraus

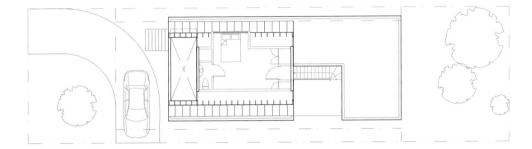

Roof plan

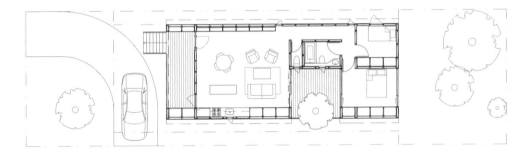

First floor

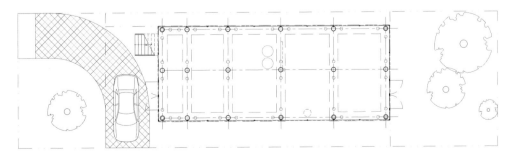

Ground floor

0 2   5   10   N

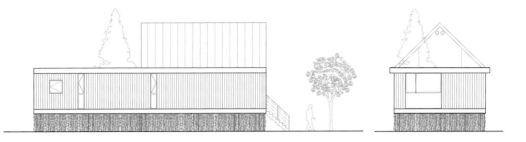

Northern elevation

Eastern elevation

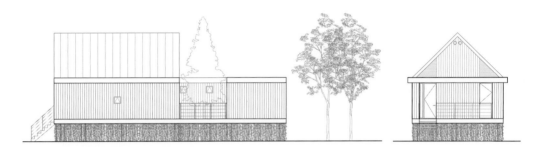

Southern elevation

Western elevation

Longitudinal section

Cross section

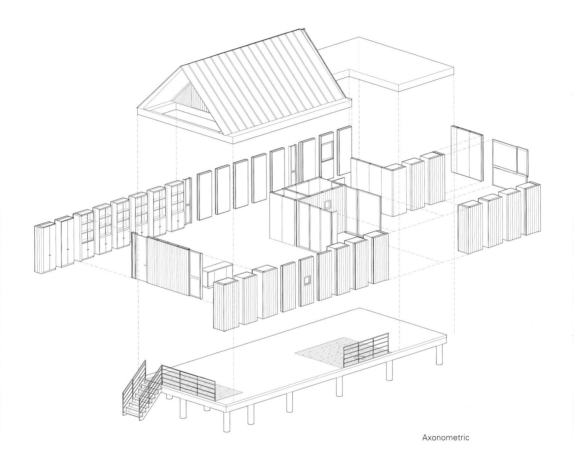

Axonometric

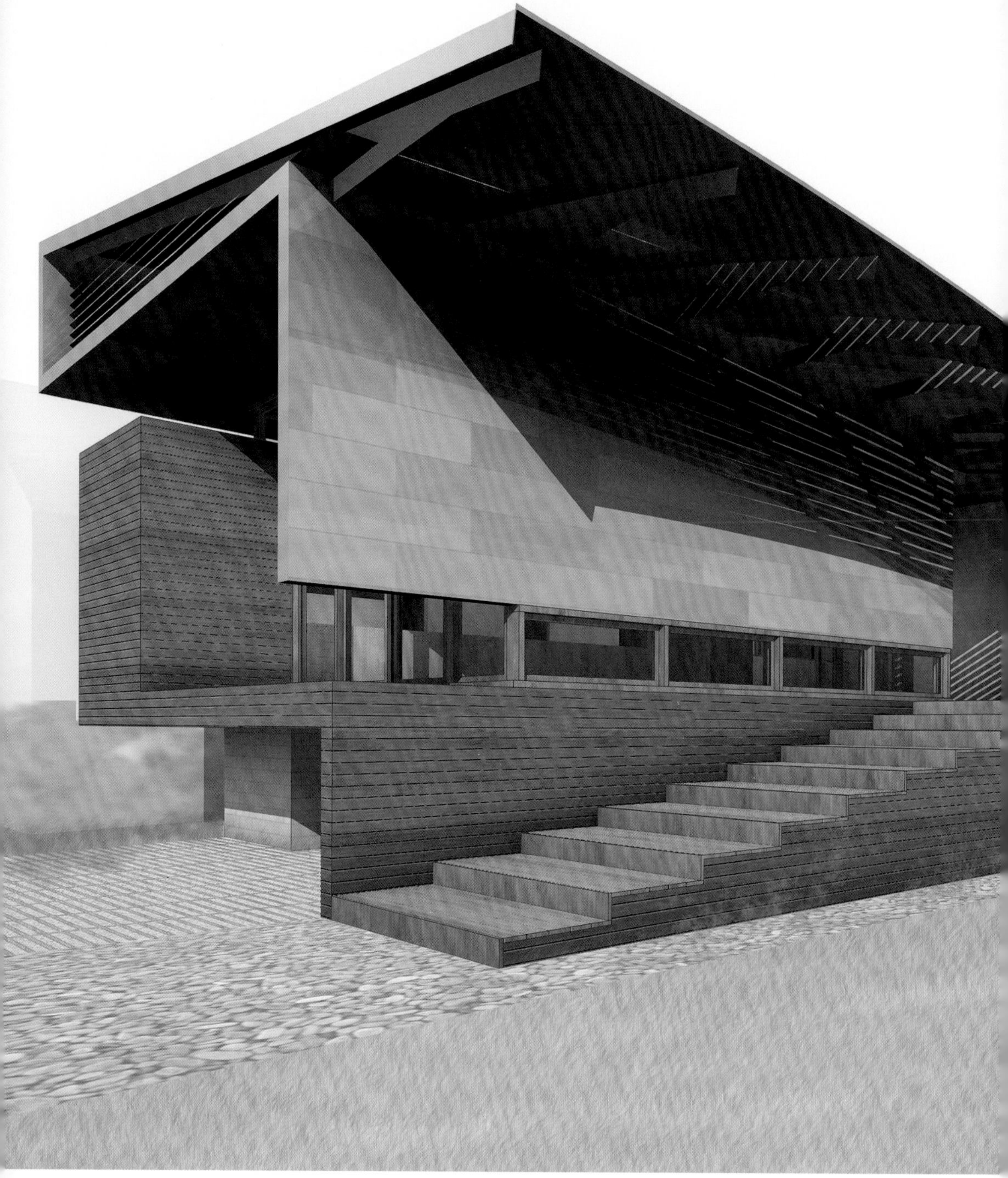

Trahan Architects
New Orleans, LA

The displaced landscape left behind by the receding waters after Hurricane Katrina has allowed new opportunities for connections between figure and ground that have long been obscured. The New Orleans Shotgun house typology is the resultant of lot constraints, environmental conditions, and efficient planning. The approach to the project was to identify these main characteristics and represent them in a more contemporary vision. As the design focuses on "safe" materials and low utility consumption, the roof becomes the main architectural expression that subtly gestures at the form of the pitched roofs common to the area of the Lower Ninth Ward. While reinforcing a familiar experience of place, the roof integrates entry, circulation, and gathering spaces into degrees of outsidedness that are typical of New Orleans typologies and their emphasis on the "porch." As the roof began to evolve from practical form and function, it transitioned into a high-performance component that acts as a shading device, rain screen, water collector, solar energy collector, and solar water heater.

Trahan Architects' general approach is defined by two main architectural elements. The first element is the low-cost passive box. Here the design is driven by meeting the demands of a limited budget and use of specialized materials/assemblies addressing the project's greater sustainability goals. Being part of a larger construction site, the scale of economy dictates the construction technique of the box (i.e., stick built, modular, or SIPs). Efficiency of the plan/elevated slab is achieved by centralizing the main entry/porch and minimizing the interior corridor. The plan is striated horizontally into two main programmatic groups: living spaces and service spaces. The main entry/porch is used to reinforce visual and physical separation from public to private spaces. A 5'0" finish floor elevation was set to have the strongest connection with the living memory of place and local foot traffic. To ground the design, the box is clad and skirted along the base.

The second element is the high-performance roof. A unique identity derived from the gable roof, passive and active sustainability systems are inte-

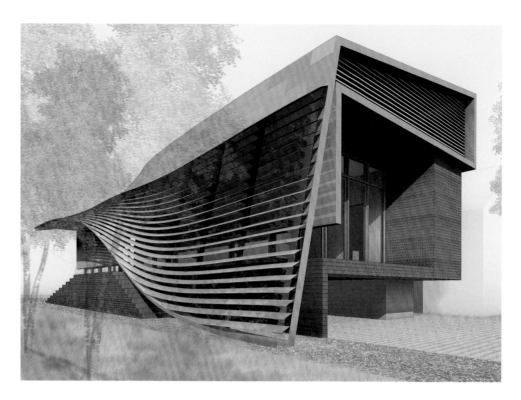

grated into a single design feature. Because of the expressive hybrid roof—low tech and high tech, integrated technical systems requiring quality control—this element is best panelized and produced in a manufacturing environment to exacting specifications. One main aspect of the roof was to address solar heat gain. The outermost roofing material will have a high solar reflective index. As the slope transitions into the "rotated gable," the south pitch begins to roll down and provide an increasing level of shade and filtered light. This south roof pitch also begins to pull apart into louvers or "gills." These louvers allow appropriate amounts of daylight as well as opportunities for air circulation and ventilation of the attic. The roof's extended overhangs on the west and east sides also provide an effective level of protection. The roof addresses the issue of water. On one hand, it serves as the conventional protection from the elements. On the other, it begins to focus on the idea of "re-using" or capturing that which the roof is diverting. The slope of the roof captures and directs water to its sloping side, where the "gills" act as small gutters. Water is channeled along these flowing "gills" into a retention system, where it can be used for gray-water purposes.

Principal: Trey Trahan, FAIA
Design Team: Mark Hash, Sean David, Stuart Helo, Michael McCune, Ed Gaskin

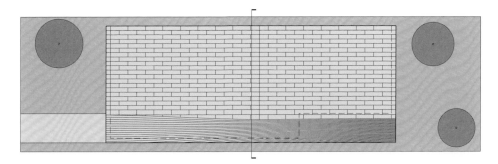

Roof plan

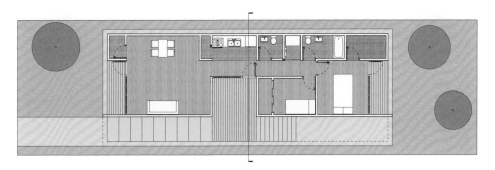

First floor

0 2   5   10   N

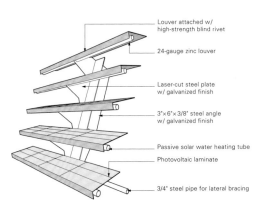

Louver detail

Louver attached w/
high-strength blind rivet

24-gauge zinc louver

Laser-cut steel plate
w/ galvanized finish

3"×6"×3/8" steel angle
w/ galvanized finish

Passive solar water heating tube

Photovoltaic laminate

3/4" steel pipe for lateral bracing

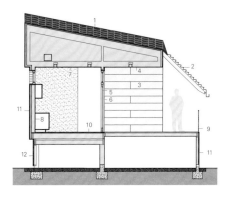

1	DLSS zinc roof system	7	Painted gypsum board ceiling
2	Zinc louvers	8	Painted gypsum board wall
3	SLSS zinc wall system	9	Galvanized steel guardrail
4	SLSS zinc soffit system	10	Wood flooring
5	Insulated low-E clear glass	11	Spanish cedar siding
6	Aluminum-clad wood door frame	12	Spanish cedar lattice

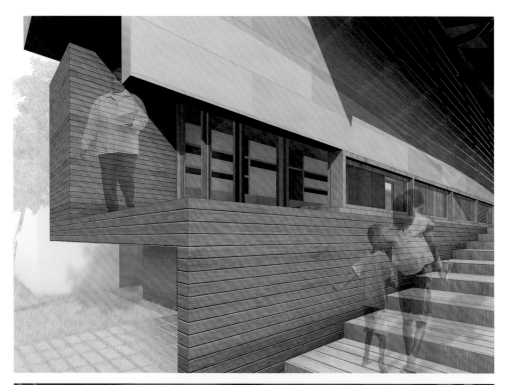

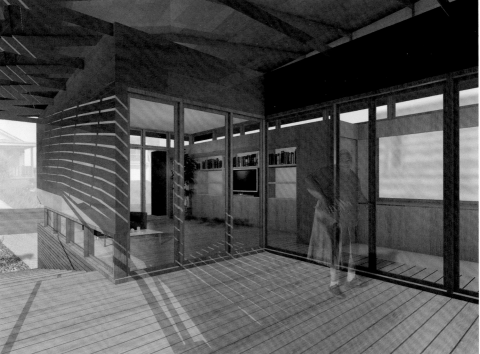

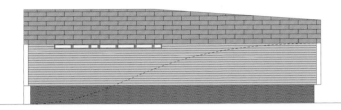

Northern elevation

Eastern elevation

Southern elevation

Western elevation

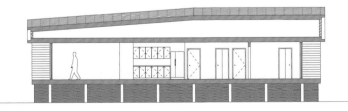

Longitudinal section

Cross section

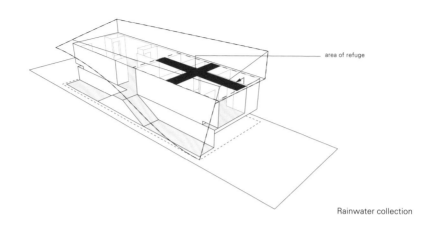

area of refuge

Rainwater collection

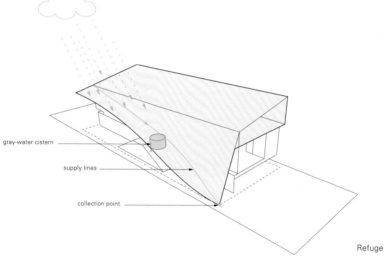

gray-water cistern

supply lines

collection point

Refuge

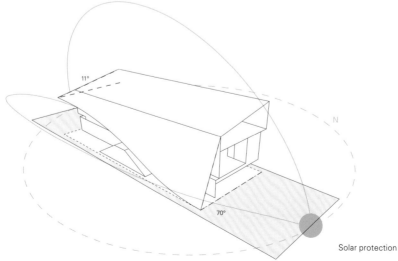

11°

N

70°

Solar protection

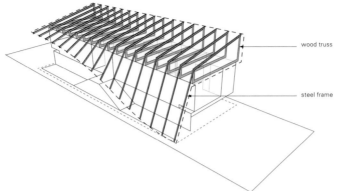

wood truss

steel frame

Framing diagram

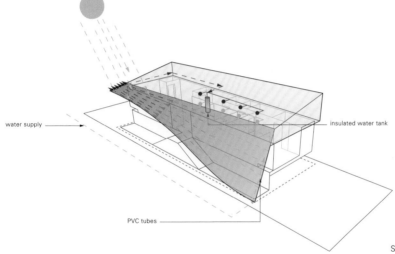

water supply

insulated water tank

PVC tubes

Solar thermal water heating
with evacuated tubes

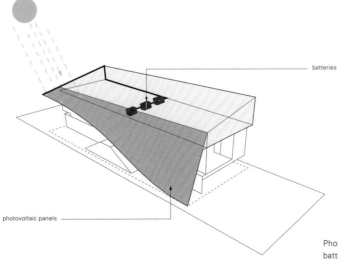

batteries

photovoltaic panels

Photovoltaic panels with
battery storage

As MIR's mission
keeps growing,
new architects
have been asked
to join the cause.
By now
the design approach
generates
interest
all over the world,
from governments and
people in need.

GRAFT

Atelier Hitoshi Abe

Hitoshi Abe

Bild Design

Will Soniat

Byron Mouton

buildingstudio

Coleman Coker

ELEMENTAL

Alejandro Aravena

Gehry Partners, LLP

Frank Gehry

Tensho Takemori

Waggonner & Ball Architects

Mac Ball

David Waggonner

William McDonough+Partners

William McDonough

Kevin Burke

Page 250

Atelier Hitoshi Abe
Sendai, Japan; Los Angeles, CA

Hitoshi Abe is chair and professor of the UCLA Department of Architecture and Urban Design. Known for architecture that is spatially complex and structurally innovative, the work of Atelier Hitoshi Abe has been published internationally and received numerous awards, including most recently the 2009 Architectural Institute of Japan Award for SSM/Kanno Museum. Principal of his own firm, he founded Atelier Hitoshi Abe in 1993 in Sendai, Japan, and recently opened a second office in Los Angeles. Some of his key projects located in Japan include the Aoba-tei Restaurant, the Sasaki Office Factory for Prosthetics, the Miyagi Stadium in Rifu, SSM/Kanno Museum in Shiogama, the 9-tsubo House "Tall" in Kana-gawa, and the Reihoku Community Hall in Kuma-moto.

Page 258

Bild Design
New Orleans, LA

Bild Design is an assembly of independent architects, designers, and fabricators that come together with their own portfolios of experience and talent—in an effort to share in the realization of built form. Founded in 1998 by Byron Mouton, architect, educator, and New Orleans native, the studio's design focus attempts to merge investigations of assembly and space with material research and regional response. Present studio investigations focus on both. In addition, recent projects are influenced by and aim to address the needs of a culture struggling with issues of decay, economic shortage, preservation, and progress. Many Bild collaborators are academically involved through the Tulane School of Architecture. In addition, close associations with other related disciplines and professions help to maintain an effective network of design-build relationships, successfully advancing the realization of conceptual thought.

Presentation of Designs II

Page 282

buildingstudio
New Orleans, LA

Buildingstudio is a small collaborative firm whose work is regularly acknowledged for its design excellence. They've received numerous honors including a P/A Design Award for low-cost housing for "Breaking the Cycle of Poverty," Emerging Voices from the Architectural League of New York, numerous Architectural Record Record House awards, and National AIA Honor awards. Buildingstudio's work has been highlighted at MoMA, SF MoMA, Wexner Center for the Arts, the Cooper-Hewitt National Design Museum, and the National Building Museum in Washington, D.C.

Page 298

ELEMENTAL
Santiago, Chile

ELEMENTAL is a Do Tank. Our field of action is the city. ELEMENTAL is a partner of Universidad Católica and Chilean Oil Company COPEC. Its focus is the design and implementation of urban projects of public interest and social impact. If there is any agreement in the world today, is that we need to correct the inequalities of our societies. For that, the only sustainable, but long-term way is education and income redistribution. The city, if well designed, might be a shortcut. ELEMENTAL does housing, public space, transport, or infrastructural projects, operating in the city as a shortcut to equality.

Page 306

Gehry Partners, LLP
Los Angeles, CA

Page 338

Waggonner & Ball Architects
New Orleans, LA

Gehry Partners, LLP is a full-service architectural firm with extensive international experience in the design and construction of academic, museum, theater, performance, commercial, and master planning projects. Founded in 1962 and located in Los Angeles, California. Every project undertaken by Gehry Partners is designed personally and directly by Frank Gehry, and supported by the vast resources of the firm and the extensive experience of the firm's senior partners and staff. At any given time, the partnership has as many as twenty-five projects in various stages of development from design through construction, which vary in size from the large-scale Guggenheim Abu Dhabi Museum in the United Arab Emirates to projects as small as the temporary pavilion recently completed for the Serpentine Gallery in London.

Waggonner & Ball Architects is an award-winning architectural and planning firm located in New Orleans' historic Garden District. Led by David Waggonner and Mac Ball, the firm has designed projects in the educational, retail, office, religious, government, residential, and planning categories. Inspired by and familiar with New Orleans' rich and diverse array of neighborhoods from its work on projects throughout Orleans Parish, the office also participated in the post-Katrina Unified New Orleans Plan. In concord with each client's mission and program, belief in the primacy of site and the land and respect for the importance of context and culture influence the firm's approach to architectural form. Employing a modern sensibility with a commitment to sustainable design, Waggonner & Ball attempts to get to the essence of architecture, which is timeless.

Page 346

William McDonough+ Partners

Charlottesville, VA; San Francisco, CA

William McDonough+Partners view ecological issues both as the source of innovative design solutions and as a fundamental measure of quality. Thoughtful design, mirroring the regenerative productivity of nature, is used to create a built environment that is sustaining, not merely sustainable. By seeking solutions that are not just "less bad" (efficient) but actually "more good" (effective), eco-effective design embraces the pursuit of maximum value, addressing issues of economy, ecology, and social impact at all scales from the region to the molecule. Fundamental to this approach is an emphasis on the Cradle to Cradle thinking developed by William McDonough and Michael Braungart. Through an eco-effective approach, William McDonough+Partners are guided by principles that emulate natural systems, envision a solar-powered world, celebrate diversity, and anticipate design evolution.

Atelier Hitoshi Abe

Sendai, Japan; Los Angeles, CA

"Hot Links" offers many different options for smart living. Through the inherit flexibility of its organization, this house can accommodate many configurations, including single-family, multiple-family, renter/tenant, and live-work arrangements.

Two Shotgun houses are linked together and are able to open, close, or share the space between. In this way, much larger open spaces are created for private bedrooms or public living spaces. The flexible boundary between the residences can be soft and adapt to the changing needs of a family throughout the years. The array of choices gives families freedom to adapt the living size to their economic situation with little cost. If an owner desires a single-family residence, they can choose from a three-, four-, five-, or six-bedroom house. If an owner requires less space, they can split the residence into a duplex, granny unit, or a live-work unit to enable the growth of a small business. Owners are able to recreate and customize their living situation as needed. The economic benefits of a flexible structure also translate into ecological benefits of a reusable or repurposed structure.

The façade of the building has been developed following a strategy of flexibility as well. It can absorb different colors, sizes, and quantities of siding depending on the availability of materials or economic conditions at a given time. Weaving different colors into one façade and taking advantage of this adaptability creates a new identity and residential fabric.

Hitoshi Abe, Midori Mizuhara, Ryohei Koike, Joe Willendra, Carmen Cham

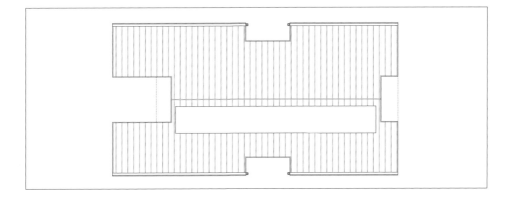

Roof plan

First floor

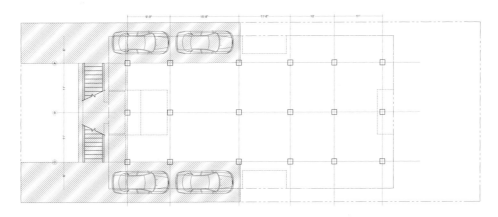

Ground floor

0 2   5   10   N

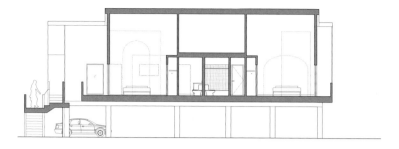

Longitudinal section

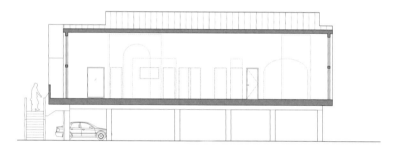

Longitudinal section

Cross section

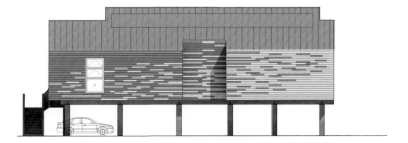

Southern elevation

Northern elevation

Western elevation

Eastern elevation

Variations matrix

Bild Design
New Orleans, LA

In response to the deficiencies illuminated by Hurricane Katrina, homes are being raised an increased distance from the ground. This is not unusual, since the most reliable building types of the region already sit upon piers, and occupants are accustomed to an elevated existence. However, in New Orleans the public activities of the neighborhood are rarely distanced from the private activities of the home; the shallow and thin spaces between inside and outside are often busy. Neighbors frequently sit upon the front porch or stoop of the home engaged in conversation with friends and family. Outdoor dining is a common activity of the culture, and eyes are often on the street. Through the presence of these events, community members provide security for and investment in their neighborhood.

While it is now required that Bild Design build at an increased distance from the ground, this duplex proposal also attempts to maintain the familiar connection between the home and neighborhood. One unit of the strategy is reduced in area and maintained at a closer proximity to the ground, while the second unit is developed with increased area and is raised at a higher elevation in anticipation of the threat of flood. While a reduced portion of the dwelling is put at risk attempting to maintain a link to the social network of the street, a larger portion of the dwelling is elevated to provide an added sense of security and permanence. If the city is again devastated by flood, the lower/reduced portion of the structure may need repair, but the upper components of the home are preserved.

The efficiency unit may be utilized as a rentable apartment to aid in the financing of the entire duplex, or as a unit for an ailing family member. It may also be used as a future extension of the primary three-bedroom unit. In fact, a young family could initially live upstairs and rent out the lower portion of the structure; as the family grows, it could expand into the entire structure by simply removing the party wall and converting the duplex into a single-family residence. This is already a common condition of New Orleans. The familiar Double-Shotgun house type of the region is often passed down from generation to generation and

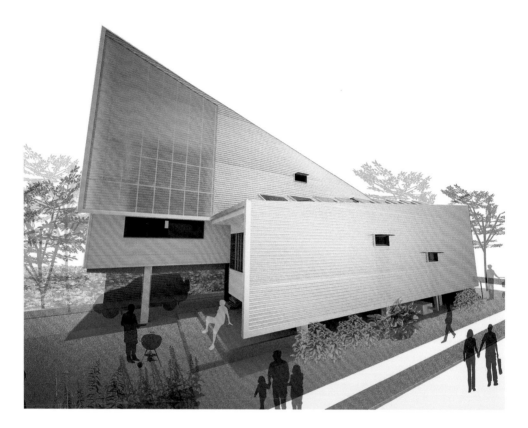

altered to accommodate fluctuations in changing family lifestyles.

The underside of the scheme's larger raised component acts primarily as the upper unit's side entry portal as well as a location for vehicles; however, it may also be used as a site for the semi-public activities of the home such as a "play area" for kids, and shelter for community engagements. In support of the shared urban activities of community, priority is given to the visible site of side-yard activities rather than the concealed site of rear-yard activities.

In addition, upper-level components of the proposal are equally developed with connection to the outdoors. The street face of the primary unit houses a second-level porch so that occupants of that home also have a public presence. The rear garden is viewed from a second-level master bed-room suite and the third level is provided with a balcony to be used in connection with the laundry room and upper bedrooms. The lower roof of the efficiency unit houses the solar energy system, and is easily accessible and serviceable via a second-level window.

Building with dependence upon an unreliable ground is an oxymoron in New Orleans, but it is a familiar condition. Many of the city's vernacular types have evolved in response to the limitations of climate and a very specific neighborhood culture, a social culture of the street and garden that is dependent upon an intimate relationship with the ground. We are not simply being asked to rebuild homes; rather, we are being asked to rebuild neighborhoods.

Project Team:
Byron Mouton, AIA / Principal + Will Soniat / Collaborator

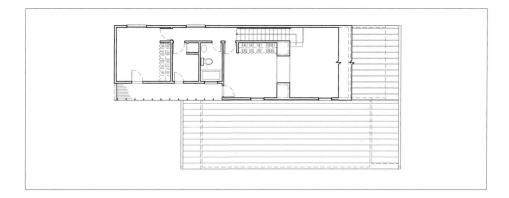

Second floor

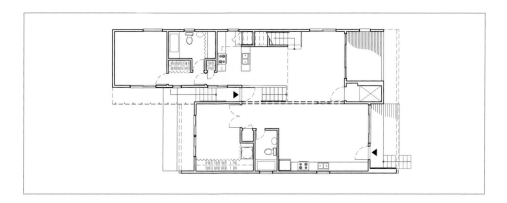

First floor

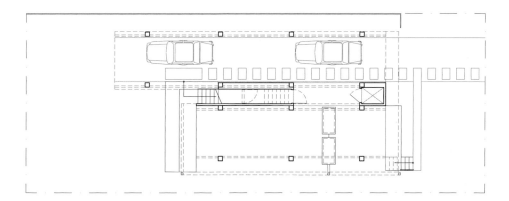

Ground floor

0 2   5   10   N

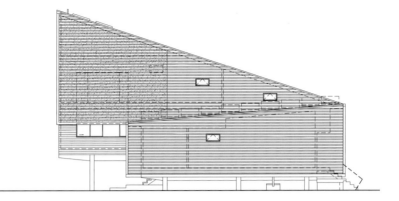

Southern elevation

Northern elevation

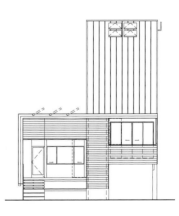

Western elevation   Eastern elevation

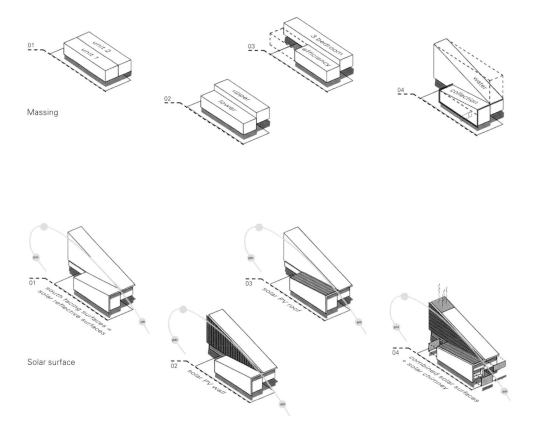

Massing

01 — unit 2 / unit 1

02 — upper / lower

03 — 3 bedroom / efficiency

04 — water collection

Solar surface

01 — south facing surfaces = solar reflective surfaces

02 — solar PV wall

03 — solar PV roof

04 — combined solar surfaces + solar chimney

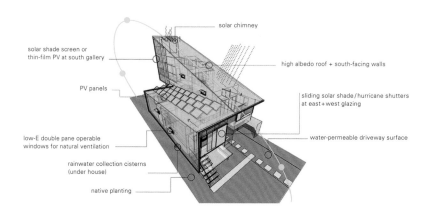

solar chimney

solar shade screen or
thin-film PV at south gallery

high albedo roof + south-facing walls

PV panels

sliding solar shade / hurricane shutters
at east + west glazing

low-E double pane operable
windows for natural ventilation

water-permeable driveway surface

rainwater collection cisterns
(under house)

native planting

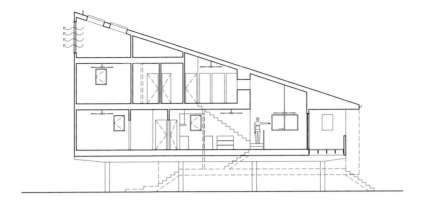

Longitudinal section

Longitudinal section

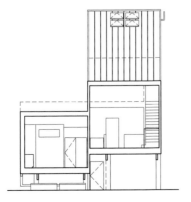

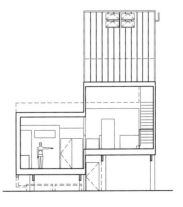

Duplex section

Single-family section

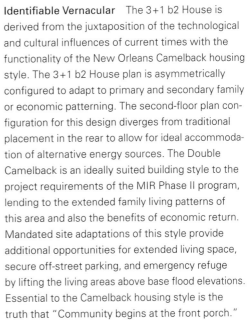

Billes Architecture
New Orleans, LA

Identifiable Vernacular The 3+1 b2 House is derived from the juxtaposition of the technological and cultural influences of current times with the functionality of the New Orleans Camelback housing style. The 3+1 b2 House plan is asymmetrically configured to adapt to primary and secondary family or economic patterning. The second-floor plan configuration for this design diverges from traditional placement in the rear to allow for ideal accommodation of alternative energy sources. The Double Camelback is an ideally suited building style to the project requirements of the MIR Phase II program, lending to the extended family living patterns of this area and also the benefits of economic return. Mandated site adaptations of this style provide additional opportunities for extended living space, secure off-street parking, and emergency refuge by lifting the living areas above base flood elevations. Essential to the Camelback housing style is the truth that "Community begins at the front porch."

Sustainable Design The 3+1 b2 House models the latest technology and building planning concepts incorporating alternative energy sources, plumbing and air conditioning systems that reduce water and energy needs, and a high-performance envelope system that contributes to low overall power consumption. Key sustainable design strategies will include minimizing southern-exposure fenestrations, maximizing northern-exposure daylighting, rainwater harvesting, Cradle to Cradle materials selections, and use of solar PV panels.

Rebuild Smart The 3+1 b2 House follows this firm's commitment to community preservation, building long-lasting value in the structures, and advancement of the art of building. The office looks to the community for design inspiration and cultural reinforcement in the design of the 3+1 b2 House, facilitating comfortable, contemporary living. The use of low-cost, durable materials and proven construction techniques assures value to returning homeowners. The house attempts to explore new alternatives to construction efficiency in envelope design and massing simplicity.

Richard S. Kravet, AIA, NCARB; Gerald W. Billes, AIA, NCARB; Rachel Chotin, LEED-AP; Lauren Hickman

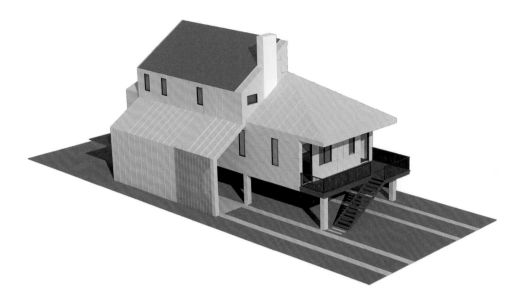

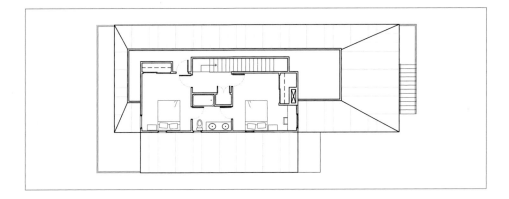

Second floor

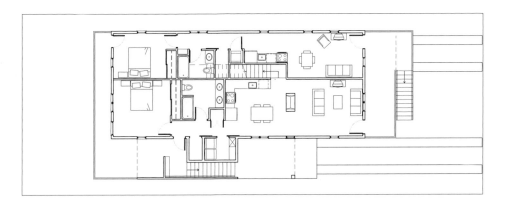

First floor

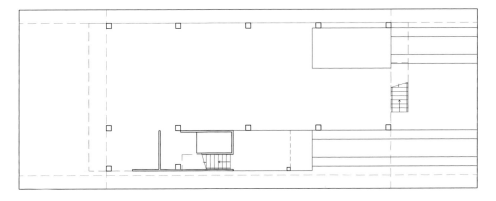

Ground floor

0 2 5 10 N

Concept diagram

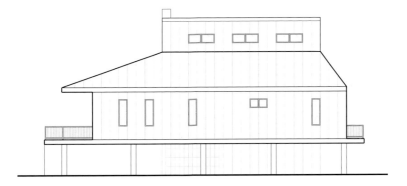

Southern elevation

Northern elevation

Western elevation

Eastern elevation

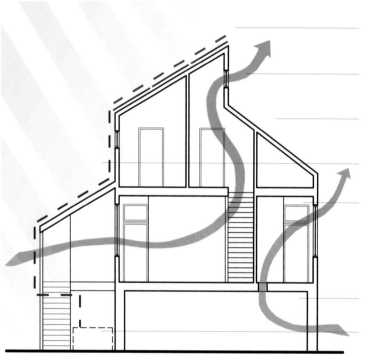

Photovoltaic panels
35-degree, south-facing camelback
roof provides +500 sq. ft. of solar
panels.

Stack ventilation
High ceilings and operable
windows allow hot air to rise and
vent to exterior.

Daylighting
North-facing windows allow
abundant indirect daylight while
limiting heat gain.

Deep overhangs
Reduce heat gain and provide
sheltered outdoor spaces.

Cross ventilation
Longitudinal hallway pulls east-west
breezes through house. Floor vents
allow cool air to enter from below and
exit through operable windows.

Raised structure
Allows air to circulate under
the building.

Rainwater cistern
Use of pitched roofs sheds water
expeditiously and collects rainwater
in cistern for non-potable uses.

Sustainability section

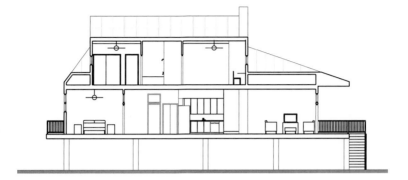

Longitudinal section

Cross section

Duplex section

BNIM

Kansas City, MO

BNIM believes that many sustainable, climate responsive and valuable cultural characteristics are to be found in the architecture of the city of New Orleans. The proposal is based on the New Orleans Creole Cottage house type. Traditional features such as the front porch, a large roof and dormer window presented to the street, the "cabinet" housing services, and a private court are reinterpreted as the basis of the design. In addition, the idea of a main house on the street with secondary buildings to the rear is transformed into a main three-bedroom, two-bathroom, two-story unit at the front, and a one-bedroom, one-bathroom apartment in the rear. The rear unit could be used by a member of the extended family or rented out. The two units are easily linked together to form a four- or five-bedroom single-family house. The house could be raised either eight feet or five feet above the ground. If raised five feet, both parking spaces would be provided in tandem in the southern side yard. Both the parking spaces and the rear garden are secured by gates. Sliding window shutters further enhance security.

The house is set back from the southern property line to optimize solar orientation for the central raised outdoor living court, which is the heart of the house. Windows are shaded by porches, sliding shutters, or vegetated screens. Rooms and windows are arranged to maximize cross ventilation in both the east-west and north-south directions. Natural ventilation is supplemented by ceiling fans. Sloping and vaulted ceilings, high windows, and a dormer induce stack ventilation.

Plumbing cores serving kitchens and bathrooms are tightly grouped in close proximity to the rainwater cistern for maximum efficiency. The south-facing roof of the rear apartment accommodates photovoltaic panels and solar tubes as a source of renewable energy. Ground-source heat pump wells, or loops, are located beneath the raised house so that digging in the garden will not cause damage to the system. Rainwater from the east-facing roof is collected in the cistern and used for toilet flushing and site irrigation. Additional rainwater falling on the house and site is collected in the garden through a series of channels, bioswales, and rain gardens that will reduce the load on the neighborhood stormwater

drainage system and help irrigate the site so that a productive "edible landscape" could be supported.

Construction is proposed in structural insulated panels (SIPs) and dimensions are carefully coordinated to avoid waste. This allows for the off-site prefabrication of components and rapid assembly on site. The house is clad in fiber cement boards and panels applied as a rain screen. Roofs are prefinished standing-seam metal. Windows are double-hung, double-glazed units that allow the operation of shutters when they are open. The windows do not require the use of impact-resistant glass, as the shutters provide

storm protection. This combination of materials assures a highly efficient building envelope that reduces cooling and heating loads and requires minimal maintenance.

Sustainable, healthy, and low-maintenance materials are proposed throughout the interior, as are efficient appliances and heating and cooling equipment.

Design team:
Steve McDowell, Mark Shapiro, Rick Schladweiler, Aaron Ross
Model:
Christian Hoxie, Josh Hemberger, Sam DeJong

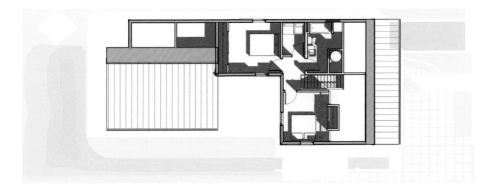

Second floor

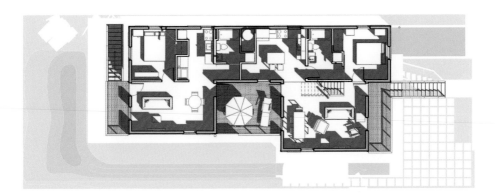

First floor

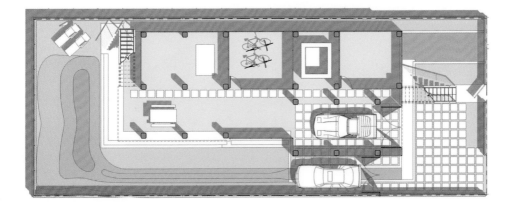

Ground floor

0 2   5   10   N

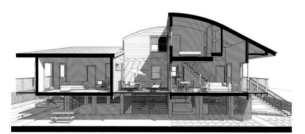

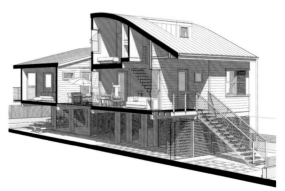

Perspective sections

Southern elevation

Northern elevation

Western elevation

Eastern elevation

Two units

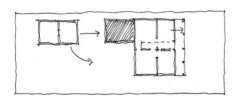

Creole Cottage

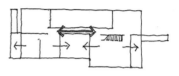

Units linked

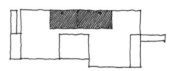

Wet cores

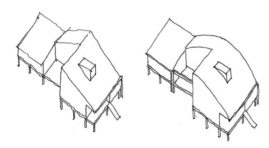

First-level open space

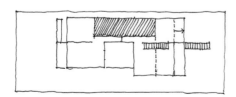

Transformation

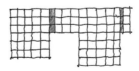

SIPs module

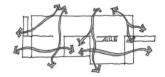

Cross-ventilation plan

Cross-ventilation section

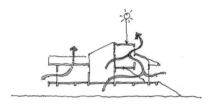

Stack ventilation

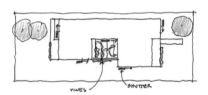

Shading

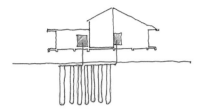

Ground-source cooling & heating

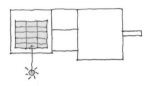

PV & Solar tubes

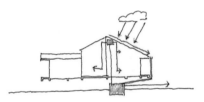

Rainwater collection and reuse

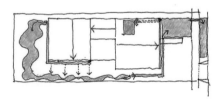

Stormwater management

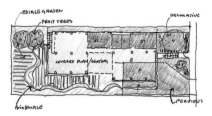

Ground floor uses

buildingstudio
New Orleans, LA

The design is shaped with two goals in mind. First, the scheme is intended to benefit from the area beneath the house to provide comfortable outdoor living spaces. The second approach is meant to offer maximum flexibility for various family groupings. The design is readily adaptable so it can be built as a three-bedroom with efficiency, a four-bedroom with efficiency, or even a two-bedroom double.

Outdoor Living   Since New Orleans has relatively mild seasons the aim is to take full advantage of the area under the home to encourage outdoor living. To make the area below the house as engaging as possible the central third of the plan is opened to the sky so sunlight can penetrate into the ground level's inner reaches. This middle area is set aside for courtyard landscaping where tall plants reach up to the second-floor level. On either side of this central space there are two distinct spaces for outside relaxation.

Fronting the street there is a large screened porch with ceiling fans. Here homeowners have the opportunity to sit in a shaded outdoor space that's protected from summer insects. This street-facing porch offers the opportunity to interact with neighbors as they pass by on the street. Toward the rear of the home there's a more private covered area for seating and barbecuing. Behind this and toward the rear yard there's a fenced outdoor storage space for bicycles, grills, and gardening equipment.

Adaptability   The scheme provides flexibility by being designed in such a way that interchangeable floor plans are possible within the same overall house form. If a potential home buyer likes the general approach of the design but doesn't want a particular floor plan, they can choose from several options that fit the same footprint and square footage. There's the basic three-bedroom, two-bath with a separate efficiency. The efficiency may be used by a family member or, with its separate entrance, can be rented out by the homeowners for additional income. As an alternate, the master bedroom in the three-bedroom scheme (along with its private balcony) can be converted to a four-bedroom, two-bath residence, still with its efficiency. Another option would be side-by-side doubles that have two bedrooms and a bath and a half each.

Since all schemes have separate parking and entrances, they offer privacy for those living in different households.

Likewise there's plenty of flexibility for the home's exterior metal siding when it comes to color choices. The vertical bands of color are inspired by quilt patterns sewn by the women of Gee's Bend, Alabama. Their work has been ex-hibited nationally in galleries around the country as "The Quilts of Gee's Bend." These led to the color patterns of the exterior cladding which are easily adapted to a variety of color choices.

Project Team Members:
Coleman Coker, David Dieckhoff, Varuni Edussuriya, Tom Holloman, Kristian Mizes, Jonathan Tate

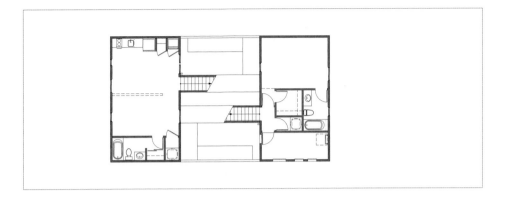

Second floor

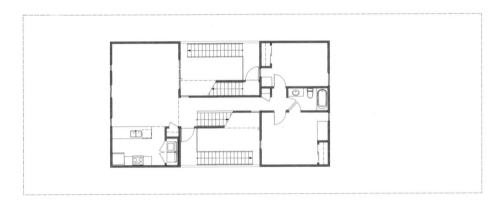

First floor

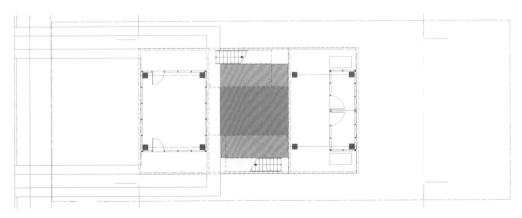

Ground floor

0 2 5 10 N

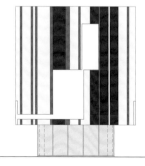

Western elevation (court)

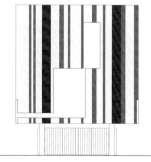

Eastern elevation (court)

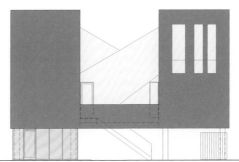

Southern elevation

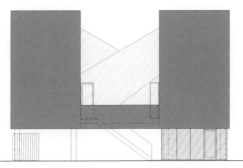

Northern elevation

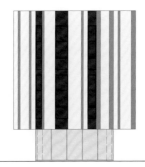

Western elevation

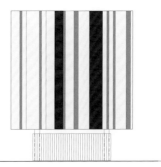

Eastern elevation

A Adaptable structural system (smart framing, SIPs, etc.) to minimize lumber use.

B Energy-efficient appliances (highest SEER rating).

C Operable windows using low-E insulated glass and thermally broken frames.

D Windows on opposite sides of rooms for cross ventilation and natural cooling.

E Ceiling fans help reduce air conditioning needs.

F Pier foundation minimizes disturbance to site.

G Shaded exterior living spaces allow more time outdoors reducing inside cooling needs.

H Courtyard landscape areas reduce stormwater runoff and provide shade.

I Water collected in cistern irrigates landscaping instead of city water.

J Cisterns collect rainwater from roof to prevent stormwater runoff.

K Cistern's gray water reduces demand for potable water when flushing toilets.

L Open courtyard allows more breezes into living areas.

M High-recycled-content metal siding (C2C approved) requires little long-term maintenance.

N Porch provides overhang to eliminate south-facing heat gain at glazing.

O Solar panels reduce dependency on fossil fuel-generated electricity.

Constructs LLC
Accra, Ghana

For the first phase of MIR, the office traced the origins of the Shotgun house to its roots in Yoruba land, West Africa, and how slaves from this region introduced this architecture to the Caribbean and Louisiana. The Yoruba house had the Shotgun structure but without porches. In Yoruba language the word "togun" means house and "sho-gun" means god's house. This proposal has an animated circulation of a "street" through the house, inspired by the city grid shift in the Lower Ninth Ward. It was an attempt to bring the outdoors within the tight confines of the program.

"Shogun 2" takes the notion of open space and circulation to new heights by combining the firm's trademark gestural entry stairs (of MIR 1) with a series of interconnecting decks and voids to define the two parts of the program, and create a more unique experience while moving seamlessly through indoor and outdoor spaces. One of the key elements of this project is the roof—expressive bird-like form, which is a reinterpretation of the classic gable roof to demonstrate the dynamism which New Orleans represents, which is often expressed in the traditional building textures, color, and wrought iron detail. Exterior wall finishes are a panoply of color and materials of wood siding, stucco/plaster, and cement fiber boards used to create a harmonious balance of practicality and playfulness.

The ground floor, with eight feet of headroom, has been designed to be a seating area around a series of landscape zones, with gravel pathways leading to the barbecue zone, seating area, and elevator for the physically challenged.

The entry stairs go up nine feet along the "nanny flat" and then to the deck which connects to the entry door of the main house, and is an experience. Wooden treads are held up by wood slats and steel rods on one end, and a stone clad wall on the other with a bench on the landing; this "space" sets the tone of how outdoor spaces and voids play a critical role in shaping the design of this home.

The entry door of the main house flanks the courtyard or "heart," and is in the middle of the entire home. Living room, dining room, and kitchen are organized around this sun-filled courtyard which has a tree growing through it. Operable windows allow

one to touch nature and get cross ventilation through the home, which would reduce the need for air conditioning all year round. Decks off the kitchen complete the outdoor experience.

Level two is reached via a "jewel box" stairwell off the main living space. This proposed non-conditioned space consists of walls of vertical and horizontal glass louvers of different colors, which becomes an art piece, or is tapestry-like in itself.

Level three is where the family can really enjoy the outdoors and congregate. The bedrooms all open up to the tree-filled courtyard void and the roof deck, protected by a functional, animated roof which brings in sunlight via clear acrylic panels, directs water, and supports solar panels.

Sustainable solutions   For the office, sustainable solutions are not only in the technologies of solar and green products, but in the design itself, the use of voids to create cross ventilation, the importance of landscape in shaping a design philosophy inspired by how people want to live. Buildings matter but experiences endure.

Josephine Dadzie, Hans Sachs, Kathleen Carthy, Rami Erapohja, Gabriel Appo, Sefako Gbomita, Kofi Akakpo, Phanuel Okrah, Mariama Abdulai, Sophie Morley

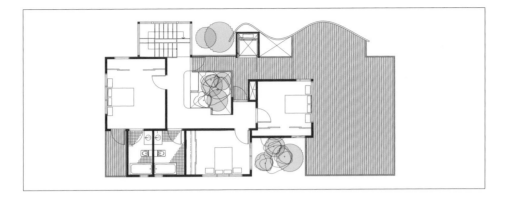

Second floor

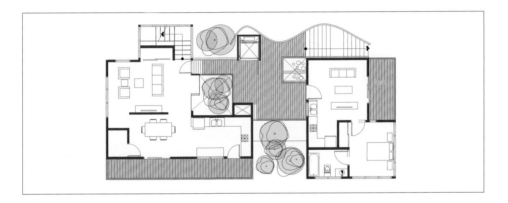

First floor

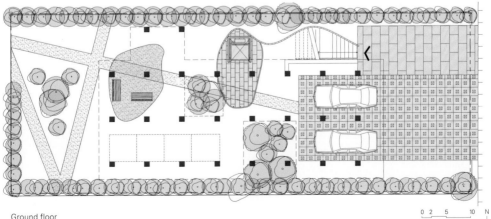

Ground floor

0 2 5 10 N

Southern elevation

Northern elevation

Western elevation

Eastern elevation

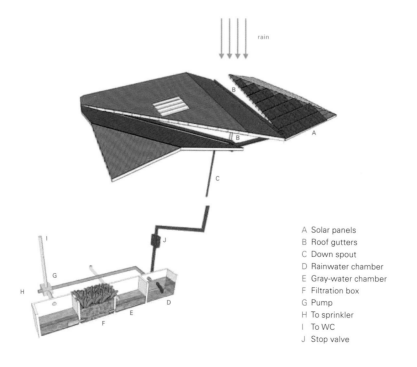

rain

A Solar panels
B Roof gutters
C Down spout
D Rainwater chamber
E Gray-water chamber
F Filtration box
G Pump
H To sprinkler
I To WC
J Stop valve

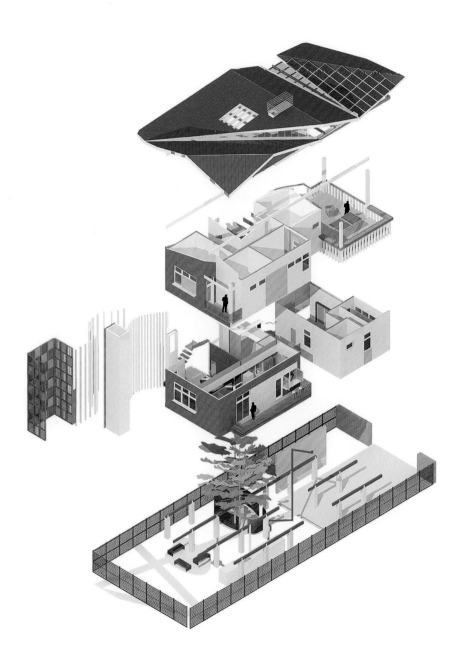

ELEMENTAL
Santiago, Chile

Pride is the community's greatest asset.
ELEMENTAL's proposal is based on two points:

1. What doesn't kill you only makes you stronger!

Architecturally speaking, this means that people deserve a house capable of matching this new status and able to capitalize on this potential. The first step of the long journey in which this new life is going to flourish is to Make It Right!; but at the end of the road, it is important to make it better. ELEMENTAL designed a house capable of being a departing point with a broader horizon within which families can develop and express themselves.

2. Who are we to tell people how to live?

Architecturally speaking, this means that an open system has to be created rather than a closed design, a structural framework and technical support that is responsible for difficult, complex duties and operations, but that allows for personal interventions and customization. Taking care of those aspects of construction that are more difficult to do individually, it is up to the families to adapt, complete, and develop their homes to their own needs, aspirations, and preferences.

The proposal is to design a house that can expand from 1,800 sq. ft. up to 2,700 sq. ft., within a safe structure, efficient and sustainable infrastructures (bathrooms, kitchens, and mechanical equipment), and under a tested roof. From this point, the "do-it-yourself culture" should take over. The design is prepared to change over time, just as family needs and aspirations do.

To achieve this, the office defined a layout which considers expansions as part of the project and just designed the most difficult part of a future 2,700-sq.-ft. house, so that expansions can be done in an easy, economical, quick, and safe way.

Increasing the families' assets   The office started by occupying the maximum available footprint for the thirty-foot-wide lot, then it built the maximum possible volume for that footprint, which in two stories allows for, potentially, 2,700 sq. ft. Half of the volume became interior space in order to accommodate the required program. The second half is initially a big porch that already considers the structure and the roof to host customized

expansions. This is the space for the expression of the families' own cultural and living traditions.

The office anticipates that in order to pay for the structure, infrastructure, and roof of a final, bigger house, some concessions in the initial phase will be required. The experience with more than 1,000 houses already built and intervened on by fam-ilies is that if a participatory process is conducted to define priorities, the design is going to be able to deliver everything that is more difficult for a family to achieve individually.

Project Team Members:
Alejandro Aravena, Diego Torres, Rebecca Emmons, Felipe Combeau, Victor Oddó

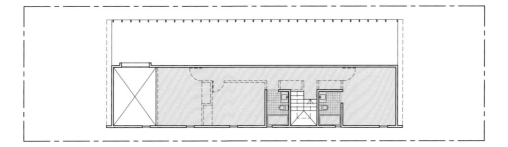

Second floor – Open plan and self-built bedrooms

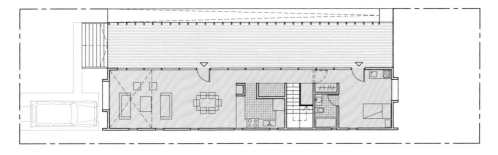

First floor

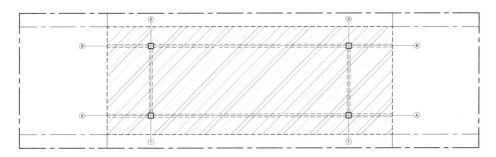

Ground floor

0 2 5 10 N

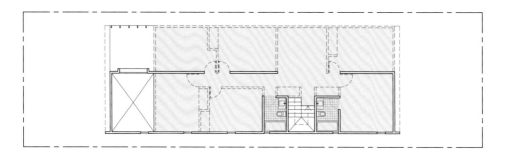

Second floor + Extensions

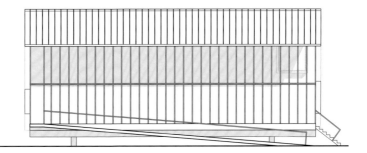

Southern elevation

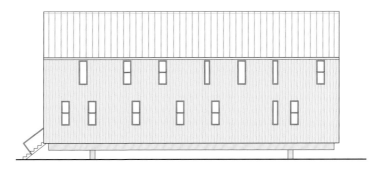

Northern elevation

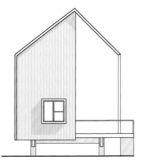

Western elevation

Eastern elevation

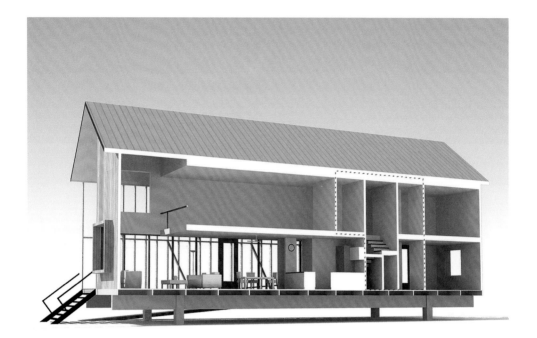

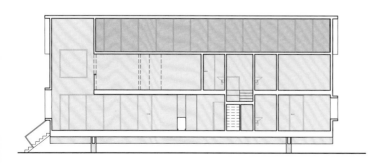

Longitudinal section

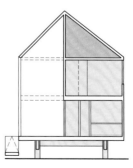

Cross section

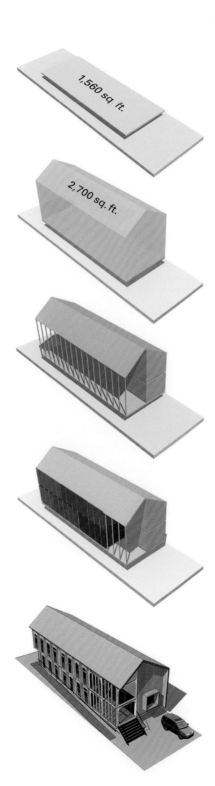

Maximum footprint
30-foot-wide lot

1,560 sq. ft.

Maximum footprint
Two-story volume

2,700 sq. ft.

Two-story house
+ big porch

Expansion scheme
2,700 sq. ft. + porch

House + Expansion

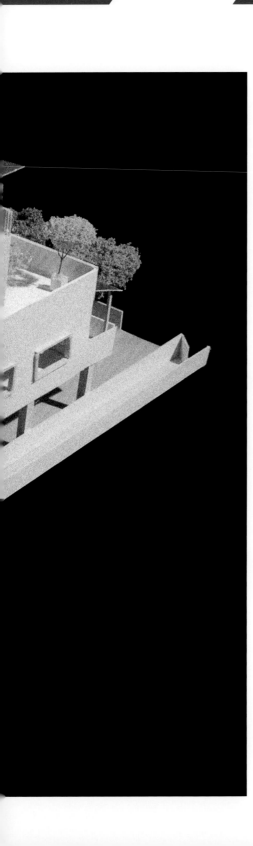

Gehry Partners, LLP
Los Angeles, CA

The design for the MIR two-family home began with the initial community feedback meeting and a study of the local typologies and proposed program. Of the components of local vernacular, the majority of the community expressed a desire for quality outdoor space, especially the garden.

Starting with this initial desire, two-story solutions were explored to reduce the overall footprint of the built structure, which would maximize available garden area, and potentially reduce foundation costs. Several basic diagrams for program organization were studied falling into two basic categories—side by side and front to back. The front-to-back organization allowed for better flow of the interior spaces, and a better proportioned single garden for each house. The front-to-back organization maximizes privacy for each house, as the area/length of the common wall is reduced.

The two-story front-to-back diagram led to additional outdoor amenities that could be provided, including porches, canopies, a second-floor terrace, and a rooftop shoo-fly for each house. The finish floor of the first level was raised to nine feet above grade to allow the area below the first floor to be usable for parking and storage areas for each house. The use of a central stairway to the second floor creates a natural solar chimney, increasing passive ventilation efficiency for each house. Rooftop solar panels, rainwater collection from the terraces, sun shading, cross ventilation, and geothermal cooling are additional sustainable strategies that have been incorporated into the design.

Each house maintains an entry on the street frontage on opposite sides of the lot. The front house is entered through the front garden with a staircase conveniently located adjacent to the parking. A partially covered staircase leads to the front porch, which overlooks the garden. One enters the house into the central great room, using an open plan for living, dining, and kitchen to maximize efficiency of floor area. The living area has a bay window to the front porch. The kitchen has a central island, providing separation of the kitchen area without a wall. A short corridor off of the living room leads to the first-floor bedroom and bathroom, laundry area, and coat closet. The first-floor bedroom has a private canopied porch, and a corner bay window.

An open stairway leads to the second-floor bedroom and bathroom. The second-floor bedroom has a corner bay window. At the top landing, two opposing windows allow for cross ventilation, increasing the efficiency of the solar chimney. A door provides access to the second-floor terrace, which overlooks the garden. An exterior stair stacked on top of the interior stair provides access to the rooftop shoo-fly, providing great views. Solar panels are placed above the shoo-fly to double as a shading device for the rooftop terrace. The rear house is accessed via a path in the side yard to a staircase adjacent to the rear garden and to parking for the rear house. The sequence of rooms for the rear house is identical to the front house.

The plan for each house is identical, rotated 180 degrees, allowing for construction efficiency. Bathrooms on both levels are stacked, bedrooms are stacked, staircases are stacked, and the great room concept for living, dining, and kitchen have all been employed to gain construction efficiency.

The final visual appearance of the two-family home is a simple expression of the solution to the design goals and parameters.

Design Partner: Frank Gehry
Project Partner: Tensho Takemori
Project Designer: Brian Zamora
Project Team: Meaghan Lloyd, Jeffery Sipprell, Samantha Triolo, Danny Bazil

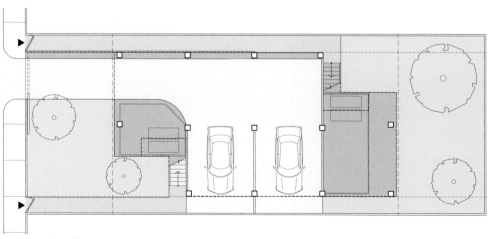

Ground floor

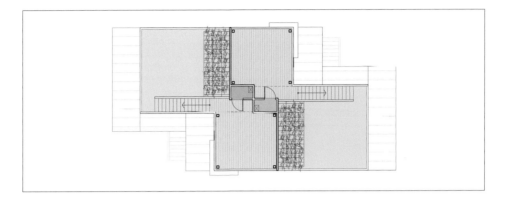

Third floor

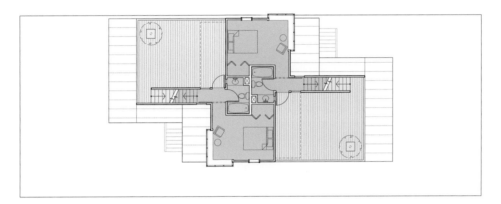

Second floor

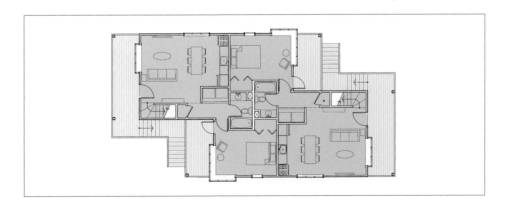

First floor

0 2 5 10 N

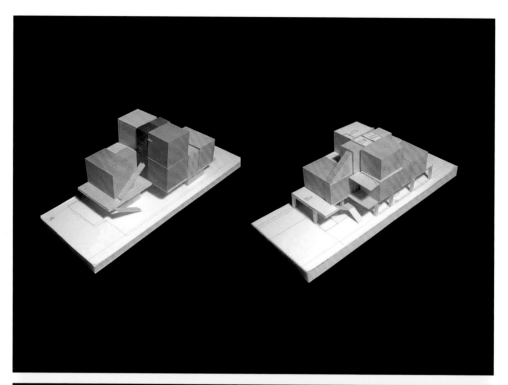

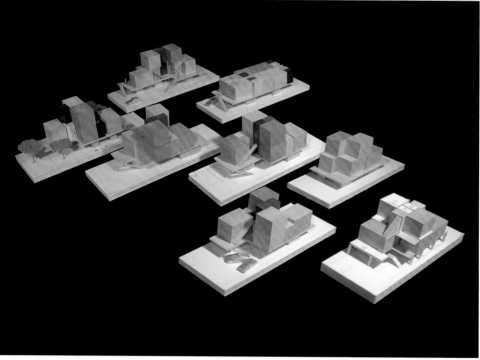

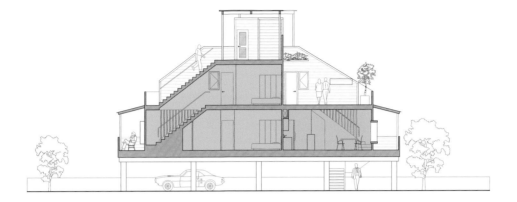

Longitudinal section

Longitudinal elevation

Cross elevation

Cross section

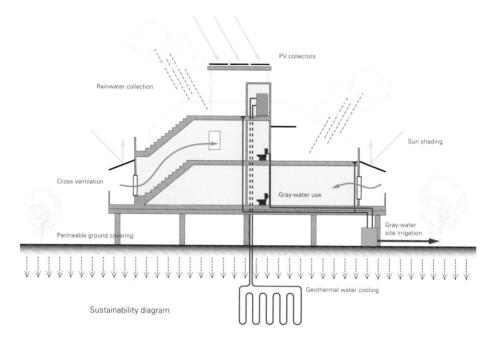

Rainwater collection

PV collectors

Sun shading

Cross ventilation

Gray-water use

Permeable ground covering

Gray-water site irrigation

Geothermal water cooling

Sustainability diagram

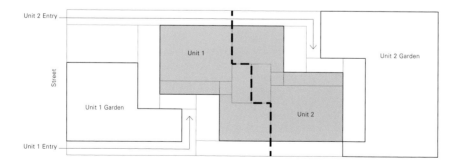

Unit 2 Entry

Unit 1

Unit 2 Garden

Street

Unit 1 Garden

Unit 2

Unit 1 Entry

Plan diagram

GRAFT

Los Angeles, Berlin, Beijing

GRAFT intended to make a strong visual connection to the round-one house in order to bring a consistency and character to the neighborhood that will continue to be populated by these types of houses. In this case the office drew from the Camelback Shotgun typology as inspiration, which historically emerged as a way for residents to add a partial second story to a residence in order to gain more space at the rear of a structure. The design utilizes the Camelback strategy to stack a second efficiency unit above a first-floor Shotgun house.

To establish a strong connection between the private interior program of the house and the shared public space of the street in front, the primary challenge lies in negotiating the 8'0" first-floor height that is required to make the houses safe from future flooding with the street level. The broad and spacious deck located in the front yard mediates the relationship between public and private by raising the deck level to 5'0" above grade. This offers a welcoming gesture to the street while at the same time creating a semi-public/private space for the inhabitants of the house to enjoy. Residents may enter the house from the side porch landing into an open living/dining/kitchen space. The lower unit has a flexible three-bedroom layout that can be converted into a two-bedroom + office layout with the use of a sliding door in the front room. The master suite near the rear of the house contains an en-suite bathroom that shares a common wet wall with the unit's other bathroom making a cost-efficient plumbing core.

Moving upward, an exterior stair carries the inhabitants of the efficiency unit up to a rooftop terrace/entry deck. This secondary deck level can be utilized as a private deck for the upper dwelling. It provides a generous outdoor living space, views of the neighborhood, space for a small vegetable or herb garden, and easy access to the solar panel array for maintenance. The upper unit itself is designed to be a simple one-bedroom dwelling with a living room/dining area facing the backyard. Here the efficiency kitchen mirrors the bath and forms a cost-efficient plumbing core as well as a circulation corridor through the unit.

Lars Krückeberg, Wolfram Putz, Thomas Willemeit, Alejandra Lillo, Tim Sola, Brian D. Nelson, Marcus Friesl, Rob DeCosmo

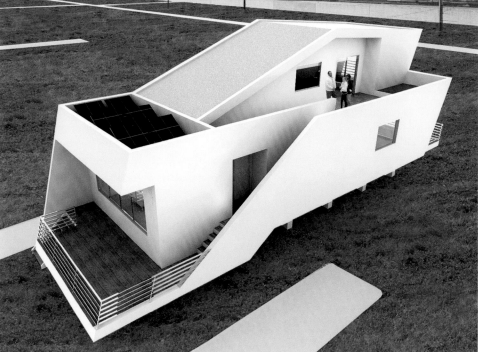

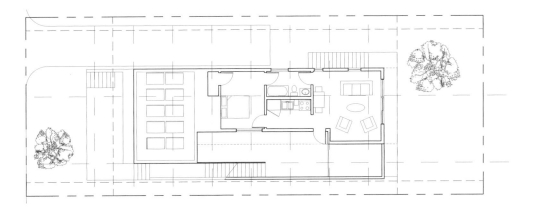

Second floor

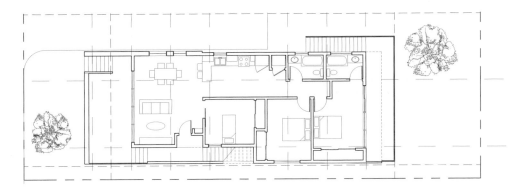

First floor

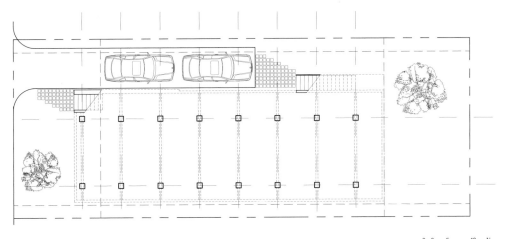

Ground floor

0 2   5   10   N

Longitudinal section

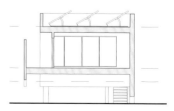

Cross section

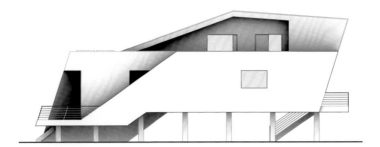

Southern elevation

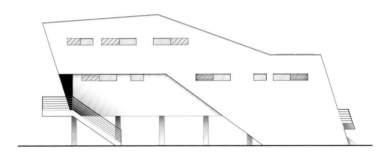

Northern elevation

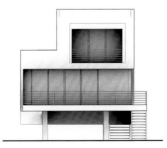

Eastern elevation

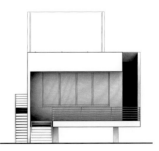

Western elevation

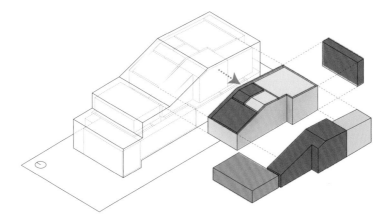

Second floor – one-bedroom unit

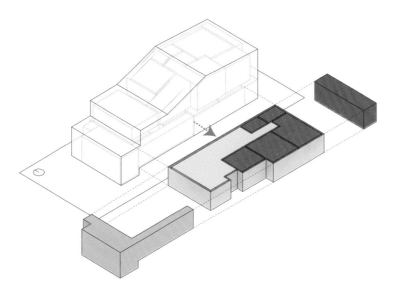

First floor – three-bedroom unit

	Interior – public
	Interior – private
	Exterior – public
	Exterior – private
	Green zone
	Solar zone

Rainwater collection system
Water drains from the rear of the site
along the second story deck to the filter
holding tank.
Water is pumped back into the home for
use in toilets and laundry.

water drain

Solar panels
Optimal orientation is assured through
the placement of the solar array within an
architectural element.

Solar shading
The exaggerated eaves allow for shading
of all major glazing including the southern
and western directions.

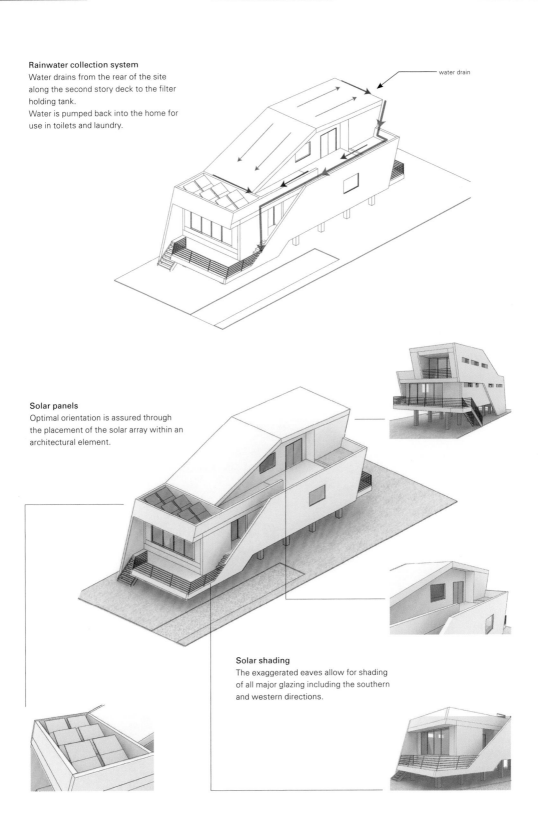

MVRDV
Rotterdam, The Netherlands

New Orleans   Because of New Orleans being below sea level, like the Netherlands, the city protects itself from floods by levees. To accept the flood as a likely future happening, new build houses are raised above flood level.

Shotgun   MVRDV highly appreciates the existing ancient houses of New Orleans. The Shotgun with its pitch roof, its wooden shutters, its front porch, its linear organization. The office uses all these elements in a very straightforward way. No unnecessary additions are made.

Double House   Instead of covering the whole lot with one house split into two houses, we propose two identical individual houses. They are similar in their volume and materialization. They are copies of each other like identical twins. Their position on the lot make them different. They start to act to each other. The lower house is more related to the garden by its easy access. A split level creates an exciting interior space. The upper house gives a view over the neighborhood and has a horizontal floor.

Landscape   By stacking the two houses, part of the lot is left free for more green. A tree can be planted along the house. Besides a front garden and a rear garden, the houses have an open garden along the house, mainly shadowed by the houses and the tree. The parking entry is paved, as well as the entry to the stairs and the rear entrance of the bottom house.

Access   The two houses share a lot. They share the garden. They can have separate accesses though. For the bottom house, one can park the car right under the house at the street side. One can access the house on the rear side. The top house is accessed from the front side of the house by an open staircase.

Layout   Since the lower house is tilted it has one split level. One can enter the house at five feet high where the living room and the kitchen are also located. Ascending to eight feet one finds the bedrooms and the bathrooms. The upper house has a horizontal floor. It is accessed at eighteen feet by an open staircase through the bottom of the house. One enters directly into the living room.

Both houses have a front and rear porch. Each has one connected to the living room and one to the master bedroom.

Sustainability The sufficient amount of an approximately 30-percent-sloped roof provides surface to locate solar panels. All rainwater can be collected from those roofs as well. The garden surface is increased by stacking the two houses. An extra tree can be planted.

Lot Orientation When the orientation of the lot is switched to east-west instead of west-east, the houses are mirrored over the north-south axis. When the orientation is switched to south-north instead of north-south the houses are mirrored over the west-east axis. When the houses are located alongside a road, the hallway can become the porch and the front and rear porch become interior space.

MVRDV
Winy Maas, Jacob van Rijs, Nathalie de Vries, with
Stefan de Koning, Gijs Rikken, Di Miao, Manuel Galipeau

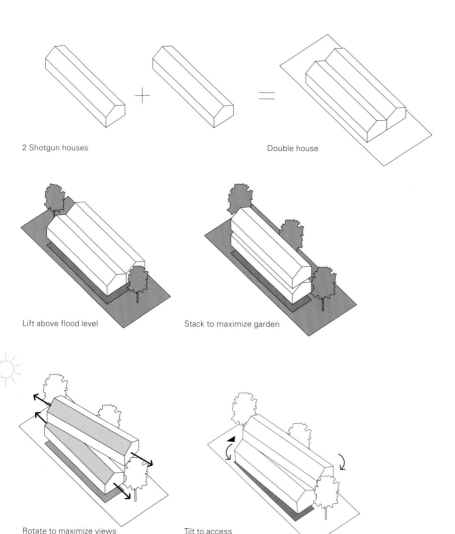

2 Shotgun houses

Double house

Lift above flood level

Stack to maximize garden

Rotate to maximize views

Tilt to access

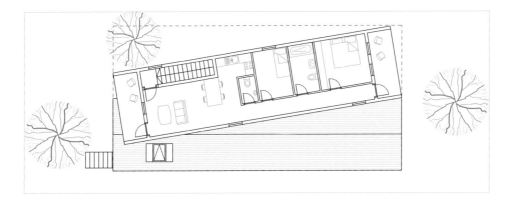

Second floor

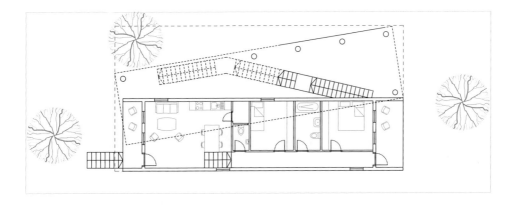

First floor

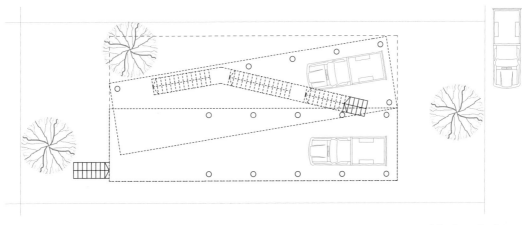

Ground floor

0 2   5   10   N

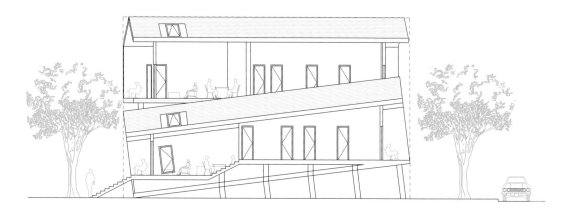

Longitudinal section

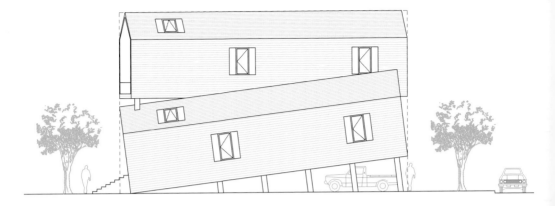

Southern elevation

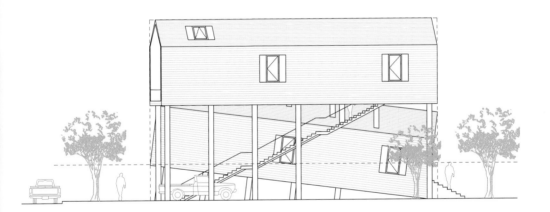

Northern elevation

Eastern elevation

Western elevation

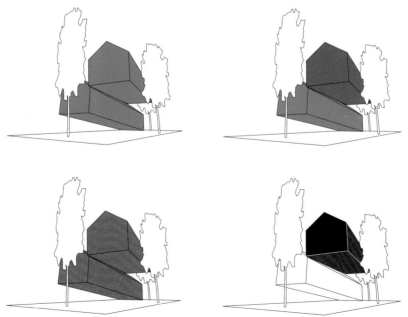

Color scheme

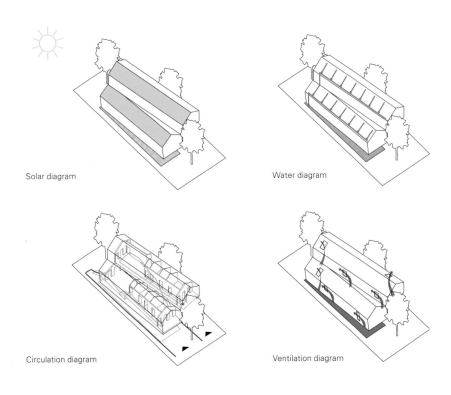

Solar diagram

Water diagram

Circulation diagram

Ventilation diagram

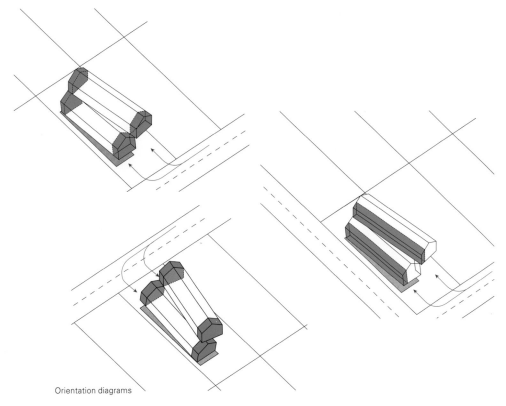

Orientation diagrams

Pugh+Scarpa Architects
Santa Monica, CA

This Right home seeks to redefine the concept of a home into a flexible, multi-functional, and adaptable space addressing the needs of today's modern family on a limited budget.

The central concept of the new duplex home is the restoration of "pride of place" to those districts hardest-hit by the hurricane.

The house accomplishes this with several significant design moves:

The overall scale of the house, topping out at thirty-eight feet above grade, is meant to achieve a presence and make the home a focal point for the neighborhood. The scale is purposefully large and commodious, both without and within. The roof pitches upward at an angle that both announces the home to the street and induces airflow upwards through clerestory windows set just below the roofline. On the exterior, vertically oriented, patterned paneling reinforces the home's height. Inside, a double-height space brings light, airflow, and a sense of commodiousness to the living room.

The verticality and focal strength of the home is emphasized by the presence of a twelve-foot-high cook pit attached to the front porch, facing the street. The cook pit is made for barbecues, with open flames visible from the street at eye level, and a rotisserie enclosure accessed from the porch. A chimney extends from the hearth enclosure past the roofline, acting as the home's axis mundi and providing the armature for the required egress ladder for rooftop flood refuge.

The front porch, facing the street, provides a gathering place for neighborhood residents and relatives.

Many of the design elements play a double role; the chimney acts both as an anchor and an escape; the porch is a refuge and a social gathering place; the cook pit is both a private and public hearth. The organization of the overall plan mediates between public and private objectives in a relatively small space. On the ground floor, the back porch and yard have a significantly more private and enclosed feel than does the front porch and yard, yet movement between the two is fluid along the south side of the house. Residents of each unit can use the other's porch without passing through the associated unit.

The two units are connected by a small exterior porch and by a pair of individually locked doors that can be opened to expand the two units into one for larger gatherings. The disposition of these units is ideal for extended families that still require a level of privacy.

Pugh+Scarpa's approach to Cradle to Cradle sustainability begins with passive solar design strategies such as locating and orienting the building to control solar cooling and heat loads; shaping and orienting the building for exposure to prevailing winds; shaping the building to induce buoyancy for natural ventilation; and shaping and planning the interior to enhance daylight and natural airflow distribution. The building responds to the specific conditions of the New Orleans climate in several ways:
– On the south side deep overhangs provide passive solar protection for the building's interior.
– Similarly, openings on the east and west sides are protected with deeper overhangs and porches.

– The north side is allowed to be flat and exposed, which affords daylighting with a minimum of solar heat gain.
– The roof is sloped to induce airflow.
– High ceilings and abundant cross ventilation allow heat to escape the building's interior. Cooling airflow inside the home is enhanced by ceiling fans, a direct-drive exhaust fan, and operable windows, which create abundant cross ventilation.
– All materials selected are commercially available, cost-effective, and eco-friendly.
– All appliances are Energy Star rated.
– The home's high ceilings promote an airy, spacious ambiance, and will be less reliant on electric lighting than a conventional home.

Lawrence Scarpa, AIA, lead designer; Brad Buter, designer; Nicole Allen, designer; Silke Clemens, designer

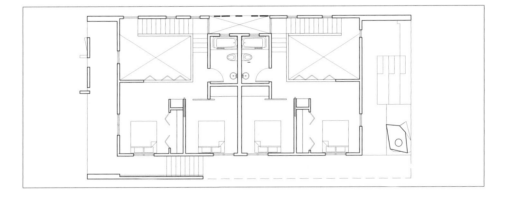

Second floor

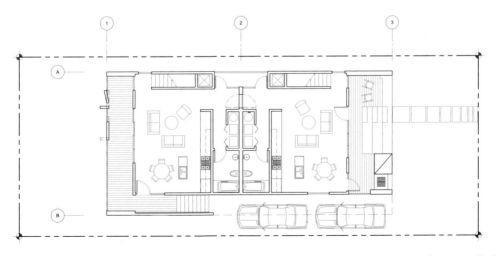

First floor

0 2 5   10   N

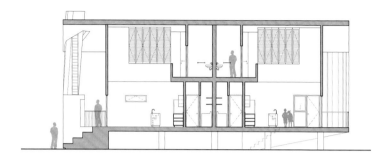

Longitudinal section

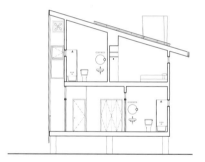

Cross section

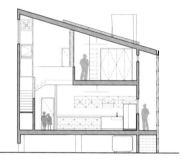

Cross section

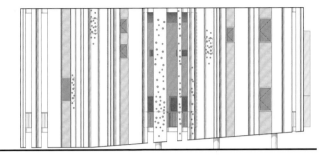

Northern elevation

Eastern elevation

Western elevation

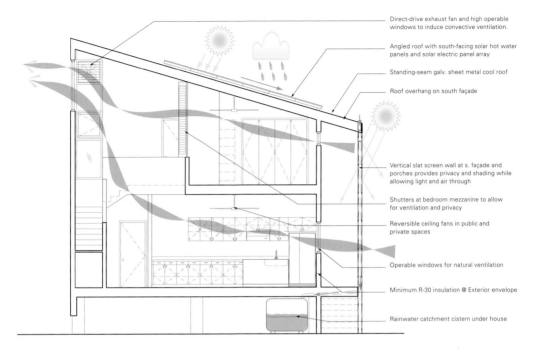

Direct-drive exhaust fan and high operable windows to induce convective ventilation.

Angled roof with south-facing solar hot water panels and solar electric panel array

Standing-seam galv. sheet metal cool roof

Roof overhang on south façade

Vertical slat screen wall at s. façade and porches provides privacy and shading while allowing light and air through

Shutters at bedroom mezzanine to allow for ventilation and privacy

Reversible ceiling fans in public and private spaces

Operable windows for natural ventilation

Minimum R-30 insulation @ Exterior envelope

Rainwater catchment cistern under house

Solar systems building section

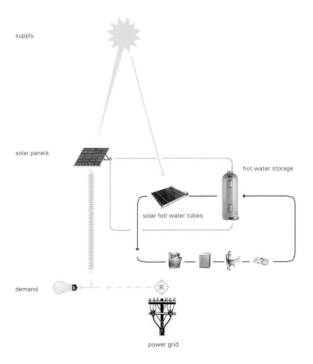

supply

solar panels

hot water storage

solar hot water tubes

demand

power grid

Solar systems diagram

Waggonner & Ball
Architects New Orleans, LA

This two-family home is loosely based on a vernacular prototype found only in New Orleans—the Camelback Shotgun. Simulating a house constructed in stages, the building is a composition of sheltering roof forms and interlocking plans that make the structure legible as a two-family home. The design is sited with its long axis on an east-west direction in order to address the issues of shading, daylighting, and solar orientation. The building's massing is composed of two nestled forms: a two-story, three-bedroom unit that is L-shaped in section joined to a one-bedroom unit that is L-shaped in plan. The small unit can be occupied by an elderly in-law or a young adult. The building can easily be converted to a single-family house by means of a single new door opening.

The main unit is entered at the midpoint of the house by means of a shared front stair that also serves the one-bedroom unit off a common porch. This entrance stair meets the street as a small deck area that serves as a place to sit, wait for a friend or a school bus, or to visit with neighbors. The larger living unit has two bedrooms on the main floor that share a full bath. The main living/dining/kitchen spaces act as a generously proportioned great room with exposure to the exterior on three sides, affording excellent views of the street and neighborhood. The smaller unit has a loft-like living room and efficiency kitchen with a rear porch for outdoor dining and a west-facing master bedroom and bath.

The building has been designed with a galvanized standing-seam roof with generous south-facing slopes at a 30-degree angle for the installation of PV panels. The roofs have also been designed to collect rainwater into a premanufactured cistern located in the backyard. Harvested rainwater, supplemented by recaptured lavatory and shower water, is intended to be used for irrigation and toilet flushing.

Clad in cement board siding and rain screen panels, the house, with its cantilevered front porch, is scaled to buildings found in New Orleans' richly diverse and unique residential neighborhoods.

Mac Ball, David Waggonner, Catherine Smith,
John Kleinschmidt, William Marshall

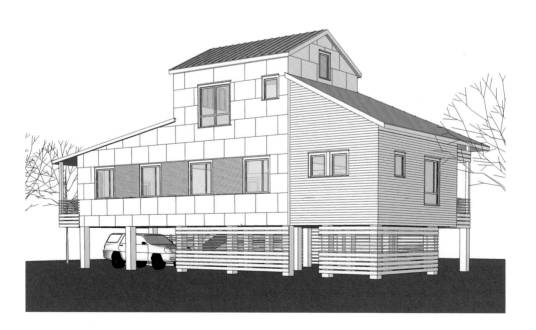

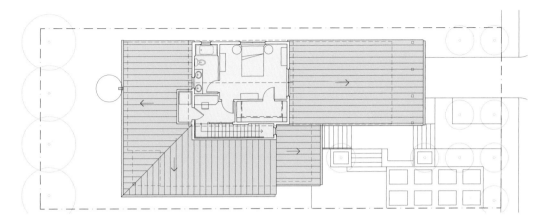

Second floor

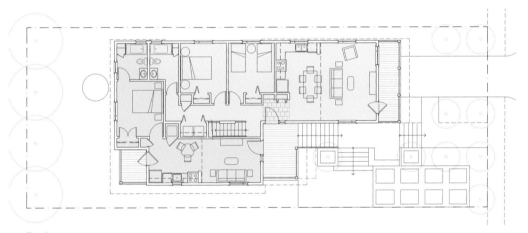

First floor

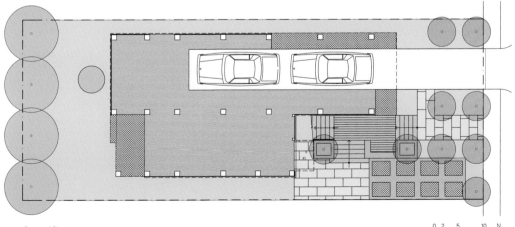

Ground floor

0 2   5   10   N

Longitudinal section

Cross section

Southern elevation

Northern elevation

Western elevation

Eastern elevation

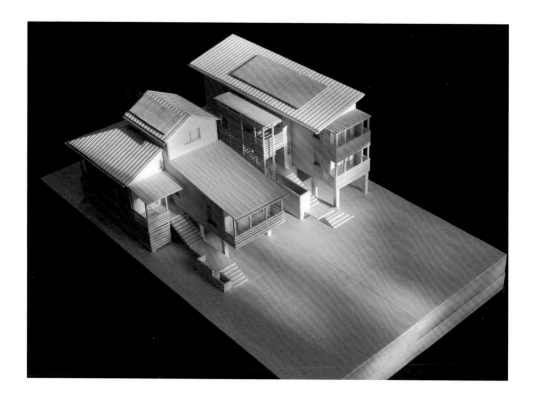

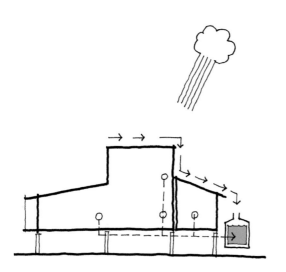

Harvesting rain

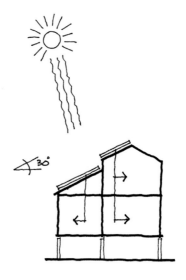

Harvesting sun

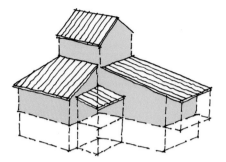

Sheltering roofs

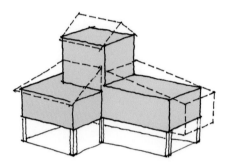

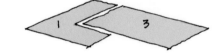

Nesting forms

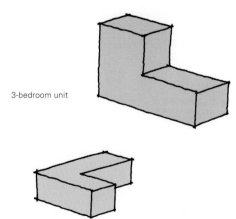

3-bedroom unit

1-bedroom unit

William McDonough+ Partners Charlottesville, VA

Flow: A Cradle to Cradle prototype house

Flow House celebrates Earth's abundance, promoting and nurturing connections between human and natural communities. The design looks to natural systems for inspiration and relies on the belief that all design decisions should support the creation of community and family. Embodying the ideas and ideals of the Lower Ninth Ward and New Orleans, through the Flow House the office strives to create a safe and healthy environment, both natural and built, with all material nutrients returning safely to biological or technical cycles—manifesting a true Cradle to Cradle residential icon.

Becoming native to place   Flow House re-engages people with their natural surroundings, embedding the house within its context, site, and community through diverse exterior rooms that become extensions of interior living spaces. The house becomes a connective and responsive organism—fostering and making visible human patterns and the rituals of daily living while engaging in the evolution of local culture and tradition. Flow House aligns architectural form and the various flows of nature (energy, air, water, light)—rendering this confluence visible through material processes that impact the quality of life of its occupants with positive effects.

The design is conceived as a "3+1" type that reimagines and combines local architectural typologies such as the Shotgun, Camelback, and "dogtrot." The primary residence at the street and a secondary rental or granny unit with an independent entrance towards the rear create a generous open landscape and rain garden while minimizing the overall building footprint. Deep overhangs and a southward-massing "shift" on the upper-floor bedroom mass dually provides access to daylight for adjacent neighbors and shade for the lower living floor. An open exterior "dogtrot" separates each unit while also providing effective natural ventilation and accommodating flexible expansion space to meet the requirements of diverse situations, family structures, and living arrangements over time.

The experience of the house begins at a live oak tree. With a simple wood bench that becomes the entry stairs, a gathering space underneath the tree canopy defines the first step into the house. With the elevated front porch, this becomes a dynamic interchange between the public and private lives of the house. Defined by an open living space, the interior of the primary unit spatially and visually connects the front porch through to the "dogtrot" or "shade" deck. Framed by generous sliding doors, the living room fully extends to the front porch, allowing views up and down the street to promote a more secure and connected community. Upper bedrooms open onto exterior deck spaces— the "sun" deck adjacent to the master bedroom suite and the "view" deck which is accessed from a common corridor and can accommodate rooftop gardens, private family gatherings, and sleeping under the night sky.

Solar and water flows   Roof surfaces are "photosynthetic," generating energy through building integrated thin-film PV, hot water through solar thermal hot water tubes, and green roof systems that filter water, support biodiversity, and provide habitat while slowing stormwater runoff. Water is visibly celebrated and collected through an integrated system of scuppers and cisterns.

Project Team Members:
William McDonough, Kevin Burke
Jose Atienza, Kathy Grove, Alexander Jack, Alastair Reilly, Matthew Wagner

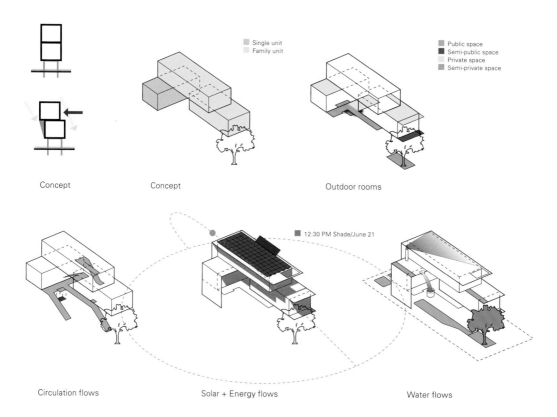

Single unit
Family unit

Public space
Semi-public space
Private space
Semi-private space

Concept   Concept   Outdoor rooms

12:30 PM Shade/June 21

Circulation flows   Solar + Energy flows   Water flows

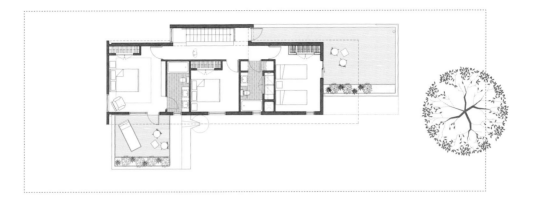

Second floor

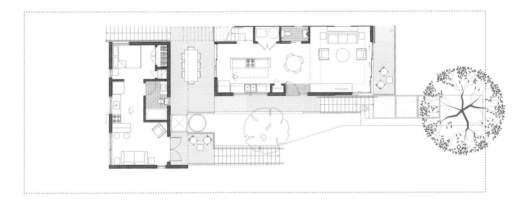

First floor

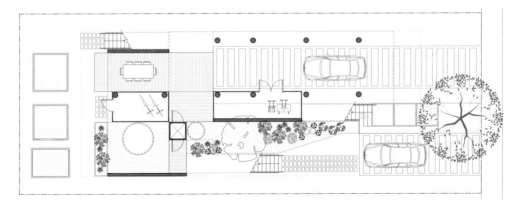

Ground floor

0 2 5   10   N

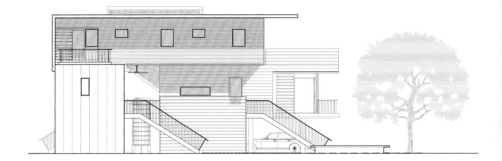

Southern elevation

Northern elevation

Western elevation

Eastern elevation

Nutrient flows Composed of three 16'0"-wide modular living units that are constructed off site, Flow House is designed and aspires to be 100-percent Cradle to Cradle with component parts that can be safely disassembled and returned to the Earth within biological cycles or to industry within technical cycles. Although material advancements have been made in recent years, the residential building industry is still challenged to replace key substrate components like plywood, a "non-nutrient" whose binders prevent it from being properly disassembled. This creates great obstacles for architecture to fully achieve the vision of Cradle to Cradle. To overcome this, the strategy here is to minimize the number of materials to a few key components that are safe and healthy for ecological and human health and are either inspired by or are Cradle to Cradle certified. Wall and roof assemblies are conceived as metal structural insulated panels (SIPs) (technical nutrients) while foundations, exterior cladding, and millwork are specified as wood (biological nutrients). Wood will either be FSC certified, formaldehyde-free, and responsibly harvested for millwork, or (non-toxic) acetalyzed for exterior cladding, structural columns, and foundation piles. Interior walls will be finished with gypsum-free, mold-resistant, and low-VOC drywall (biological nutrient).

Flow House is a life support system in harmony with both energy and material flows, human souls and other living things, embodying the interdependency between the built with the natural.

MIR DNA Analysis

Element	Class	Material	Description	Surface ft^2	Volume CF
Structure					
A Columns	Biological Nutrient	Wood	Non-toxic fusion of glass and wood	613	101
B Metal Framing	Technical Nutrient	Steel/Light Gauge		4,724	87
C SIPs	Technical Nutrient	Steel SIPs/EPS	Steel exterior with expanded polystyrene insulation	10,968	2201
D Concrete	Technical Nutrient	Concrete	Concrete with high fly ash content	309	71
E Floors	Biological Nutrient	Wood	Recycled or reclaimed wood	988	103
F	Technical Nutrient	Wood	Engineered wood panel containing no added Urea Formaldehyde and is FSC Certified	4,320	270
G Roof	Technical Nutrient	Steel SIPs/EPS	Steel exterior with expanded polystyrene insulation	5,031	1054
Openings					
H Windows	Product of Service	Glass, Metal, Sealant		939	28
I Glazing	Technical Nutrient	Glass	Large operable openings	226	19
J Door	Technical Nutrient	Metal	Metal door	241	8
Walls					
K Interior Walls	Technical Nutrient	Drywall	80% post-industrial recycled waste, no gypsum	4,127	217
L Exterior Cladding	Biological Nutrient	Wood Siding	Sustainably sourced, non-toxic, acetylated wood	2,655	216
M	Biological Nutrient	Paneling	Bio-composite exterior cladding material from post-consumer products	486	30
Stairs/Railings					
N Treads/Risers	Biological Nutrient	Wood	Sustainably sourced, non-toxic, acetylated wood	724	40
O Stringers	Technical Nutrient	Steel	Steel	227	49
Interiors					
P Cabinets	Biological Nutrient	Wood	Reclaimed or rapidly renewable wood	601	24
Q Counter Tops	Technical Nutrient	Solid Surface Counter	Cement countertop with 100% recycled-content glass	107	6

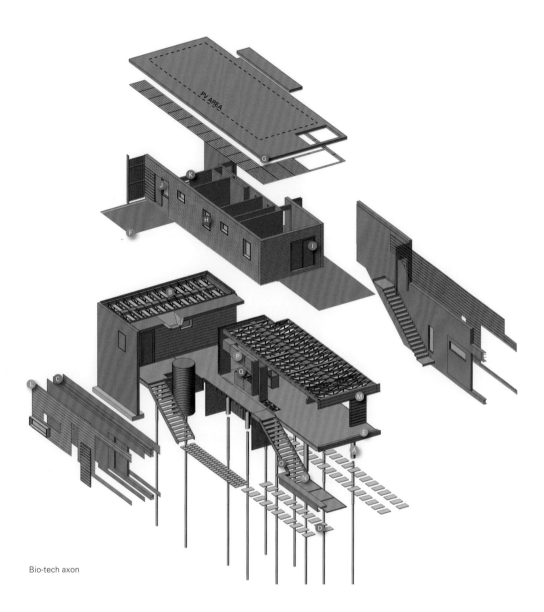

PV AREA

Bio-tech axon

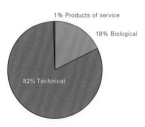

1% Products of service

18% Biological

82% Technical

Nutrient flow

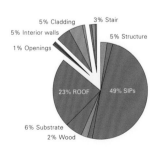

5% Cladding

3% Stair

5% Interior walls

5% Structure

1% Openings

23% ROOF

49% SIPs

6% Substrate

2% Wood

Category

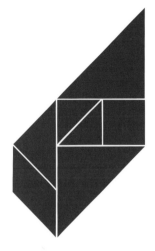

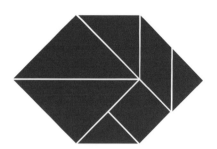

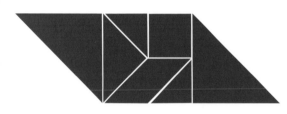

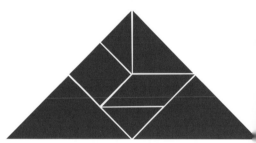

Why pink? —
Because it screams the loudest.

Brad Pitt

The Pink Project

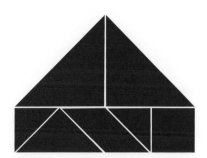

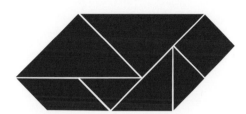

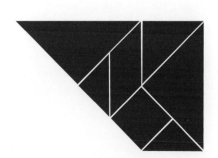

164 tons of steel scaffolding and 40,000 lbs. of recyclable aluminum

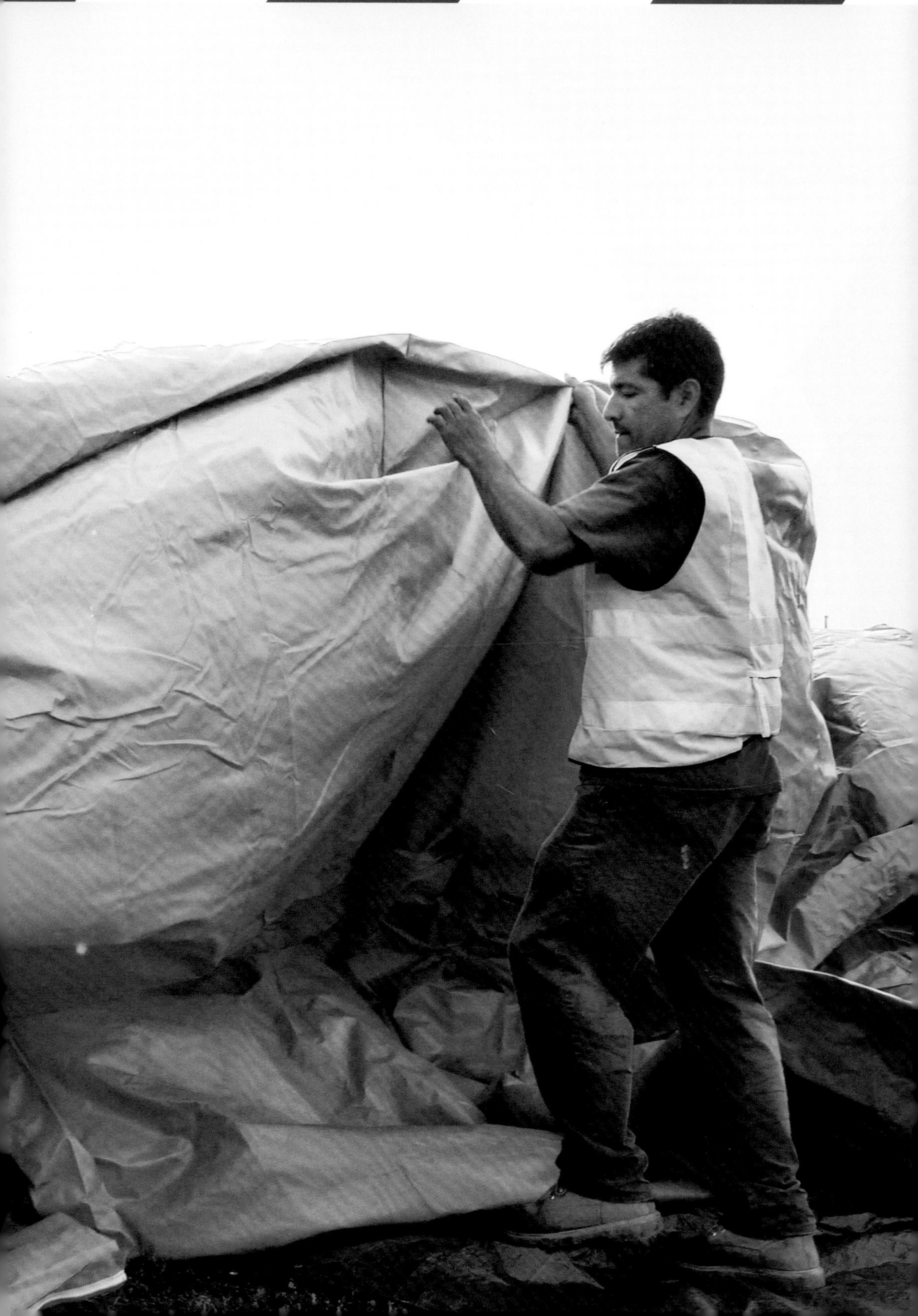

"I warned that we would be turning their neighborhood into a circus.

They explained, "our neighborhood is already a circus."

Brad Pitt

55,000 sq. yds.

environmentally friendly, 100-percent recyclable pink fabric

Basic Forms

House Types

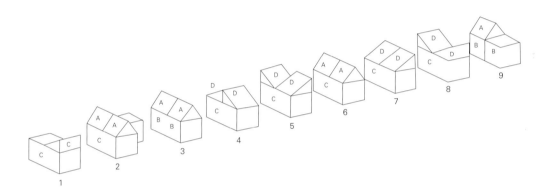

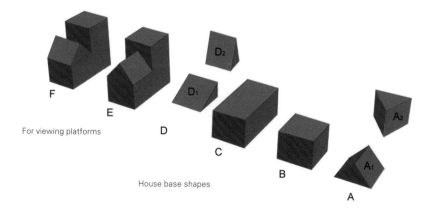

For viewing platforms

House base shapes

Random Structure

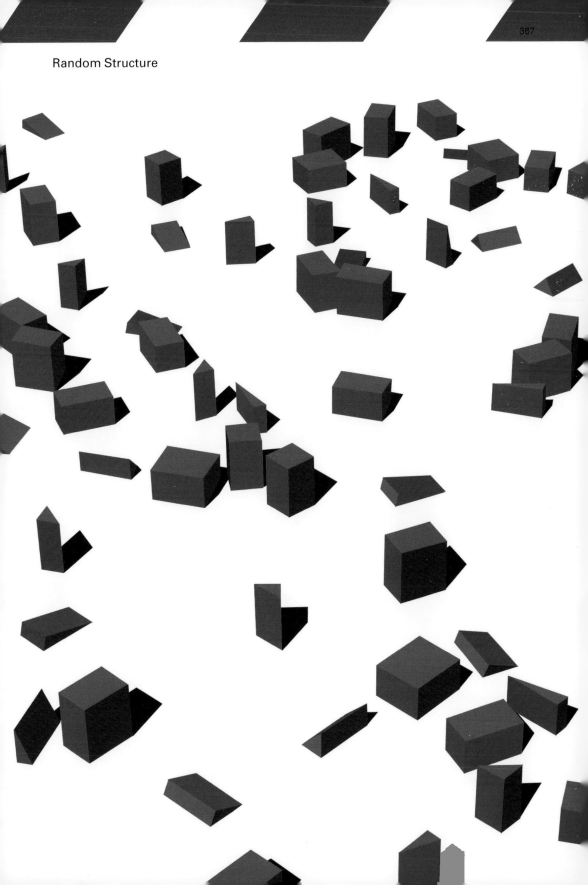

Structure

Site plan – day one

N

Ideal site plan on the last day of installation and completed fundraising

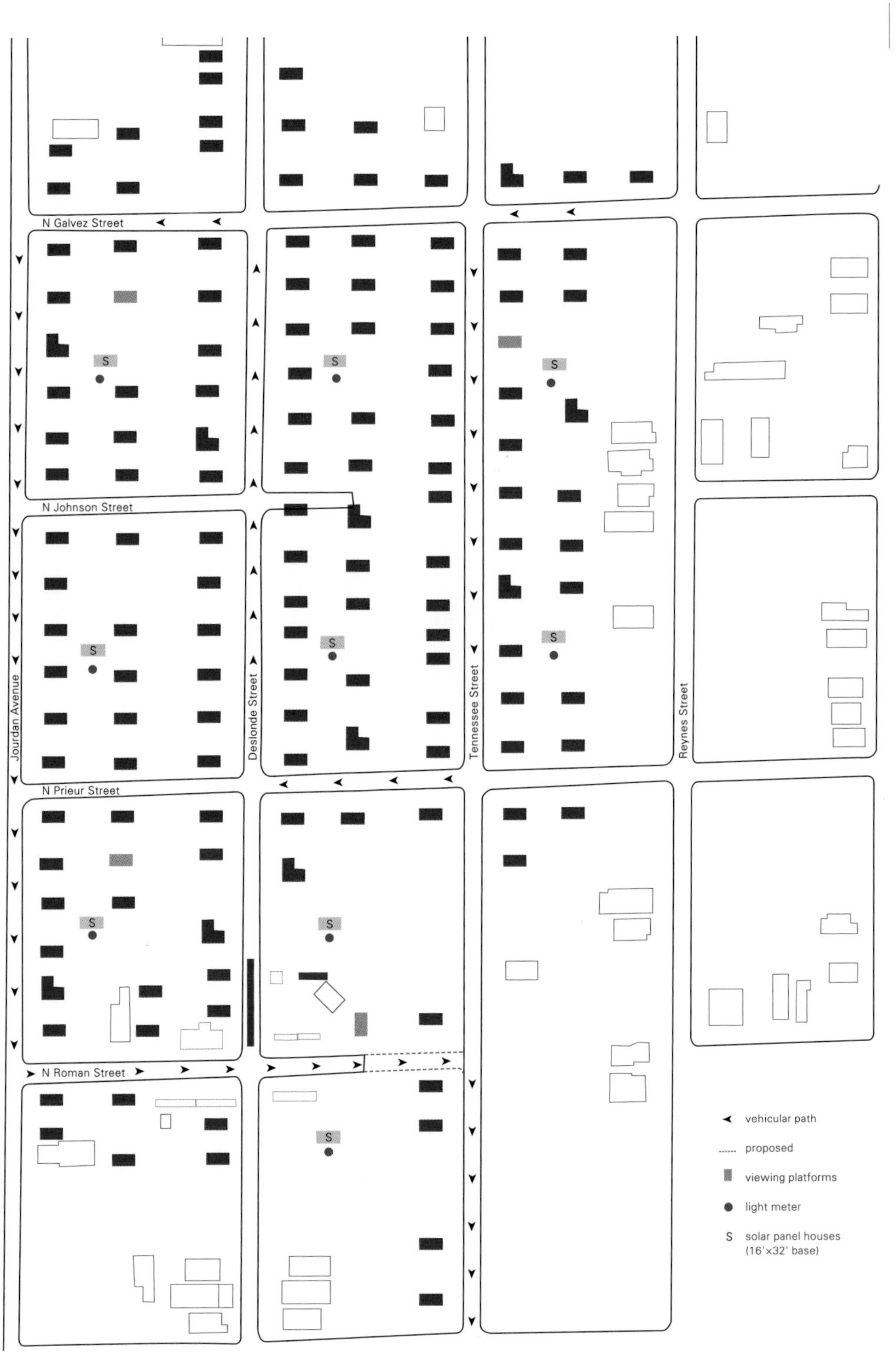

N

N Galvez Street

N Johnson Street

N Prieur Street

N Roman Street

Jourdan Avenue

Deslonde Street

Tennessee Street

Reynes Street

◄ vehicular path

...... proposed

▮ viewing platforms

● light meter

S solar panel houses
   (16'x32' base)

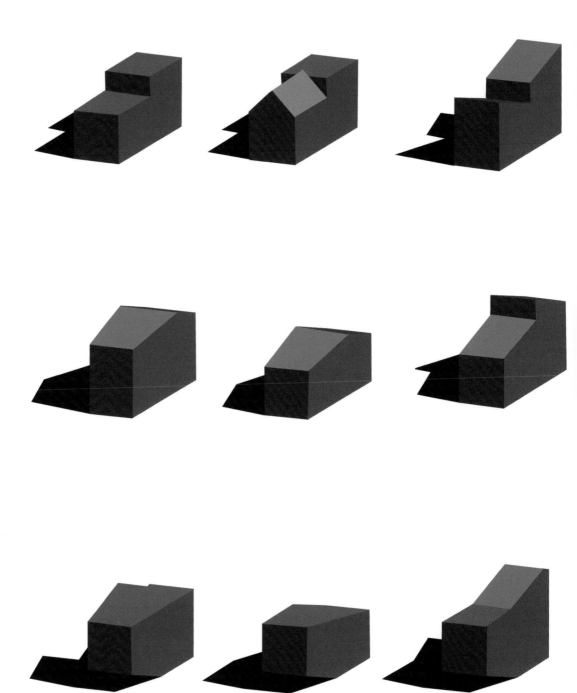

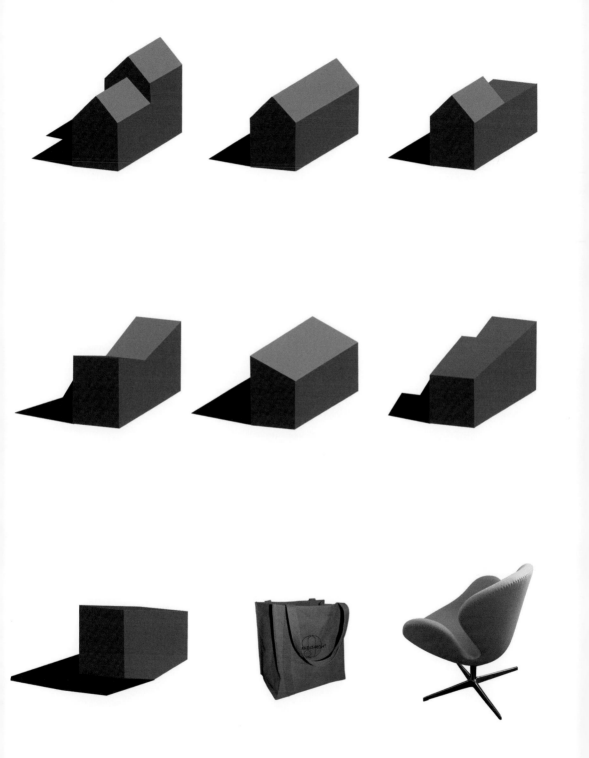

Brad Pitt

Idea, Concept, and Construction of Pink

On the set of *The Curious Case of Benjamin Button* I found myself staring at this two-story fluorescent pink silhouette of a house sitting amongst the trees. Director David Fincher explained his plan to later computer-generate a house within the outline. They had painted it day-glo pink because it was the most unnatural color in the landscape and therefore less confusing for the computer process.

I found it beautiful … fanciful … whimsical. Mesmerized, I envisioned a whole neighborhood of them … grand in its scope … beautiful. But it would have to serve a greater purpose. As the day concluded I had the story of what would become the Pink Project. The idea was this: we'd litter the neighborhood with bright pink geometrical shapes as if tossed like dice by the hand of God. This would represent the aftermath of the storm. We would then hit the airwaves to ask businesses, congregations, and individuals of America to, in essence, adopt a house, solar panel, maybe a toilet, a brick—whatever their means would allow. As each house was adopted, we would reassemble them one by one until the entire neighborhood was complete—symbolically we would right the wrong. I called my partners at GRAFT that very night.

This art installation/political messaging device/fundraising tool would have to operate under the same tenets as the MIR houses, meaning it must be sustainable and accomplished at a price. This was no small feat. And it was GRAFT's expertise that "cracked the code."

The idea of the Pink Project felt sufficiently ambitious but never outlandish, yet whenever I would present it to someone else, I was met with baffled bemusement. Ironically, when presenting to the community, the native New Orleanians saw nothing strange in it. I warned that we would be turning their neighborhood into a circus. They explained, "our neighborhood is already a circus."

After nine months of preparation we put our installation up in a matter of days. It wasn't until I walked on site amongst the mass of pink structures did I realize why so many found it daft … because it was a bit daft. But, simultaneously, it was glorious, it was whimsical, and most of all, it was fun.

The DNA of the Pink Project worked much like a *tangram,* an ancient Chinese board game and dissection puzzle, which consists of seven flat shapes, called *tans,* which can be put together to form a multitude of 10,000 different shapes and figures.

Destruction meets Hope

We had 429 pink components lay haphazard at the outset of the installation, able to ultimately cluster into groups of three or four components, each cluster forming a single pink house. Collectively, there were twelve house types represented on the site, echoing the intention to retain individual expression. The construction of the five-week installation was executed with environmentally responsible materials. The house components were assembled with standard rented scaffolding, the gabled roof components recyclable aluminum with rented Kee Klamp attachments. These structures were clad with pink Earthtex fabric, a 100-percent recyclable Cradle to Cradle-certified material, which is now put to work as merchandise material for MIR bags, carrying on the message in the hands of our supporters. Four-foot exterior fluorescent lights glowed softly in the evening within the structures, powered by nine solar units mimicking the south-facing rooflines. These solar units now live on in the first homes built.

We scheduled operation from Thanksgiving to Christmas as a driving tour for the holidays. Hervé Descottes provided the final poetry for the piece. His lighting design captured the warmth of home and the glow of life that would return. To further tell the story he covered the ground with a thousand candlelights in tribute to the lives that were lost and in a pattern that mirrored the constellation of stars on that tragic night.

February 11, 2007, at Brad Pitt's house in New Orleans:
first mock-up of the Pink Project using kids' Play-doh.

In the days to come I would hear people discussing the reason for pink. Some said it represented "little pink houses for you and me," as in the quest for the American dream. Others said it spoke for the pink elephant in the room, the indictment that was Katrina, though little if anything was being done about it. Most just thought it was my favorite color. For me it was pink because it screamed the loudest.

As an art installation I wish it would have been cost effective to build them in a more solid manner mimicking the crisp corners of a monopoly house. As a fundraising tool we received millions in support from American families, but interestingly enough very little from businesses, congregations, or groups of any kind. As an outreach device it was highly successful in its message that little has changed but, "We are still here and we're coming home." As an act of social disobedience … it was just right.

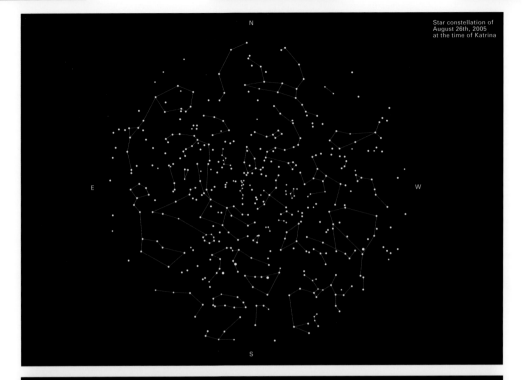

Star constellation of
August 26th, 2005
at the time of Katrina

Lighting principle for site: Stars and Sparkle

Lighting concept for week six developed by
L'Observatoire International

Mirroring the stars' constellation 1,000 solar candles glowed,

commemorating the lives that were lost during the catastrophe.

Hervé Descottes
Lighting designer of the Pink Project

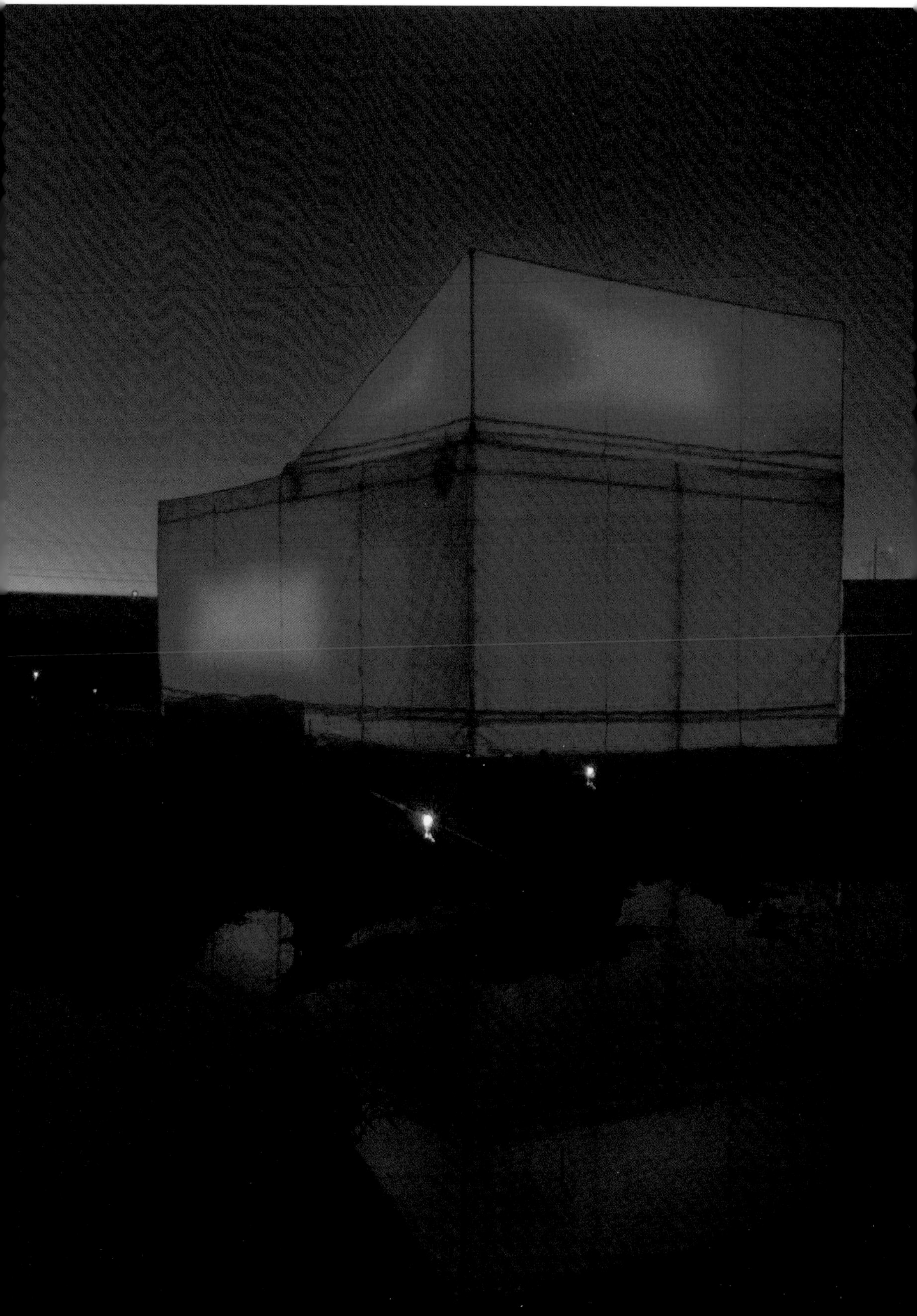

Lighting
powered by solar energy
Reuse of
photovoltaic
systems
for the new houses

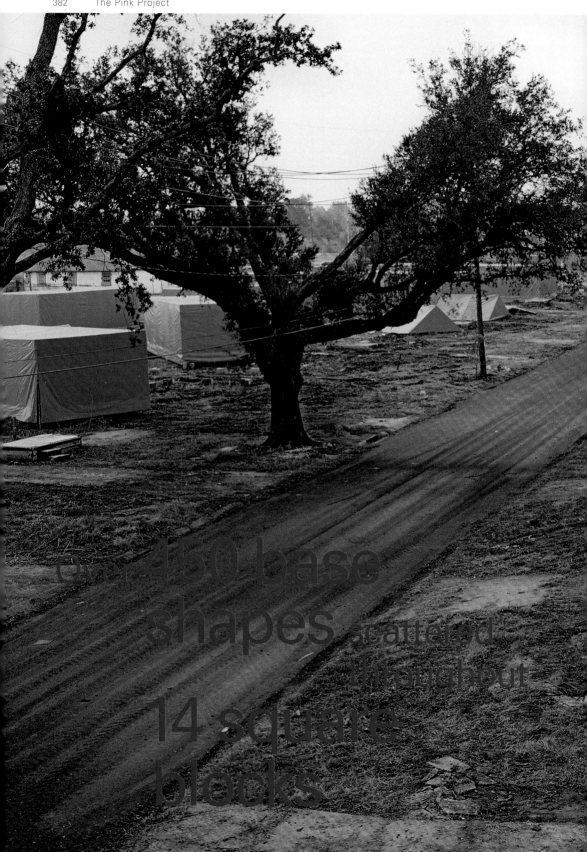

over 450 base shapes scattered throughout 14 square blocks

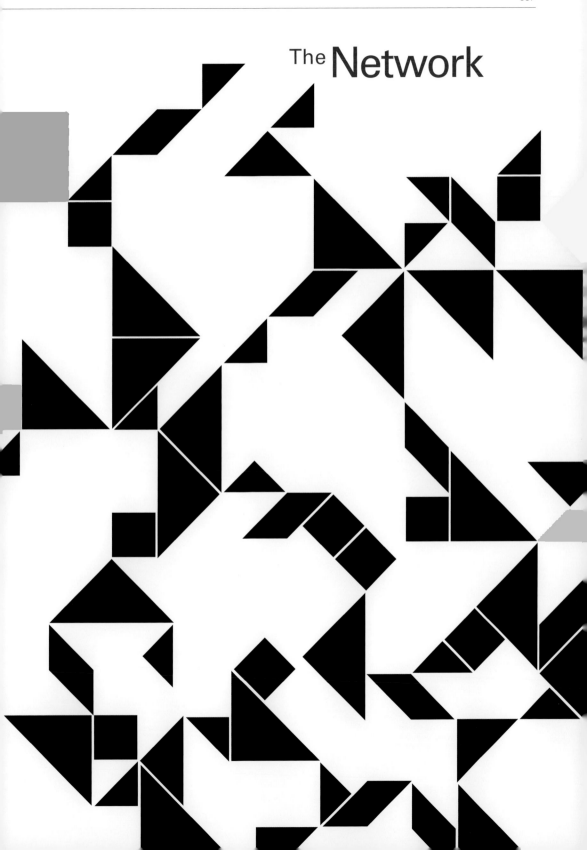

The Network

I'd like to see someone try and stop these folks from returning home. Brad Pitt

Make It Right, like so many other private organizations and community and church groups, is doing its part to move the Gulf Coast further on the path of recovery.

Hillary Rodham Clinton, U.S. Secretary of State, in 2008

The Make It Right (MIR) Team

Tom Darden, MIR

Make It Right (MIR) personnel located in New Orleans focus attention on project management including home construction, homeowner services, and general project promotion and communication. Formally recognized in August 2007 as a nonprofit entity, MIR developed a presence on the ground to function in coordination with core partners directly enacting the foundation's initiatives. In the winter of 2007, Tom Darden, having recently completed real estate projects at his own development company Arbor Equity, volunteered to come to New Orleans with his partner Mathias Linden. Together they began initial site research to determine where MIR might make the most positive impact.

For the purpose of finding potential MIR homeowner candidates and explaining MIR's mission locally, engaging the Lower Ninth Ward community became a primary imperative. New team members Ajamu Kitwana, Brandon Young, and Ware Smith joined MIR in the spring of 2007 under the leadership of Darden in his newly established role as executive director. Their objective was to concentrate efforts to reach out to former Lower Ninth Ward residents as well as political and community group leaders in order to establish neighborhood partnerships and encourage collaboration. In June 2007, Brad Pitt and MIR signed an unprecedented memorandum of understanding with a coalition of nine nonprofit Lower Ninth Ward advocacy groups with the special objective of restoring their neighborhood though shared resources; accordingly, MIR continues to work closely with this Lower Ninth Ward Stakeholders Coalition.

As MIR will continue to identify potential homeowners throughout the project, the enlisted support of homeowner counseling agencies like NeighborWorks America has been of significant advantage. These organizations specialize in community revitalization to provide opportunities for affordable housing. They will assist in the process of introducing residents to MIR and evaluating, case by case, family circumstances to determine how MIR might best benefit each resident.

In parallel with the process of community outreach, home construction will also be ongoing. MIR construction director Jon Sader joined the local team in the winter of 2008 to lead logistical rebuilding efforts in conjunction with local executive architect John Williams and MIR core partner William McDonough. Together with GRAFT they are generating construction documents for all MIR designs, determine which technical systems and materials equip the homes, and execute all elements of vertical construction. Construction methodologies vary depending on systems of cost and eco-efficiency, but initially include traditional site-built homes, structural insulated panel (SIP) framing, and modular configurations. All MIR home designs are chosen by the residents. The first MIR homes were completed at the end of summer 2008.

Publicity generated by the MIR project has been orchestrated by local New Orleans public relations firm Beuerman Miller Fitzgerald (BMF). Through media outlets local, national, and international, BMF strategically manages all MIR press releases and media events. As relates to receiving and responding to any general incoming communications and opportunities, MIR invites all inquiries through phone and website-based e-mail at www.makeitrightnola.org and has developed a unique database system to appropriately address each query. As the MIR project advances, so will MIR personnel expand and evolve. The ultimate goal is to help as many families as possible return home safely and responsibly to the Lower Ninth Ward. With the continued support and expertise of dedicated MIR partners, the future offers promise of a renewed New Orleans.

Organizational Diagram

Board of Directors	Board of Advisors
Sam Whitt	Brad Pitt
	William McDonough
Executive Director	Tom Darden
Tom Darden	Lars Krückeberg
	Thomas Willemeit
	Wolfram Putz

Analyst
Sarah Marks

Chief Operating Officer	Director of Communications	External Affairs	Director of Development	Legal
Veronica Taylor	Kim Haddow	Ware Smith	Steve Ragan	Cherokee
	—	—	—	
Office Manager	E-communications Coordinator	**Analyst**	**Sr. Associate**	
Grace LaGrazie	Jaime Peters	Sarah Marks	LaToya King	

Support Services	Dir. Homeowner Services		Dir. Construction Services	Architects Coordination
	Ajamu Kitwana		Jon Sader	GRAFT
	Veronica Taylor			
Office Manager	—			
Grace LaGrazie	**Outreach Coordinators**		**Administrative**	
—	Zakenya Perry		Paulette Pierce	
Receptionist	TBD			
Joyce Williams		**Product Acq. and Warehouse Mgmt.**	**Product Acquisition**	
	Administrative	Jodie Bua	Cesar Rodriguez	
Finance Manager	TBD	—		
Annette Thigpen		**Product Asst./ Warehouse/Est.**		
—	**Homeowner Services Analyst**	Josh Primmer	**Site Assistants**	
Acountant Specialist	Delia Woods		Bill Lawton	
Jaime Guillory			Julian Orr	
—		**Architect**	John Stough	
Warehouse Coordinator	**Homeowner Counseling Mgr.**	Tim Duggan		
Belinda Choina	TBD		**Construction Analyst**	
	—		Pierre Moses	
IS Manager	**Senior Counselors**			
Scott Freeze	Ashley Aubrey			
	Dena Rodriguez			
	Dale Sabatier			
	Jolita Tolbert			
	Customer Care Coordinator			
	Willie Murray			

GRAFT

In the summer of 2006 GRAFT was approached by Brad Pitt to help develop the idea for Make It Right. Brad Pitt's commitment and desire to ameliorate the circumstances facing New Orleans' displaced residents through a grassroots, privately funded initiative, resonated deeply with GRAFT. Brad Pitt's and GRAFT's collective goal was to create an innovative architectural role model for developing a coherent community under restrictive conditions—in this case, the aftermath of a natural disaster. A few months later in December 2006 all core team members were assembled to found Make It Right.

GRAFT's team, spearheaded by the partners Gregor Hoheisel, Lars Krückeberg, Alejandra Lillo, Wolfram Putz and Thomas Willemeit, began its efforts by studying the urban and architectural heritage of New Orleans and the greater Louisiana region. With the help of Nina Killeen, John Williams Architects, Tulane University, and many other contributors, GRAFT's team, led at various stages by Neiel Norheim, Christoph Rauhut, and Nora Gordon, researched New Orleans' iconography and particularities, specifically the urban matrix and predominant residential models of the Lower Ninth Ward (pp. 100–8).Simultaneously, GRAFT established a dialogue with the community as a means by which to understand the region's "taste culture," the psychological impacts of their loss, and their impressions of existing reconstruction efforts within the community. These were fascinating, sometimes heated discussions, hinging upon a variety of issues, such as whether or not this tragic loss called for a pure, nostalgic reconstruction of what once was. Despite the pain it brings, destruction also holds a chance for improvement, for modernization, for blending the quality of the past with the innovations of the future.

It became apparent in the midst of dialogues with the residents and research of the city that the situation best called for a rich diversity of architectural approaches. The diverse origins of the authors served to reflect the diversity of the residents. This led to the inclusion of local, national, and international architects and expanded GRAFT's role from sole architectural author of the single-family homes to that of curator for all of MIR's design components (pp. 121–29).

As the inaugural event for MIR, the Pink Project (pp. 354–85), initiated by Brad Pitt and produced by Stefan Beese at GRAFT, provided the backdrop upon which an exhibition of the thirteen proposals occurred. This exhibition, organized by Verena Schreppel, in which the projects were publicly revealed for the first time, cogently communicated the promise for future housing.

The roles of design curator and MIR advisory board member has presented unforeseen challenges. GRAFT has enthusiastically embraced these challenges, learning through this ambitious project how to diplomatically balance the authorship and generosity of gifted colleagues while simultaneously streamlining the designs to fit within MIR's organizational structure. Regardless of the challenges with which the MIR team was confronted, we persistently encountered the beauty of the collective spirit within every single member of the team to feel and do the simplest human thing—to provide help in times of need.

It is our hope that the challenges encountered and the solutions provided by the MIR team can assist in establishing similar organizations with like-minded goals in other parts of the world. With this in mind, as well as the ideological and financial support of Brad Pitt, GRAFT initiated the making of this book with renowned architectural writer Kristin Feireiss as editor.

Cherokee Gives Back Foundation and Sam Whitt

In December 2006, Cherokee Gives Back was invited to a charrette sponsored by Brad Pitt to discuss the feasibility of rebuilding homes in one of the hardest hit areas of New Orleans. After a spirited exchange of ideas, the group established a goal to build 150 homes in the economically disadvantaged Lower Ninth Ward, a community devastated by Hurricane Katrina. Brad Pitt's passion for the people of New Orleans was evident, and Cherokee Gives Back, the philanthropic arm of Cherokee, agreed to help turn Pitt's vision into a reality.

For the next two months, Cherokee Gives Back devoted time and resources to determine whether a revitalized community was a feasible objective. Is land available? Could homes be constructed amidst the devastation? Will the rebuilt levees endure the next storm? What is the environmental condition of the land? Is there adequate infrastructure, and can it support 150 homes? Will residents of the area return? Is insurance available? These questions and many more had to be analyzed before the project could move forward.

In early 2007, Cherokee reported its findings to Brad Pitt. Following an extensive question-and-answer session, the group decided that, while the task was challenging, the obstacles could be overcome. Based on commitments at that meeting, Cherokee agreed to provide project management expertise and organizational support to advance the project and build homes. In this role, Cherokee helped forge community relationships, lead the construction process, and manage the donations and project finances.

Cherokee Gives Back, along with Brad Pitt, GRAFT, and William McDonough+Partners formed the core group of partners—each providing time, talent, and resources to the project. Recognizing the need for on-site representation, Cherokee looked internally for a person who could move to New Orleans and manage the work. There were no internal candidates, but Tom Darden was wrapping up two of his own real estate projects and volunteered to help out. Cherokee continued to give behind-the-scenes support by providing engineering and environmental remediation assistance, and budgeting, corporate governance, and legal support.

As the project matured, the team reorganized and officially formed the Make It Right Foundation in August 2007. Cherokee created this new entity and continued to manage the finances. GRAFT, as the curator of MIR, oversaw the architectural research and development. Brad Pitt and William McDonough provided vision and leadership. As executive director of Cherokee Gives Back, Sam Whitt served as the interim executive director of MIR, and Cherokee worked with Shearman & Sterling's pro bono legal department to obtain MIR's determination letter from the Internal Revenue Service in October 2007.

As the project advanced, Cherokee took an ever-increasing role in helping to staff MIR. Tom Darden moved to New Orleans. Ajamu Kitwana, a summer intern with Cherokee, deferred his Wharton Business School education to help with the project. Brandon Young, a student at the University of North Carolina, provided valuable IT skills. Meanwhile, Cherokee also helped to form a board of advisors. The board provides strategic guidance and includes Brad Pitt, Bill McDonough, and representatives from Cherokee, GRAFT, and Steve Bing's office. Upon creation of the board in December 2007, Tom Darden was promoted to executive director, and Sam Whitt became a member of the board of directors.

Nearly twenty Cherokee staffers have provided support to MIR, helping to ensure the success of the project. We look forward to seeing the residents of the Lower Ninth Ward return and experience the rebirth of one of America's greatest cities.

William McDonough+Partners

Architecture and community design firm William McDonough+Partners is part of the Make It Right core team. The firm is helping to guide the design process and the material selection process. The project's mission embraces the core principle that products of human design can have positive impact and emulate natural systems, as defined in William McDonough and Michael Braungart's 2002 book, *Cradle to Cradle: Remaking the Way We Make Things*. For Make It Right, William McDonough+Partners developed a framework of strategies for the project that are inspired by Cradle to Cradle thinking to address climate and the Lower Ninth Ward location, eco-effectiveness, affordability, replicability, and support of the local economy. These strategies are incorporated in the design guidelines used by the architecture firms preparing prototype designs for Make It Right. William McDonough+Partners collaborate with these firms to ensure a synergy between their designs and the eco-effective systems and materials selection used during construction of the houses.

William McDonough+Partners and project executive architect John C. Williams Architects have assembled an integrated design team for the project to develop high-performance systems for the houses. Successful systems integration ensures that the houses optimize use of key resources including water and energy, such that over time the houses will become an equity-building tool for the homeowners. The integrated team includes New Orleans-based Moses Engineers, global design and consulting firm Arup, and the not-for-profit Solar Electric Light Fund. A key measure of success for the project is the ability to deliver these high-performing, eco-effective homes on a budget. To that end, systems frameworks and passive strategies are leveraged to deliver a 30 percent savings over typical energy and water use of a similar-sized, con-ventionally constructed home in the region. "Add-on" strategies, such as solar electric installations and large-scale rainwater harvesting, could further optimize the houses to perform at 90 percent savings in energy use and 53 percent savings in water use over conventional design.

Construction material selections for Make It Right are evaluated by William McDonough+Partners using a holistic understanding of place, performance, and human and environmental health. Material selection includes chemical assessment by McDonough Braungart Design Chemistry (MBDC) using their Cradle to Cradle protocol. The Make It Right houses will incorporate appropriate certified products, along with a preference for materials composed of ingredients supportive of human and environmental health that can be safely and repeatedly recycled. The list of project materials under review is extensive, and will evolve as the project is developed, as designs are refined, and as new materials become available and affordable, in line with the project's goal to inspire positive change in the design, construction, and building products industries over time.

Community meeting during the creating and design
of the project

June 16, 2007, signing of the Memorandum of Understanding

One of the first meetings where the 13 different architectural
designs were shown

The people of the Lower Ninth Ward examine the first designs

The Lower Ninth Ward Community

The project would only work if it were community driven. First we must earn their trust. Brad Pitt

The community leaders have been working with Make It Right since the launching of the planning process. They meet once a week to collaborate on efforts to rebuild a strong, sustainable Lower Ninth Ward. Some groups have already had experience in cooperating before and after the storm. The Lower Ninth Ward Stakeholders Coalition was formed after consulting with key neighborhood leaders, being convened as the Lower 9th Ward Neighborhood Empowerment Network Association (NENA). Their primary motivation, besides rebuilding the Lower Ninth Ward, is to build relationships over time, delivering on their commitments as outlined in the group descriptions (pp. 406–10). By following through on these goals, they continue to keep the trust between them and the people of the Lower Ninth Ward intact.

In the process of rebuilding, the biggest problem encountered was the lack of resources supplied to residents who were injured by the government's gross negligence. No alternative housing was provided. Infrastructure broke down. The government's red tape,[1] ignorance, and lack of expertise on multiple levels impeded efforts to help. The Lower Ninth Ward Stakeholders Coalition addressed these facts to MIR and clarified the need to draft a memorandum of understanding between the Coalition and MIR to formalize the already established relationship.

The purpose of this agreement was to outline collaboration for the goal of rebuilding approximately 150 homes for returning homeowners in the Lower Ninth Ward. The driving principle of the Coalition is to support and advance the interests of the people of the Lower Ninth Ward and their community. The Coalition's overarching belief is that residents must have the opportunity, both directly and through organizational representatives, to participate in determining how their community is rebuilt.

The Coalition and Make It Right agreed to promote neighborhood affordability and sustainability. Furthermore, all redevelopment efforts are aimed at building local organizational capacity, utilizing local contractors, and working within a broad framework for equitable and participatory rebuilding. The partners decided that employment and business opportunities should first be given to Lower Ninth residents and then branching throughout the city when necessary.

A critical component of this effort is rebuilding homes that are safe, exhibit high-quality design, and incorporate innovative, sustainable building technologies. Towards this goal, the Make It Right Project provides Lower Ninth residents with access to a range of expertise in sustainable building and design, and all homes developed under this project incorporate state-of-the-art eco-friendly components.

The creation of the Memorandum of Understanding and its adoption by all partners on June 16, 2007, helped in thinking through the process, clearly identifying specific roles, expectations, and responsibilities of all the parties. It was a long and painful process accompanied by both frustration and laughter. Nevertheless, the Memorandum of Understanding furnished a sturdy foundation for rebuilding the Lower Ninth Ward to be a place of choice as a vibrant and sustainable community.

1 "Red tape" is a derisive term for excessive regulation or rigid conformity to formal rules that is considered redundant or bureaucratic and hinders or prevents action or decision-making. It is usually applied to government, but can also be applied to other organizations like corporations. Red tape generally includes the filling out of seemingly unnecessary paperwork, obtaining of unnecessary licenses, having multiple people or committees approve a decision, and various low-level rules that make conducting one's affairs slower, more difficult, or both.

The Lower Ninth Ward Stakeholders Coalition

Charles E. Allen, III

Willie Calhoun, Jr.

MSPH, President,
Holy Cross Neighborhood Association
(HCNA)

Founder, New Life Intracoastal
Community Development Corporation
(NLICDC)

The assistant director for external relations and director of the Research Academy at the Center for Bioenvironmental Research (CBR) at Tulane and Xavier Universities, Charles E. Allen, III attended Xavier University of Louisiana and received his master's degree in public health from Tulane University. Since Hurricane Katrina, Charles E. Allen has spearheaded efforts to guide the restoration and recovery of the Holy Cross/Lower Ninth Ward community. He is involved with many organizations, including the U.S. Green Building Council.

A soon-to-be retiring FAA inspector of non-federal airports, Willie Calhoun attended George Washington Carver Sr. High School and Southern University of New Orleans. He is a lifelong resident of the Lower Ninth Ward and a Baptist minister. He founded the New Life Intracoastal Community Development Corporation during the 1990s to encourage community development and to create affordable housing in the area. Since Katrina, he has been diligently working to help his community recover.

Holy Cross Neighborhood Association (HCNA)

New Life Intracoastal Community Development Corporation (NLICDC)

Founded in 1981, the Holy Cross Neighborhood Association's (HCNA) mission is to improve the living conditions and serve the needs of its residents in Holy Cross New Orleans, preserve cultural and architectural heritage, serve as a clearinghouse for information, and actively represent the interests of the neighborhood with city, state, and federal agencies, private businesses, community organizations, and individuals for the purpose of actively improving the community.

New Life Intracoastal Community Development Corporation (NLICDC) is a nonprofit organization that was founded in September of 1993 with the vision of building affordable housing for residents of the Lower Ninth Ward. The board members are all community-minded residents of the Lower Ninth Ward. Prior to Hurricane Katrina, NLICDC successfully built five homes for Lower Ninth Ward families. Since the Hurricane, NLICDC has been providing home-buyer training, design services, and information to residents.

Mary Croom-Fontenot

Executive Director,
All Congregations Together
(ACT)

A native New Orleanian and resident of the Ninth Ward, Mary Croom-Fontenot is a graduate of the New Orleans public schools and received her bachelor's degree from Southwestern Louisiana University. A mother of three daughters, she found the conditions of the Lower Ninth Ward to be deplorable after Hurricane Katrina and uses her strong leadership to empower people to improve their quality of life and the Lower Ninth Ward.

All Congregations Together (ACT)

All Congregations Together is a congregation-based community organization dedicated to empowering people to affect change and improve the quality of life of families and communities in Greater New Orleans. ACT does this by developing leaders in member congregations and teaching them to organize. Sponsored by the New Orleans Interfaith Sponsoring Committee (NOISC), ACT works to utilize faith to allow people of diverse backgrounds to help each other recover from the devastation of Hurricane Katrina.

Pamela Dashiell

President, Lower Ninth Ward Center for Sustainable Engagement and Development (CSED)

A resident of the Lower Ninth Ward for the past nineteen years, Pamela Dashiell is the former president of the Holy Cross Neighborhood Association. She now directs the Lower Ninth Ward Center for Sustainable Engagement and Development. After Hurricane Katrina, she relocated temporarily to St. Louis where she continued to advocate for her community. Back in New Orleans since December 2005, she helps Lower Ninth Ward residents rebuild through her work with CSED.

Lower Ninth Ward Center for Sustainable Engagement and Development (CSED)

The Lower Ninth Ward Center for Sustainable Engagement and Development is an initiative of the Holy Cross Neighborhood Association that seeks to stimulate civic engagement and restorative rebuilding in the community. CSED strives to encourage repopulation, sustain natural systems, assist community leadership, and preserve resources in the Lower Ninth Ward. The CSED provides access to sustainable resources for returning residents and works towards the sustainable regeneration of the Lower Ninth Ward.

Linda Jackson

President, Lower Ninth Ward
Homeowner's Association

As president of the Lower Ninth Ward Homeowner's Association, Linda Jackson coordinates
efforts to help homeowners in the community
rebuild. She organizes neighborhood watch security
of the Lower Ninth Ward through block captains,
seeks monetary resources to help reconstruct
homes, and advocates throughout the nation, state,
and the City of New Orleans to obtain help in
rebuilding. She also informs residents of policy
changes through monthly meetings and connects
them to legal aid and counseling resources.

The Lower Ninth Ward Homeowner's Association

The Lower Ninth Ward Homeowner's Association,
located in the heart of the Lower Ninth Ward
community, has been working diligently to rebuild
and revive the community. The goal is to restore
the Lower Ninth Ward to the thriving, loving,
and caring community it was before the disasters
of poverty, crime, and Hurricane Katrina. The
Homeowners Association has spent countless
hours helping their neighborhood by organizing
residents and maintaining community contiguity.

Vanessa Johnson-Gueringer

Chair, Lower Ninth Ward Association
of Community Organizations for Reform
Now (ACORN)

A lifelong resident of the Lower Ninth Ward,
Mrs. Johnson-Gueringer has been a member of
ACORN since 2001 and during September 2005
became chair of the Lower Ninth Ward ACORN.
Upon returning home after Hurricane Katrina, she
was distressed by the lack of interest in rebuilding her community. Her leadership role has allowed
her to actively lobby for her community, meet
with elected officials, lead protests, and confront
political leadership about foul treatment of the
community.

Lower Ninth Ward Association of Community Organizations for Reform Now (ACORN)

ACORN and Lower Ninth Ward homeowners
have begun an unprecedented partnership that
has allowed them to be able to work together
to advocate for Lower Ninth Ward residents. They
have worked together to advocate both nationally and locally while working with public and private partnerships to improve conditions for those
affected by Hurricane Katrina. They have developed
community-based plans to rebuild the neighborhood and have facilitated the rebuilding process
through volunteer-led demolition and development.

Patricia Jones

Executive Director, Lower 9th Ward
Neighborhood Empowerment Network
Association (NENA)

As executive director of the Lower 9th Ward
Neighborhood Empowerment Network Association, Patricia Jones works to rebuild the Holy
Cross / Lower Ninth Ward community. With a
bachelor of science degree from the University
of New Orleans, Patricia Jones is currently
pursuing a master's of business administration
degree. A highly active member of the community, she works with many organizations to
help the Lower Ninth Ward recover from Hurricane Katrina.

Lower 9th Ward
Neighborhood Empowerment Network
Association (NENA)

The Lower 9th Ward Neighborhood Empowerment Network Association (NENA) is a resident-
based community development organization
established after Hurricane Katrina to play a leading
role in rebuilding New Orleans' Lower Ninth Ward.
NENA works to address destruction caused by
the storm, and the institutional neglect and disin-
vestment that plagued the neighborhood long
before Katrina by utilizing outreach to residents,
volunteer coordination of those who wish to
help, residential case management services, and
grassroots advocacy.

Alice Craft-Kerney

Executive Director, Lower 9th Ward
Health Clinic

A New Orleans native, Alice Craft-Kerney, RN,
BSN, is a product of Orleans Parish public schools.
She graduated with a bachelor's degree in biology from Southern University of New Orleans and
a bachelor's of science degree in nursing from
LSUHSC School of Nursing. She is executive director of the Lower 9th Ward Health Clinic founded
by herself and other community members as
a result of inadequate primary healthcare in the
Lower Ninth Ward post-Hurricane Katrina.

Lower 9th Ward Health Clinic

The Lower 9th Ward Health Clinic is a nonprofit,
community-based resource that arose out of a
desperate need for primary healthcare in the Lower
Ninth Ward and surrounding areas post-Hurricane
Katrina. The clinic provides high-quality, cost-
effective, culturally sensitive healthcare services
regardless of ability to pay. The staff provides all
clients with the support and knowledge they
need to successfully care for themselves, and also
advocates for patients in healthcare and quality
of life issues.

Vera McFadden

President, Lower Ninth Ward
Neighborhood Council, Inc.

President of the Lower Ninth Ward Neighborhood Council and resident since 1951, Vera
McFadden is the secretary at Dr. Martin Luther
King, Jr. Charter School for Science and Technology, where she worked pre- and post-Katrina.
Through her activities with the Lower Ninth Ward
Neighborhood Council, Mrs. McFadden is an
outspoken advocate to help her neighborhood
recover.

Lower Ninth Ward
Neighborhood Council, Inc.

The Lower Ninth Ward Neighborhood Council,
Inc. is a nonprofit organization created on November 23, 1966, to serve residents, especially low-
income residents, within the boundaries of the
Industrial Canal, the Orleans Parish line, Florida
Avenue, and the Mississippi River (the Lower
Ninth Ward). The council works with various organizations to assist residents and improve the local
quality of life. After Hurricane Katrina, the focus is
to advise the dispersed and encourage residents
to return home.

Malik Rahim

Founder, Common Ground Relief

Raised in New Orleans' Algiers neighborhood,
Malik Rahim founded and operated the Algiers
Development Center and Invest Transitional
Housing. He is co-founder and outreach organizer
of Housing is a Human Right in San Francisco,
California, and co-founded Common Ground Relief
in September 2005 with Scott Crow and Brandon
Darby. Since Hurricane Katrina, nearly 13,000
volunteers have gutted over 3,000 homes in the
Ninth Ward of New Orleans through their efforts.

Common Ground Relief

Common Ground's mission is to provide short-
term relief for victims of hurricane disasters in the
Gulf Coast region and long-term support in rebuilding the communities affected in the New
Orleans area, recently shifting focus to the Ninth
Ward. It is a community-initiated volunteer
organization offering assistance, mutual aid, and
support. It gives hope to communities by working
with them to provide for immediate needs and
emphasizing mutual cooperation to rebuild their
lives in sustainable ways.

Ajamu Kitwana

Financing the Vision

The Make It Right (MIR) program is designed to provide healthy, environmentally sustainable, and affordable homes for Lower Ninth Ward homeowners who were displaced by Hurricanes Katrina and Rita. MIR makes its homes affordable by providing "gap" financing to cover the difference between the home price and funds available to the property owner. Available funds may come from disaster recovery funds, mortgage loans, the homeowner's personal resources, or a combination thereof. Gap financing will be provided according to need via financing products made possible by charitable contributions to the Make It Right Foundation. Actual home prices will depend on the size of each home and its sustainable features. In addition to helping finance the cost of a new home, it is MIR's intent to ensure long-term affordability by establishing a guideline that limits the house payments of MIR households to no more than one third of gross monthly income—including principal, interest, taxes, and insurance.

Financing Sources   MIR anticipates that various funding sources will be available to finance each candidate's new home. Based on each household's financial history and capacity, candidates will have access to the following funding sources:

Disaster Recovery Funds   Homeowners negatively impacted by Hurricanes Katrina and Rita are eligible to receive disaster recovery funds or compensation to repair the damages incurred to their property. Funds are provided by various sources, including the federal government's Road Home program, homeownership and flood insurance proceeds, Federal Emergency Management Agency (FEMA) payments, etc. All MIR homeowners are expected to contribute disaster recovery funds that they have received for their MIR home. MIR counselors will work with homeowners to track disaster recovery funds received as well as to locate funds for which the homeowner is eligible but may not have received yet. Payment obligation may be reduced in cases where funds have been spent on medical expenses or essential living expenses related to the hardship of being displaced by the hurricanes.

Affordable Mortgage   Homeowners have the opportunity to utilize conventional financing at favorable terms with a local financial institution depending on the family's

Make It Right
Home Financing Structure

The example illustrates how the MIR
Loan Package can supplement a
homeowner's available resources to
cover the total costs of a MIR home.

Total Home Price

financial situation and credit history. MIR will have a list of approved lenders in the New
Orleans area of which households can take advantage.

Cash Contribution   Homeowners may contribute cash resources beyond their
disaster recovery funds and additional mortgage debt up to an affordable portion of
the homeowner's income to upgrade the size or special features of the MIR home.

MIR Gap Financing   The MIR Gap Financing is available in the form of forgivable loans
to fill the gap between the homeowner's home price and the sum of their disaster
recovery fund contribution. Clients may appeal to increase their forgivable loan eligibility
if a portion of their disaster recovery funds has been spent on approved expenses.
Approved expenses include housing costs and medical expenses. MIR's Gap Financing
will consist of a loan package that will include various loan products. Participating households will receive a MIR Loan Package calculated using various financial assessment
tools according to the following basic formula:

	Sales Price of MIR Home
–	Disaster recovery funds
–	Homeowner cash contribution
–	Mortgage from a private bank
=	MIR Gap Financing

Trevor Neilson

Raising Money to Make It Right

The most grueling task for me would prove to be financing the vision. It's simply not in my skillset to ask people for money. As instructed I embarked on the arduous fundraising circuit to little avail, dragging friends like Doug Brinkley around for backup. And though I was met with some kind support, it was clear that support would translate into few dollars. My partners at GRAFT had already been working for a year spearheading the architects and at this point were well into the design phase. I walked into a CGI meeting with President Clinton further dejected by the lack of response and the so-called Katrina fatigue. In a moment of questioning and contemplation I asked him if I was wasting everyone's time, mine included? Worse, would the levees even be properly corrected? He said to me calmly and in a kind voice something to the extent of just go forward … you will figure it out … this is needed. This became the impetus to carry on. Later that day I first called founding partner Steve Bing who committed an extraordinary contribution and would become the easiest call I was to make. Soon thereafter the Clinton-Bush Katrina fund donated one million dollars, and in a complete reversal of fortune we had begun. But ultimately, it was the kindness of strangers who would help res-urrect the Lower Ninth Ward. From our Pink Project and support on the website, to the American Idol audience, we were able to raise the necessary funds, and to that American spirit I remain grateful. Brad Pitt

When Make It Right (MIR) was created, the Global Philanthropy Group knew that fundraising needed to be approached with a sense of urgency that matched the size of the challenge. MIR was determined to not let down the families of the Lower Ninth Ward.

There are four strategies we developed to raise money:

Dinners with friends First, we asked friends to host fundraising dinners. Jane Rosenthal and Craig Hatkoff hosted the first of these events at their home in Watermill, New York, followed by a dinner at the home of Richard and Dorinda Medley. Brad Pitt and Angelina Jolie had multiple individual meetings with the dinner attendees and helped educate them about and convince them to support the project. The Ashmead Group helped organize these events which brought in several million dollars.

Securing our key partner   Second, the Global Philanthropy Group reached out to Steven Bing, a passionate advocate and generous philanthropist on environmental issues. Steve Bing became a founding partner, and with Brad Pitt's contribution created a ten million dollar matching fund MIR used to challenge others to donate.

The Clinton Global Initiative   Next, the Global Philanthropy Group asked Bill Clinton to use the Clinton Global Initiative's (CGI) annual meeting in New York, September 26–28, 2007, to announce MIR to the public and expose high-net-worth individuals to the project. Brad Pitt delivered a powerful speech to CGI members about MIR, and through a series of meetings and conversations Brad Pitt and the Global Philanthropy Group were able to secure additional commitments from these important individuals. Bill Clinton actively promoted MIR throughout the conference.

Events and massive media coverage to generate online donations through a cutting-edge website   The first of these events was conceived by Brad Pitt and GRAFT. What became the Pink Project was a large-scale public art project in the Lower Ninth Ward (see Pink Project, pp. 354–85). Using the art to draw attention, Brad Pitt did interviews with the media for two full days—over twenty in total. In each of these interviews he told viewers to go to www.makeitrightnola.org and urged them to donate parts of the house—donation levels created to coincide with costs of various components of the homes.

This was made possible through the web design work of MGX Labs, a talented team of people who created a three-dimensional online home that supporters can "walk" through online. This gave supporters a strong personal connection to the homes and project, resulting in a high percentage of visitors donating.

In March 2008, Bill Clinton and 600 university students from around the country joined Brad Pitt for the groundbreaking ceremony. The students volunteered to prepare the site for construction. Once again major media coverage resulted in increasing web traffic—8,000 hits as opposed to typically 2,500 hits per day—and donations.

The next major event was Brad Pitt's and Make It Right's appearance at the "American Idol Gives Back" show. Michelle Kydd Lee with the Creative Artists Agency (CAA) was extremely helpful in negotiating Brad Pitt's appearance on "American Idol Gives Back," which brought critically important funding and visibility to Make It Right.

During the shooting of the *American Idol* feature

MIR raised millions of dollars that came in as a result of the show—money that helped to reach the overall goal of $30 million.

What comes next   As of April 2009, Make It Right has raised approximately $32 million. While the Global Philanthropy Group and MIR are proud of this success, we know that it is a tiny fraction of the money needed to rebuild New Orleans. What happened to the people of New Orleans was wrong—it was one of the greatest moral failures in the history of the United States. MIR will build the 150 homes they have committed to build, and will then look for the next opportunity to help Make It Right.

Press conference during the opening event of the Pink Project

December 3, 2007, CNN's Larry King interviews Brad Pitt in
New Orleans' Lower Ninth Ward

GRAFT

The Network Phenomenon

The ever-increasing ability and desire of human beings to interrelate with one another at all geopolitical scales has generated a wide assortment of results, ranging from efforts seeking the eradication of disease to the engagement in decentralized modern warfare. Within this ample spectrum of collective efforts, regardless of ethical bearing, practically no act of sustainable potency would be attainable without the presence of intricate, intentionally formed social networks.

Having witnessed the state and federal governments' slow response in amelio-rating the conditions for residents of New Orleans, Brad Pitt felt a moral imperative to provide a solution; his first action was to "put the smartest people together in a room" to find this solution. This initial grouping of people created the core MIR network. Each core member of the MIR Team, Brad Pitt, William McDonough + Partners, Cherokee Gives Back Foundation, Trevor Neilson, and GRAFT, brought sub-networks of their own and the generosity of spirit to put these to excellent use. All core members of the MIR team are highly specialized individuals with broad social networks ranging from the philanthropic, political, architectural, and academic, to the vocational.

Three primary points of interest have existed within the MIR project in respect to how it functions as a network: firstly, the relationship between the idea and leadership roles; next, the relationship between the initial idea and the subsequently established goals; and finally, the evolution of the network's shape and functionality. There are both virtues and weaknesses inherent within this grassroots, non-hierarchical growth pattern, as there also are within top-down structured hierarchies.

The core MIR team was comprised of leaders from a wide variety of professions. Notably however, during the first phases the project organized itself through a democrat-ic approach where all parties participated in generating plausible solutions, rather than through a top-down hierarchy. Arguably, leadership in this case was provided by a self-evident idea so powerful that it needed not be driven by the individual but rather by the idea itself. Certainly leadership has played a key role in logistical organization and management, but for a concept to be replicable elsewhere the value of the idea is critical as the primary driving force and strongest leader.

A defined goal or series of goals must be established in order for a network to func-tion efficiently, particularly in respect to networks whose modus operandi is atypical, such as MIR. The difference between the ideas and goals must be properly defined before enacting an overall strategy. Ideas flow from an initial abstract condition, and are centered upon a specific sense of purpose as an overarching concept in relation to this condition. Goals are concrete objectives. As goals are meant to be actualized, they typically inform methods of implementation. In essence, ideas deal more with "what" while goals rest more in the realm of "how." Any successfully pursued idea progressively concretizes, first becoming a concept, and later folding into an overarching strategy comprised of goals and the associated tactics necessary to meet them. For Make It Right the overarching idea, that initial catalytic kernel, was the revitalization of New Orleans as a justice call, beginning with the tangible goal of building 150 safe, affordable, sustainable, well-designed homes.

By testing the viability of the concept through research and scenario planning, the pertinence of the goal may be identified at an appropriate level of specificity. Once agreed upon and established, the goal in many ways becomes the king that rules the network. Vague goals run the risk of generating communication breakdowns, inefficiency due to information redundancy, competing fiefdoms, and discrete, overly personalized operations. Strict goals whose resolution is prematurely or excessively defined may stifle innovation. Strong, mutually agreed-upon goals that lay down basic and necessary restrictions generally lead to robust, collaboratively produced solutions.

Brad Pitt's determination to assist in enabling the re-growth of the city of New Orleans began in a loose, primarily non-hierarchical fashion. Grassroots and democratic in nature, no clear hierarchical rules of engagement were established, opting instead for a free-form think-tank mentality. This model helped generate incredibly interesting dialogue between individuals of all walks of life. All input was given equal consideration and all network members could access input easily, without pre-established communication protocol. As the tactics and strategies to achieve MIR's goal grew so did the network necessary to achieve them. The non-hierarchical network necessarily evolved into the more structured organization that we see today primarily due to the scale of the network.

Ideas and goals carry the potential to easily corrupt one another if not kept in check. Due to the looseness and freedom associated with idea formation, oftentimes certain real-world constraints are necessarily eschewed. There is a rhythm or pace that must be kept between the development of the infrastructure enabling the system to operate and the imposition of guidelines and operative constraints: there is a sweet spot. The further the project proceeds, the more the goal can be viewed in detail, and the more specific the innovation can become. It is at this point that highly specialized individuals

From left to right:
William McDonough, Brad Pitt, Wolfram Putz, Tom Darden

will focus upon their core competency. For this very reason it is critical to constantly refer to the overarching idea as a check-and-balance exercise to ensure the project does not veer off course. In order to build an infrastructure robust enough to fulfill the objectives, the organizational structure must adjust organically as the project moves forward.

The path to attainable innovation generally contains greater-than-average pockets of frustration accompanied by minor inefficiencies. It is typically through trial and error that goals, tactics, and networks can be adequately assessed, more often than not in hindsight, to ensure they are supporting the initial idea or concept. If they are not operating synergistically, the potency of the idea is compromised, the goal must be retooled, or the network infrastructure must be modified. In the case of MIR, the goal of 150 homes additionally called for these to be sustainable, affordable, and safe and well-designed homes. These constraints impact one another significantly, and as such the project has called for a constant valuation process oftentimes favoring one condition over another and making equal concessions in all categories. In order to ensure a balance between all components, during the onset of the project it was critical for each of these pillars to have an advocate. Over time this balance has become so integral to the process that guardianship or advocacy has become obsolete, the entire network understanding the value in each mandate and working collectively to ensure them.

Within the petri dish of minimal guidelines and creative thinkers many incredible opportunities for innovative problem solving emerge. Examples such as the Pink Project, whose model falls outside the operational norms of fundraising, would likely have not been pursued. The Pink Project was initiated by Brad Pitt as an invaluable tactic to meet a fundraising goal. Pink succeeded in raising awareness, lending credibility to the cause, stimulating a wave of grassroots donations, and generating momentum for larger sponsorships. Similarly, the design guidelines for the houses left sufficient flexibility for the designers to produce innovative proposals. Had the MIR team favored utilizing pre-existing building techniques, the variety and uniqueness in the thirteen projects would not exist, nor would the extraordinary construction innovations have occurred.

The organic growth of the MIR model within an initially non-hierarchical network led the team down avenues of extraordinary beauty as well as frustration, all the while navigating our way towards the goal of building 150 environmentally responsible, safe, affordable, well-designed homes for the residents of the Lower Ninth Ward. This project's positive effects have been acknowledged on a global scale, most notably apparent through the international interest expressed to replicate the MIR model in response to unfortunate global catastrophes, including the recent earthquake in China, the devastating fires that have swept Australia, the hurricane disasters in Haiti, as well as the increasing problem of homelessness in the United States. Concerned citizens have expressed interest in the project through monetary and intellectual donations and have augmented the network of imaginative solutions. Speaker of the United States House of Representatives Nancy Pelosi, in her suggestion that MIR is a model for the nation, has bolstered our convictions to continue to find innovative ways to solve the problems that face us as a people.

Contact Addresses for Donations

Make It Right
P.O. Box 58009
New Orleans, LA 70158
Phone: (888) 647-6652
www.makeitrightnola.org

Churches Supporting Churches
Reverend Dwight Webster
President and National Project Director
Pastor - Christian Unity Baptist Church
1700 Conti Street
New Orleans, LA 70112-3606
Phone: (504) 522-3493

Common Ground Relief
P.O. Box 6128
New Orleans, LA 70174
Phone: (504) 304-9097
commongroundrelief@gmail.com
cubc89@bellsouth.net
www.cscneworleans.org

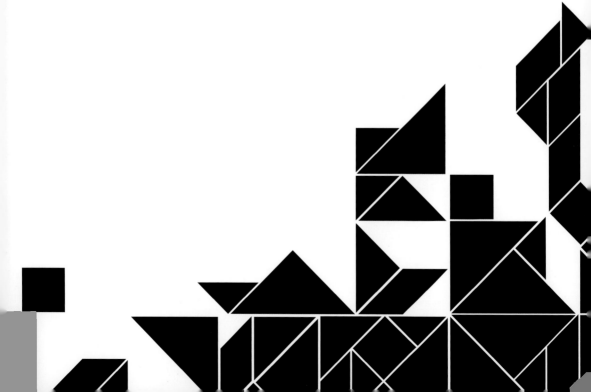

Building the Future

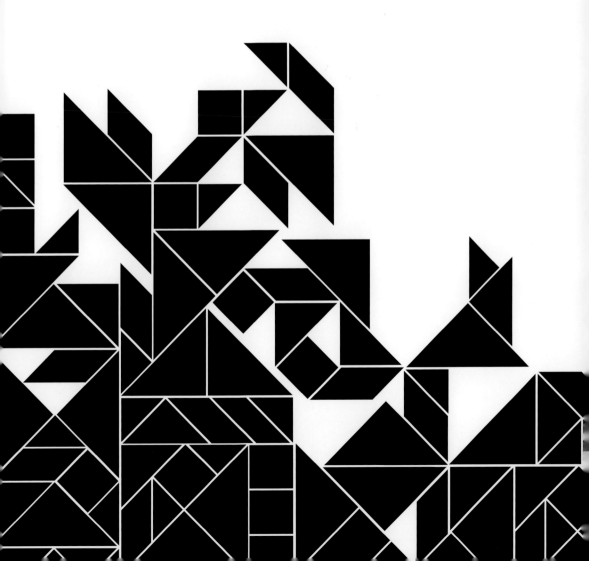

To rebuild here it is absolutely essential to create something that is equitable, fair,

and offers dignity for the family within. Brad Pitt

Green technology has been considered a rich man's toy, but to truly be viable it must be **efficient** at all levels.

Brad Pitt

Tom Darden

Homeowner Counseling

It's said the road to hell is paved with good intentions. You can author all the great ideas in the world but you need a pragmatic voice of reason to guide those ideas to fruition. We would simply not be here today if not for Cherokee, specifically the all-star team of father and son Tom Darden II and Tom Darden III (secretly known as T2 and T3).   Brad Pitt

Outreach Process

Hurricane Katrina and the resulting breach in the Industrial Canal levee devastated the homes of the Lower Ninth Ward. Very few former residents have the wherewithal to rebuild. In order to gauge the interest of displaced homeowners in the initial target area in rebuilding with MIR, they first have to be identified and contacted. In order to identify former homeowners in the initial target area, MIR has resolved to partner with local community organizations.

MIR relies on community partners throughout the outreach process to communicate with residents who elect to participate in the MIR project. In the event community partners cannot locate certain residents, MIR staff works with these groups to re-evaluate the strategy. Given that these community nonprofits have contacts and existing relationships with residents of the neighborhood, through a Request for Proposal (RFP) process MIR has partnered with community groups interested in connecting MIR to individuals who meet the project criteria.

**Community partners who have
agreed to participate in MIR outreach include:**

Common Ground Relief (CGR) (p. 410)

Lower Ninth Ward Center for Sustainable
Engagement and Development (CSED) (p. 407)

Lower Ninth Ward Homeowner's
Association (LNWHA) (p. 408)

Lower Ninth Ward Neighborhood
Council, Inc. (LNWNC) (p. 410)

New Life Intracoastal Community Development
Corporation (NLICDC) (p. 406)

Homeowner Counseling

Homeowners in the MIR target area face many obstacles to rebuilding that make recompensing the dollar value of their destroyed homes woefully insufficient. Some of those obstacles include dramatically increased construction costs, utility costs, insurance costs, and property taxes. Many homeowners in the MIR target area are retired and/or disabled and unable to work. Property tax exemptions and other conditions that made homeownership affordable before Hurricane Katrina are unlikely to be adequate in the future. The unique challenges among homeowners in the MIR target area require that MIR considers carefully how to make MIR homes truly affordable. The process of homeowner counseling helps to achieve this end.

Homeowner counseling is the process through which Lower Ninth Ward residents who work with MIR choose, finance, and prepare to own their new homes. Through the intake process, candidates that are determined to meet MIR program eligibility requirements are referred to a homeowner counselor. The counselor works with clients to assess their financial situation, choose a home design that meets their needs and preferences, and assemble a financing package. Financing options include a contribution from the client, outside financing sources such as a mortgage, and grants and MIR forgivable loans to meet any outstanding financial need. Through the homeowner counseling process, MIR helps each homeowner acquire resources they can contribute to their new home, including arranging for MIR forgivable loans. These means help to ensure any remaining financial gaps are bridged and a MIR home is affordable to each displaced Lower Ninth Ward homeowner.

The vast majority of homes in the MIR target area have been leveled. These homes represented valuable assets to families, many of whom had little or no income but who managed to maintain the equity of their homes. Increased costs of construction and insurance make rebuilding, even to pre-Katrina conditions, unattainable for many homeowners. Many have not received enough compensation from Road Home or insurance claims to cover current rebuilding costs. Many would also be overwhelmed by ongoing insurance costs, property taxes, and maintenance costs even if MIR provided a new home for free. Homeowner counseling provides MIR an opportunity to evaluate what affordability means for each homeowner in the initial target area and, subsequently, to develop a plan and the necessary support structure to ensure that MIR homes are affordable for residents.

In order to respect the value of homeownership and resistance to outside investors within the Lower Ninth Ward community, MIR is not seeking to acquire land until adequate trust has been established. MIR therefore is seeking site control by working with each landowner independently. The aftermath of Katrina presents several challenges to this approach, including lost ownership documentation, undocumented succession, post-Katrina transfers of ownership among family, and difficulty for elderly and handicapped homeowners displaced to other cities to return to New Orleans to work with MIR. However, many resources are available to homeowners who lost homes in the Lower Ninth Ward. All levels of government, private foundations, religious institutions, and generous individuals are reaching out to provide aid. Homeowner counseling plays the keenly important role of assisting each property owner to assemble all available outside resources. Ultimately, this step is critical in reducing the cost of MIR forgivable loans necessary for each household, and in turn enabling MIR to build more homes.

In addition to financial support, homeowner counseling helps homeowners face the practical challenges of building a new home. Counselors ensure that candidates understand the energy-saving technology and the unique home designs that MIR is offering. Determining the space where one's family lives is a very important decision. The challenge of considering a unique and innovative proposal in the aftermath of a tragedy like Hurricanes Katrina could easily become overwhelming. Ultimately, homeowner counselors enable MIR homeowners to make informed decisions about their new homes.

MIR intends to partner with local nonprofit organizations to conduct homeowner counseling. In so doing, MIR bolsters the capacity of the local community to help residents return home throughout the Lower Ninth Ward. Working with local, community-based nonprofits also enables MIR to utilize the resources of those who know and understand the Lower Ninth Ward community, as well as to maximize the effectiveness of MIR homeowner counseling services.

The process that each Make It Right homeowner will go through is described in the following Homeowner Road Map:

Homeowner Road Map Steps

Outreach – Contact to Make It Right
Residents learn about MIR through word of mouth, MIR's local community partners, through the internet, via news media, or through direct outreach by MIR staff.

Orientation and Application
Residents take the first step toward coming back home by attending a MIR Orientation Session and completing the preliminary application form.

Intake Session
Residents attend an individual session with a Housing Counselor who provides details about the program, answers questions, and collects the household information required to determine eligibility. Eligible residents will be assigned a Housing Counselor who will provide support and stay with them from intake through move-in.

Eligibility Assessment
Internal process during which MIR staff determine residents' eligibility for MIR.

Design/Financial Session
Residents review home design options and select one that meets their needs, lifestyle, and budget. The initial cost is calculated. The residents are scheduled for a comprehensive needs assessment, and receive a list of participating mortgage lenders who can be approached for financing.

Comprehensive Needs Assessment
The Housing Counselor explores residents' counseling needs, makes referrals where appropriate, and develops a list and schedule of financial counseling sessions.

Financial Counseling Sessions
The Housing Counselors work with the applicant to develop a need-based financing package that ensures that a MIR home is affordable by supplementing the family's resources with MIR Loans and helps the resident to become mortgage-ready.

Home Selection Session
Residents select a home design to meet their needs, aesthetic preferences, and lifestyle. The Housing Counselor puts together final building and financing package.

Pre-closing Session
Resident attends a pre-closing session to review closing documents so they understand what they will be asked to sign at closing.

Closing Session
At the Closing Meeting the resident signs all the construction and mortgage loan documents.

Pre-Construction Workshop
MIR residents attend a group workshop to learn about the construction process, being introduced to the major players involved in building the homes and receiving a general overview regarding progress benchmarks and timelines.

MIR Home Construction
MIR homes are built using sustainable materials that are healthy for families and the environment. MIR Counselors will track and monitor progress and keep homeowners informed of the home construction, ensuring the work quality meets their satisfaction. This includes a number of site visits during construction.

Move-In
A MIR Counselor will conduct a "how to" walk-through with residents focused on the energy-saving features of their home, how they work, and how they are maintained. Residents will also receive a Green Vendor Resource List detailing green appliances and materials.
Residents will be encouraged to get involved in activities that ensure long-term viability of the neighborhood. All MIR residents will receive a Hurricane Planning Guide which includes detailed instructions regarding pre-evacuation preparation, evacuation routes/procedures, and post-evacuation guidance. Certificate of Occupancy is issued and the new owners can move in!

Group Workshops

Financial Fitness 101 Workshop

- All MIR program participants are invited and encouraged to attend a Financial Fitness workshop designed and delivered by NeighborWorks® America.
- The Financial Fitness course focuses on basic money management skills, avoiding the pitfalls of predatory lenders, how the home can be a wealth-building vehicle, accessing mainstream financial tools, and other subjects aimed at helping MIR families become informed consumers.

"Green House = Green in Your Wallet" Workshop

- Maximizing the benefits of the green features in your MIR home
- Enhancing the health of your family and community by living "green"
- Teaching children the benefits of protecting the environment and how they can lend a helping hand

Sustaining the Gain: What You Need to Know About Basic Home Maintenance

- Cost-saving benefits of preventative home maintenance
- A "how to" guide for basic home maintenance
- Using the seasonal maintenance calendar to stay on track
- Tips for addressing home repairs
- The connection between home maintenance and reduced insurance premiums

Creating a Sustainable Community Workshop

- Investing in Your Community: Short-Term Investments, Long-Term Rewards
- Playing a Leadership Role in Your Neighborhood
- Homeowner as Catalyst for Helping Neighbors Back Home
- Simple Strategies for Keeping Your Neighborhood Safe
- Involvement in the Neighborhood Association
- Creating a Tool Lending Library
- Creating a Neighborhood where Children Thrive

Overview of the curriculum for the Make It Right Homeowner Counseling program:

Pre-Construction Counseling

The pre-construction counseling provides the foundation for an ongoing trust relationship between the counselor and the homeowner which is essential for success. The counselor's work in this phase supports the eligibility, needs assessment, and financial packaging processes, and ensures consistent outcomes.

During Construction Counseling

The counseling sessions conducted during construction prepare families for the ongoing responsibilities/benefits of homeownership, and provide support as they make the transition into the new neighborhood. Counselors will do status checks as construction progresses and provide guidance to MIR families as they monitor the ongoing development of their homes/neighborhood. This phase of counseling will support families' active involvement in the construction process/neighborhood planning, teach them financial skills/management to ensure sustainable homeownership, and help them learn about preventative maintenance as a vehicle for reducing insurance and energy costs.

A customized counseling plan will be developed for each MIR family based on a comprehensive needs assessment (from the Initial Intake Session). The number of sessions conducted during this phase can range from three to nine depending on the family's goals/circumstances.

1. **Construction Management**
   - Meeting the Key Players
   - Monitoring the Construction Progress
   - Preparing for Move-in Day
   - Participating in Neighborhood Visioning/Planning

2. **Financial**
   - Developing a Family Budget
   - Creating a Debt Reduction Plan
   - Building a Solid Credit History
   - Dealing with Income/Employment Issues
   - Developing a Family Emergency Fund
   - Establishing Family Financial Goals
   - Opening an Individual Development Account or Savings Account

- Maximizing the Benefits of Earned Income Tax Credits
- Preparing for the Closing Meeting
- Steering Clear of Predatory Lenders
- Sustaining the Gain; Avoiding Financial Pitfalls

3. Home Maintenance

- Conducting Preventative Maintenance
- Dealing with Home Repairs
- Learning the Basics of Living in a "Green" House
- Getting the Most out of Energy-Saving Features
- Saving Money on Insurance Premiums

Post-Construction Counseling

The post-construction counseling provides support services to families as they transition from their existing post-Katrina housing arrangement into their new home and neighborhood. There are two key elements to this phase: the post-occupancy site visit and attendance at the "Sustainable Community" workshop. At the site visit MIR families will learn how to operate all systems in the new home and will receive a customized, user-friendly schedule for conducting routine maintenance. The workshop will suggest ways in which MIR families can participate in the ownership and growth of their neighborhood/community. The workshop will identify a wide range of options for involvement, so that residents can choose those that are consistent with their interests, skills, and lifestyle.

1. Post-Occupancy Site Visit –
"Getting to Know Your New House"
The "How To" Walk-through:

- Electrical System
- Heating/Air Systems
- Water and Plumbing
- Energy Features
- Windows and Doors
- Lighting Fixtures
- Appliances
- Exterior Elements
- Routine Maintenance Schedule
- Hurricane Preparation and Evacuation

Exhibition of first design of first-round architects
during the Pink Project.

Credit: Exhibition design, GRAFT

2. Creating a Sustainable Community Workshop

– Investing in Your Community: Short-Term Investments, Long-Term Rewards
– Playing a Leadership Role in Your Neighborhood
– Homeowner as Catalyst for Helping Neighbors Back Home
– Simple Strategies for Keeping Your Neighborhood Safe
– Involvement in the Neighborhood Association
– Creating a Tool Lending Library
– Creating a Neighborhood where Children Thrive

Jon Sader

The Ground Game
The Process of Construction

On December 6, 2007, when the Make It Right project was announced with the
Pink Project in the Lower Ninth Ward, the foundation began to offer thirteen different
designs, conceived by internationally acclaimed architects, to the homeowners living
in diaspora. It was now time to develop the designs and build the homes while adhering
to the four principles established by the founders:
- the use of environmentally intelligent Cradle to Cradle[SM] materials
- ambitious high design
- providing safety
- maintaining an affordable single-family residence

There were also the goals of being a catalyst for positive development, using innovative
engineering techniques, and making the innovations replicable for global application.
Usually these concepts are mutually exclusive, but MIR was determined to find ways to
combine as many of these concepts as possible together, without leaving any behind.
I became the director of the MIR construction department and a pivotal figure in the
realization of the founders' determination to bring families back to their homes in New
Orleans while fulfilling these goals. With the help of Sarah Howell from John C. Williams
Architects, we took on this challenge: to see the opportunities that lie within the cross-
disciplines of the combined fields of expertise.

Cross-Disciplines

The agreement of the founders to maintain the four principles described above as
priority over any and all standard and widely accepted traditional construction methodologies uniquely belongs to the Make It Right construction department. Traditional
construction methodologies consist of methods that have their own profit margins which
drive cost and create competition between architects, engineers, general contractors,
and subcontractors. This competition of cross-disciplines commonly results in entities
not sharing information or purposefully providing misinformation to the end consumer.
The propagation of misinformation continues throughout the professional labor forces
and the material suppliers within the construction industry, becoming exponentially

First-round architects at
kick-off meeting in New Orleans.

Source: Make It Right Foundation

fictitious with any associated media hype regarding a particular construction method
or new material.

The development of cross-disciplines within Make It Right is the assembly of
architects, engineers, contractors, subcontractors, building officials, material suppliers,
and vendors with the moral fiber and unwavering desire to eliminate all misinformation
and to achieve the fundamental four goals. The inherent ability of the Make It Right
project to draw experts in the fields of manufacturing, implementation, and testing
brings purveyors of innovation to the project. In turn, this produces an unmatched spirit
in the collaboration of technology, creating cutting-edge construction methods and
practices. The construction site functions as a laboratory of implementation process, performance, innovation, and education.

The Drive to Affordable

MIR's holistic approach to affordability entails teaching new methodologies of
construction, implementing new combinations of technologies, and producing higher
performance at a lower cost. To achieve affordability, the economic impacts of design,
materials, labor force, contractor profit margins, insurance, legal fees, governmental

fees, economies of scale, implementation of staff, and speed of construction must be considered. All of the above have a profound effect on the affordability of the home. MIR recognizes all of these things in combination with the quality of the product received and is working diligently to achieve the factual definition of "affordable."

In designing a building or any other system, there are two possible approaches: prescriptive and performance. Prescriptive analyzes individual components of a system and performance analyzes the system as a whole. The MIR design and construction team has chosen to follow the performance approach through all of the components of the home. For example, a prescriptive-based design of an HVAC system would use a rule-of-thumb to size equipment, such as one ton per 1,000 square feet. The performance-based design of the same system would evaluate insulation, building materials, windows, and determine how much heat loss or gain there is. The furnace is sized so that it runs efficiently and has the correct capacity. MIR applies the performance approach to several components of the building.

Foundations

One example is the foundation of the home . A typical foundation follows the perimeter of the home. MIR can significantly decrease the amount of concrete by shrink-ing the foundation to support effectively the center two-thirds of the home. This causes the structure to be cantilevered over the edge of the foundation, and by doing so it decreases the amount of concrete in the foundation by over 50 percent. It also increased the speed of installation by over 50 percent, and therefore cut the cost of the founda-tion by 50 percent. The deep wooden beams under the home, and the wood fiber that goes into making them, is also significantly less because it was possible to introduce engineered floor joists. These joists contain significantly less wood fiber than conven-tional 2 × 10 floor joists. Coupled with advanced framing techniques, this innovation resulted in a 30 percent reduction of lumber used in constructing a typical Make It Right house. By evaluating the components and cladding of the building as one system, MIR implements performance-based design. This all occurred as a result of the performance engineering and is exactly the same as sizing an HVAC system for a home.

Framing

A similar approach was taken with the framing techniques. There are about fifteen different techniques used in advanced framing—all of them are done to reduce the amount of wood in the lumber package, or rather, the board fiber in the house. But inter-estingly enough, advanced framing techniques have long been resisted because build-ers, framers, and homeowners always believed that more wood equals more strength.

Foundation with over
50 percent less concrete

Source: Make It Right Foundation

Common practice in residential construction is to space wall studs 16" on center. This
is an assumption that is only recently being questioned by building science experts and
by MIR. In researching the basis of the 16" on-center standard, it became evident that
the people who build the wall section have each tested the individual components: the
strong-tie people test their strong-ties, the glue people test their glue, the wood people
have tested the wood, and the nail folks have tested the nails. But nobody has ever
tested them in combination with one another. Over at the University of New Orleans,
MIR tested the prescriptive wall, and that wall is just a normal wall nailed together like
all the framers do across the country. The performance test is to put the studs at
24"OC, use the glue as MIR specifies, and use new high-performance nails and a specified nailing pattern. The preliminaries on those tests show that MIR's 24"OC wall cross
section is roughly five times stronger than a home that is built with a normal 16"OC
wall. Another consequence that happens when jumping to a 24"OC: the amount of
insulation that is used actually increases by about 7 percent, so the home is insulated
more, which equates to a significant improvement in each category : sustainability,
affordability, and durability.

Electrical Wiring – Verve Living Systems

This product, based on a new wireless battery-less technology, gives Make It Right
homeowners a new level of control over their lighting systems. This system relies on
a small compact radio frequency to turn lights on and off and requires fewer switches,
allows the builders to do all the wiring through the attic and basement (saving material
and labor costs), and is enormously energy efficient.

Plumbing

A singular pipe in a bathroom services up to four fittings. A plumbing system called Pex allows MIR to use multiple connections at any point in the system. It reduces the number of potential leakage points by about 40 percent. Another big advantage with the Pex is that an in-home sprinkler system can be introduced. Pex lines support sprinkler heads in the house, so the expensive pressurized water system that commercial sprinkler systems need can be avoided. By having sprinklers in each room MIR is able to immensely increase safety in these homes. By looking at the home itself as a lending institution, increasing the home's durability is a wise investment. Everything from the added strength of the framing, the elevated foundation, the fireproofing, etc., can result in a significant reduction in homeowner's insurance. There is already a program that has been approved by Congress that involves certifying the houses as being "fortified" by a third party . This allows savings up to about 50 percent on insurance payments.

Sustainability

Most people think sustainability aspects undeniably add costs to a home. However, what is not taken into consideration is the longevity of material and health of people. By using only non-toxic Cradle to Cradle materials we not only extend the life span of the buildings, hence amortizing the up-front costs, but in a way do the same with the people living in them. The usage of solar panels and geothermal HVAC systems reduces the energy costs on utility bills for some houses to as little as $3 per month. Using "greener" materials can also result in decreased costs. For example, limestone aggregate found in concrete is not a natural resource in Louisiana. However, crushed concrete is. Usually if someone elevates the home they will pour concrete on the entire underside of the home, which is rather expensive. MIR uses crushed concrete under the home as a way of reducing the carbon footprint that it took to make the concrete to begin with. Concrete is about $6/sq. ft., whereas crushed concrete is about $0.50/sq. ft. The used concrete comes from demolition and construction sites around the city. Instead of this material going to a landfill, MIR stockpiles and reuses it on site.

Effectiveness

The construction methods above are examples for rethinking the way we build. The MIR construction department is driven by optimization so that the construction of MIR homes can effectively fulfill the demands of the established principles and possibly affect the construction industry as a whole.

Micro Effects

- Decrease overall home cost
- Increase speed of construction
- Increase performance of home
- Increase quality of products

Macro Effects

- Resource development
- Vendor development
- Information networking
- Education / Job market
- Change in public policy

The MIR construction department is in the unique position of acting in the best interest of the consumer with high-performance "green" technology, while holding the construction and product industry to the highest standards achievable with the unified goal of "affordable."

In spring of 2009, the first eight homes designed by world-renowned architects and a community playground were completed. The homes average 1,400 square feet, consisting of traditional site-built, structural insulated panel (SIP) and modular construction, utilizing a different general contractor for each home. All the homes achieved the U.S. Green Building Council's (USGBC) Leadership in Energy and Environmental Design (LEED) Platinum Level and the National Association of Home Builders (NAHB) Gold Level. The houses' energy performance is outstanding, as is their hurricane resistance, as proven by Hurricane Gustav, which hit just after the first six homes were completed in September 2008. They are Cradle to Cradle inspired, their average cost is $150/sq. ft. (including solar and geothermal), and their homeowners are each convinced that the design of their own home is the most beautiful. One hundred more homes will be completed by the end of the year. Our construction technologies create the market—not corner the market. MIR as a nonprofit organization has the unique ability to be a catalyst of construction technology. To actually research, engineer, educate, and implement new technologies for the entire project from the demolition of the lot to the completion of the home makes MIR a model for future construction.

Make It Right has the potential to revolutionize the green building industry and in so doing become a catalyst for building energy-efficient and environmentally sustainable homes throughout the country and around the world.

Tim Duggan

Community Beyond Housing
Micro-Farming and Landscape Design

MIR has received a grant from the LA Disaster Recovery Foundation to create a series of "open to the community" demonstration gardens. In a series of public dialogues and charrettes with the community about the ecological context of wetlands and the historical context of the agricultural community within the Lower Ninth Ward, the residents clearly stated that they would love to see these demonstration gardens relate to both wetlands and urban farms. Intensifying this dialogue specifically with the Urban Farming Coalition MIR decided to take what have historically been vacant or non-usable lots and turn them into interesting experiments of social, economic, and agricultural developments within the Lower Ninth Ward. Urban Farming Coalition provides information and instructions for citizens to acquire a vacant lot and turn it into an agricultural plot of land that is both restorative and productive. Each lot will grow a variety of fruits and vegetables that include kale, corn, beets, strawberries, carrots, etc.

Through this initiative MIR have partnered with the Blair Grocery project that teaches at-risk youth about various agricultural practices in an effort to build a micro-community that is able to cultivate the land and harvest its benefits.

Already in March 2009 two lots in the target area were dedicated as demonstration garden projects for an urban micro-farm. A curriculum will be integrated into the local schools that addresses the micro-farm concept and teaches children and neighbors how to enhance a community through gardening and farming practices. In a next step MIR envisions developing relationships throughout the neighborhood with various local restaurants that will buy this produce and help create a smaller-scale economic development engine within the community.

Contaminated Soil

The plants that are chosen for the urban farms are also aiding in the reconditioning of the soil, and in this way MIR was able to address a broader issue with the soils in New Orleans. The micro-farms' soil-improvement possibilities can help with the perception of the harmful contaminants that people talk about with the soils in New Orleans. In this way it starts an educational outreach opportunity relating to the soils and compost opportunities that were historically thought to be waste products and carted away to the landfill instead of being returned to the natural cycle locally. At the moment it is planned to establish an open composting for the community at the street front of the garden sites. Additionally, a series of contaminated soils that are a product of the site demolition are cleaned through a four-stage reconditioning and site composting program.

The majority of the water for the micro-farm will be captured from the local street runoff. It will be cleansed with a so-called rainwater buffer to remove sediments and pollutants and will be funneled by gravity into the agricultural terraces and passively irrigate the crop. In addition, MIR is also looking at creating small rainwater catchment areas that can act as rain barrels or cisterns.

Stormwater

The handling of stormwater runoff in a sustainable way is not only of interest to us in regards of water collection for the micro-farms. MIR has been working with the City of New Orleans, and specifically the director of public works, to develop a conceptual layout of the pilot streets for the Stormwater Management Project that is four linear blocks long, and is intended to create four individual models of street typologies that are related to stormwater management. Each model will have different applications: pervious pavement, rain gardens, bioswales, collection cisterns, etc. MIR is currently working on developing the logistics of the team as well as surveying, percolating, and performing geotech investigations and soils reports.

The site strategy for the MIR houses is different from the conventional engineering mindset of collect, convey, and discharge. Every parcel is treated as a zero-runoff site, and every house treats water as a resource. This also allows the elevation of the dialogue and permits the question: "Why can't everybody be handling their stormwater this way?" Because it is handled successfully at the lot level.

Standard practices have had retention approaches and detention approaches for stormwater management. Due to the clay soils and due to the difficulty for water to infiltrate, soils are amended and areas are assigned to create a retention opportunity and are overlaying a framework of detention on each one of those systems to control flooding. In this way the landscaping program is establishing a combination of both concepts. The soil itself is treated as a resource because the practice of simply digging it up and replacing it with new soil is not very sustainable. This is achieved by putting plants in the ground that allow stormwater to integrate into that infiltration layer and establish a more permeable soil layer.

It helps to imagine the flow of water on our site. It hits the roof and is then directed to a gutter and downspout system which is tied into a rainwater collection cistern which holds approximately 600 gallons. When the rainwater system accepts approximately

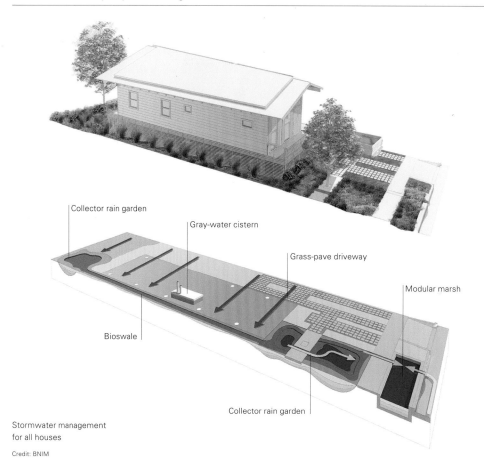

Collector rain garden

Gray-water cistern

Grass-pave driveway

Modular marsh

Bioswale

Collector rain garden

Stormwater management
for all houses

Credit: BNIM

50 percent of the roof drainage it fills up and overflows into what can be deemed a natural systems approach that integrates rain gardens, bioswales, and pervious pavement into the broader landscape design. Once the gardens and bioswales accept that water, they act as mini-bathtubs that fill up and nourish plantings that drink that water very fast so that it does not leave the site in curbs and gutters. The last line of defense, if it's really raining hard, is the perimeter of sidewalks in the neighborhood where the pervious concrete is installed. The subsurface section below the pervious concrete varies in depth so that in essence it is acting like the final detention canal around the house and the last stage in water storage. If there is even more stormwater entering the site then these systems can store this water, which would later leave the site and go to a curb and gutter.

In each of the ten initial installations of pervious concrete, the subsurface depth was changed to give more or less storage of water. It was also attempted to achieve the correct compaction in each case so that the pavement won't fail. Some of the installations have over thirty inches of storage capacity. In New Orleans, a hundred-year storm requires approximately fourteen inches of storage. If one can store anywhere near fourteen inches then it is possible to reduce the flooding of a hundred-year rainstorm, which is quite an accomplishment. Only last year the sewage and water board spent many millions of dollars pumping water over the levee with electricity that can be broken down into a per-gallon cost to the City of New Orleans. One can calculate that every block that is developed using these strategies deviates over 100,000 gallons from hitting the stormwater system. That is a very quantifiable metric that can make people understand how much money can be saved.

This innovative approach, versus the traditional curb and gutter concepts, comes with little extra cost. Right now MIR is finding that pervious concrete is about an 8 percent premium over regular concrete. That premium is good because it's a labor cost increase. It means that MIR is training and creating jobs in a green-collar approach for the local economy. If one wants to compare apples to apples then one has to look at all the other costs, which include building bigger pipes and handling much more stormwater on a much larger scale.

Modular Approaches

Stormwater is an equally urgent issue in other cities around the country. MIR hopes to figure out innovative solutions so other cities that have the same water quantity and quality issues related to stormwater management can benefit from this as well.

The City of New Orleans has been an early partner for MIR's pilot streets program and MIR is very excited about the opportunity.

One of the components that is most exciting is the idea that each one of these stormwater and urban-farming systems are modular at the site scale, but flexible enough to be integrated into a larger macro scale with respect to how MIR develops its strategies for the public. That allows long-term maintenance and visioning to be dealt with in a sustainable and economic manner. It also creates a framework which can be scaled to the size of the development tasks at hand.

MIR is creating a natural, systems-based site sustainability.

GRAFT

Learning from Mistakes

Somewhere along the way it was misconstrued that we were giving away free houses; this was not the case nor was this what the homeowners were asking for. This was never about a handout—this was about a hand up.   Brad Pitt

All smart systems try to establish a feedback loop. Everybody can only progress if we face and give criticism—and are open to learn from our mistakes.

Starting out, more people of the Lower Ninth Ward were rightfully suspicious and hesitant to believe in Make It Right—they had their hopes raised and dashed by other groups earlier. Charles Allen of the Holy Cross Neighborhood Association remembers that after the first meetings with MIR he was "pretty excited, but I also wondered how real it was. Were they really going to stick around?" Pamela Dashiell of the Lower Ninth Ward Center for Sustainable Engagement and Development observed that "people were suspicious of all the organizations who parachuted in after the storm. Being rational, people always wonder what's in it for these groups? Why would they be doing this?" And Patricia Jones, executive director of the Lower 9th Ward Neighborhood Empowerment Network Association (NENA), explains that it was important to the residents that they "were assured that this partnership would not be about impressing or showcasing Brad Pitt, but more importantly about getting people who lived in the neighborhood back home quickly into more sustainable, green-conscious, and affordable homes."

Organizations like NENA already provided case management, financial counseling, architectural services, construction administration, and volunteer labor to residents in the Lower Ninth Ward. They were willing to partner with MIR since there was interest in bringing resources to the community, finding a way to get more people home faster, and making green technologies a permanent fixture in the Lower Ninth. NENA was concerned however, "That this project could just be another façade for a developer to creep into our neighborhood," according to Patricia Jones. One of MIR's core members is the Cherokee Gives Back Foundation, a nonprofit branch of Cherokee, a leading redeveloper of brownfields and contaminated sites nationwide. Their expertise was crucial to the organization and management of an endeavor of this scale. But people were suspicious this project would be a springboard for Cherokee developments in the region. Those concerns and suspicions have proven to be unfounded.

Volunteers entering a local scenario from the outside always face the challenge of ramping up their knowledge of the local conditions and are dependant on the willingness of the local residents and community organizations to teach them. All the members of MIR started with a steep learning curve and required time to understand how to work within the Lower Ninth Ward. Patricia Jones of NENA believes that at the beginning MIR failed in "clearly identifying roles, responsibilities, and expectations." But other community leaders like Pamela Dashiell disagree, saying MIR connected by making a formal partnership with the community, by putting it in writing in a memorandum of understanding signed by the stakeholders' coalition and MIR. She says MIR was "as explicit as possible about what they were about on the front end. That was a big difference. That was something unique and welcome and really necessary to do. They reached out—and in New Orleans terms, and especially in Ninth Ward terms— this all happened with lightening speed. It happened fast and it was heartening that something was happening. They reached out and connected." Charles Allen also points out that an open dialogue is ongoing and that MIR has "been coming to the stakeholders coalition meetings every Wednesday since the beginning, keeping us updated on their progress, vetting and getting our input." He observed that when people finally saw the "splash and national attention the Pink Project generated and then saw work on the houses begin," it became apparent to them that MIR was committed and that "they were going to be around for a while."

Miscommunication can be a natural ingredient of the dynamics that make up human relationships, and the MIR project is as vulnerable to that risk as all endeavors of this kind. It takes an ongoing effort to improve the dialogue and it relies on the generosity to forgive mistakes, the willingness to learn in all partners, and the assumption of positive motivation for every individual.

One typical example comes from Pamela Dashiell. "There have been some miscommunications and some missed opportunities. As we were engaged in determining the mortgage, ownership, and heirship issues, it got confusing and unclear. Especially the communications part of it—it seemed to some folks they were not getting what they were promised. Some people were under the assumption the houses were free. I never heard anything like that from Make It Right, but some people just assumed that and there is still some confusion about that." But in reality, MIR was careful never to promise a free house to any resident. The principles of partial ownership and the contribution of the residents' personal assets from disaster recovery funds and other private sources of income were an integral part of the financial concept from the beginning. The attempt to design a fair financing system to help to bridge the funding gap (see section on finances, pp. 411–12) seems to have been vulnerable to missed or misunderstood information. Pamela Dashiell thinks that "part of the confusion comes from the fact that it is a very complex process—the financing, the personal data that's required, and changes in the processes that have occurred over time have left some folks in the community unclear—except for the people who are in the program."

While continuing to support the capacity of the Lower Ninth Ward Stakeholders Coalition, Patricia Jones and NENA also partnered with MIR to advise on the project and counseled residents who were interested in participating in the MIR program. Patricia Jones is of the opinion that the publicity for MIR's agenda created internal strains on the community's agenda. For her the question arose as to whether the partnering with MIR would be detrimental to the community's larger agenda. MIR was committed to building 150 homes in a first stage, but in the Lower Ninth Ward more than 5,000 homes were damaged. She feared there could be a struggle to maintain and grow the capacity to continue to assist hundreds of other families not getting MIR homes. While MIR has seriously committed itself to 150 homes in a first phase, its members hope to grow its program beyond those numbers. But being aware of the necessity to promise only what you know you can deliver, MIR has kept its focus on building the 150 homes it promised the community it would deliver. For other community members, therefore, the MIR program is not seen as a competing project or a limitation on the large-scale rebuilding efforts still at hand. For Charles Allen of the Holy Cross Neighborhood Association, MIR has definitely been a catalyst for generating momentum for all recovery initiatives. In his opinion it has attracted the attention of people all over the world with positive effects. "They want to hear our stories. It's kept New Orleans and what happened here in the news. This is a great and big happening to and for us. We want this to continue and to do more. I would love to see the site evolve into some economic development for the local community. I would also hope the Make It Right team would be willing to do some business redevelopment and open some stores here."

And Pam Dashiell says right now that the fact is MIR is the largest-scale development in the Lower Ninth Ward. "They have built the most energy-efficient neighborhood in Louisiana and play a pivotal role in the larger community."

Two other goals make the MIR program different from many other disaster relief initiatives and generated complex discussions within MIR and with the community. Architectural high design and an ambitious sustainable program are benchmarks for

MIR that other organizations do not pursue with similar zeal. The motivations, benefits, and tasks involved with these goals needed to be discussed at length with all partners of the process.

For Patricia Jones, the understood intent was to expose people in the community to different architectural styles and designs that addressed sustainability and survivability within the context of the Gulf Region. MIR was able to convince renowned local, national, and international architects to participate who agreed these needs had to be addressed. Patricia Jones believes the architects offered their expertise to develop designs that addressed the region's landscape, welcomed an association with a high-profile project, and were interested in putting their designs on display in the region. But she also says there were ego issues. "I believe the architects were honestly inter-ested in helping our community, but didn't necessarily like the idea of a small New Orleans-based architectural firm stamping and/or changing their designs at the local architect's leisure. In agreeing to help our community, expectations around design control were not discussed thoroughly enough before launch. There was a delay in the process because the architects weren't comfortable with losing control of the design. They were not comfortable with another architect explaining a design on their behalf to residents. They were not initially convinced that the recognition that followed ade-quately accounted for the role played and the work provided. Friction was inevitable."

While there were certainly practical aspects of the architects' motivation to become part of MIR's program, one should firstly accept and respect that all architects did par-ticipate out of a deeply felt human desire to help. They followed the call to right the wrong and to engage themselves in a lengthy and often time-consuming process with very little pay or in some cases even a voluntary relinquishment of their fees like the firm of Pugh+Scarpa. It was part of the stated MIR goal to attempt to build these designs with community collaboration, at an affordable price point, and with an innovative, sus-tainable concept. Within a demanding process like this, tensions needed to be resolved not only within the community but also within the demands that MIR made of the archi-tects to stay true to these goals. As of today, no architect has abandoned the project no matter how hard the collective learning and sacrificing has been. Charles Allen states that the design charrettes that MIR organized with the architects and the community "have really engaged the organizations and residents to get our ideas on what we want. And they listened to our ideas—the very large windows the residents were used to in their old houses were incorporated into the designs. And the length of the new houses was made more like the Shotgun houses people used to live in. People really get engaged and excited." And Pam Dashiell underlines the point that MIR focused on a direct and ongoing dialogue with the groups as a whole and with individual groups.

Community meeting and design charrette

"The community has been engaged as an active partner in finding and recruiting the people who had been dispersed after the storm so they could come home and participate in the creation of beautiful, sustainable, energy-efficient houses that contribute to the community, climate, and carbon neutrality overall." There were concerns about MIR's commitment to show that green development is attainable, affordable, and replicable by adopting Cradle to Cradle thinking. For Patricia Jones a lot of the ideas of Cradle to Cradle were still too much in theory and not enough in practice in mainstream America. She was concerned about the possibility of added costs associated with this high-profile project, and wondered if it could be replicated affordably?

In 2009 MIR will reach that goal of building affordable green buildings. Until now the conventional wisdom within the design and construction industry was that green was too expensive, but these new houses are of high design and MIR has cracked the code of making sustainable living available at an affordable cost. For Pamela Dashiell of the Lower Ninth Ward Center for Sustainable Engagement and Development the houses are leading examples in energy efficiency, provide dramatic reductions in energy bills, and are symbols of pride by having obtained the LEED Platinum certification. "It's wonderful. It fits right in with New Orleans—they have made the house as resilient as possible— wind resistant, water resistant, high over the flood plain. They are one of the leading drivers on cutting carbon and helping us reach our climate and carbon-neutral goals to fight climate change."

Look, nothing like this project has ever happened here, just like the disaster of Katrina — we're still learning lessons. Charles E. Allen, III

Make It Right has built in the Lower Ninth Ward the most advanced, resilient, sustainable neighborhood in America. Pamela Dashiell

What we are doing to revitalize our neighborhood is hard work. There are no easy answers and all lines are not black and white. Many are gray, but we press on to- wards a better environment and a better future. In the end, I'm sure no one received everything he/she wanted or expected. This work is not for the faint of heart. How- ever, when I look down Tennessee Street and see electricity bills of $20, I always find myself smiling. I shoot up a prayer and say "Thank you God for those who made it home. Strengthen us for those to come." Patricia Jones

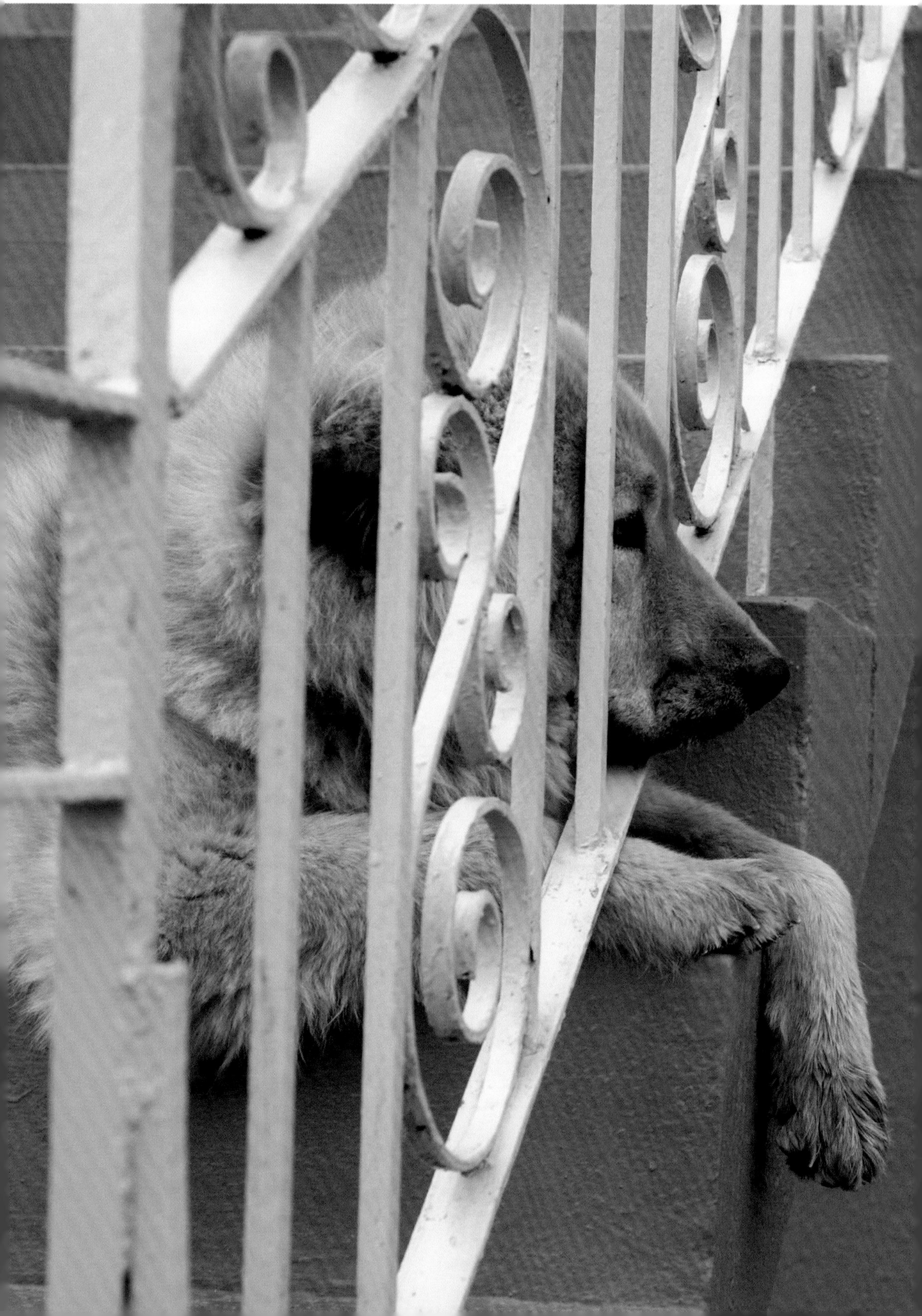

Brad Pitt

Closing

Architects are historically underpaid and misunderstood, yet it is they who shape the world in which we reside. The greatest misconception about architecture is that it is merely an occupation of aesthetics. In truth

architecture defines our daily lives ...

how we get up in the morning, how we move through our cities, in what conditions we will complete our work, and where our kids will play. We remain creatures susceptible to our environment. Whether this existence be harmonious or cumbersome,

it is architecture which hones our memories.

If you are ever able to tour one of the MIR homes, you will discover buildings of air and light, homes that have respect for the families that dwell within, homes that have respect for a parent's paycheck, respect for the health of its children, and respect for the environment at large. MIR has proven that there is no reason affordability means sacrificing quality, and care. These are homes of dignity. And isn't this architecture at its best? MIR is important to me for another reason that wasn't clear upon its inception. If you've experienced catastrophe upon catastrophe, are historically shut out, or just seemingly destined for misfortune, what becomes your definition of the world? But the moment someone comes along and helps you back on your feet through the simplest of gestures, doesn't that reshape your view of the world and your relationship with it? I have begun to believe this is Make It Right's greatest contribution.

The most exciting moment for me as of late has been watching the neighborhood take form, for it is the choice of each

individual family that will collectively define the streetscape. Therefore the final paragraph of this story of MIR is unknown to me, because it is the community that will define it. As it should be.

Already families are seeing electric bills of eight dollars, twenty dollars, twelve dollars. More importantly you can sense the pride in these families that have returned. Funny enough, each one will tell you, "our house is the best."

This neighborhood which suffered such travesty, in fact the hardest-hit spot of the hardest-hit area, the icon of all that was wrong with the recovery effort, has now become the most ecologically performing and intelligently built community in all of the United States. Someone in D.C. should come down here and seriously take a look at this.

Thank you to the members of our team who

have been here since Make It Right's conception; especially GRAFT who has been there since the beginning. Thank you to the tens of thousands of people who have given their ideas, their sweat, and their support. You know who you are and

you have my respect.

And thank you to the folks of New Orleans for your tenacity and enduring spirit. You have taught me much.

Appendix

Biographies

Charles E. Allen, III
Associate director at the Tulane/Xavier Center for Bioenvironmental Research (CBR), Charles E. Allen, III, MSPH, also helps direct the CBR's Sustainable Urban Ecosystem Initiative (UrbanEco), is president of the Holy Cross Neighborhood Association (HCNA), represents the Holy Cross Historic District as a member of the New Orleans Historic District Landmarks Commission, and is co-chair of a partnership and project known as REACH-NOLA. Mr. Allen is a proud graduate of Xavier University of Louisiana where he received his bachelor of science degree in biology in spring 1995. He is also a graduate of the Tulane University School of Public Health and Tropical Medicine where he received his master of science degree in public health in fall 1998.

Art for Wear
Art for Wear is a New Orleans-based company that strives to create and manufacture unique, high-quality, yet socially and ecologically responsible products. The Make It Right merchandise products have been developed and manufactured with consideration for the environment through each step of the process. The tees are 100% certified organic cotton. Each is printed with eco-friendly inks (no PVC's, phthalates, or solvents).

Ken Alston
Ken Alston is CEO of MBDC, the product and process design firm founded to implement Cradle to Cradle design. Since 2000 he has worked closely with William McDonough in a variety of roles. Under Alston's leadership, MBDC has launched a Cradle to Cradle product certification program, which is increasingly being taken up by leaders in sustainable product design. (Cradle to Cradle[SM] is a Service Mark of MBDC.)

Claudia Baulesch
Born in Pruem, Germany, Claudia Baulesch studied interior design at the University of Applied Sciences Trier, at the Danish Design School in Copen-

hagen, and at Kansas State University, Manhattan, Kansas. She worked as an architect at Rosenmund & Rieder Architekten, Basel, Switzerland, and as project manager in interior design at plajer & franz studio, Berlin. Since 2006 she works as a freelancer in interior design in Berlin, Germany.

Stefan Beese
Executive associate at GRAFT and the executive producer of the Pink Project, Stefan Beese studied architecture at the University of Applied Science, Kiel, and interior architecture and production design at the University of Applied Science for Design and Media in Hanover, Germany. In 1995, Stefan formed the company Beesign Production Design and has done production design for feature films, TV and commercials, as well as having designed shows, fairs, exhibitions, and sets for stage and screen in Europe and the United States. In 1999, Stefan began working with GRAFT as both project manager and production designer. Recently appointed to helm their new production design division, Mr. Beese will oversee the entirety of GRAFT's projects for film, television, music videos, and related media events.

Carrie Bernhard
Carrie Bernhard is the executive director of the Lime Agency for Sustainable Hot/Humid Design, a nonprofit architectural research and outreach organization, and a principal of Prosus Design, an architectural design office based in New Orleans, LA. She was recently the co-coordinator of *Architectural Record*'s and Tulane University's international design competitions for New Orleans. Carrie Bernhard is the co-author of the online publication "An Introduction to New Orleans House Types" and the forthcoming book *New Orleans Urban Morphology and Housing Typology.*

Dr. Michael Braungart
Dr. Michael Braungart has been a professor of process engineering at Universit Lyneburg, Germany, since 1994. Braungart is the scientific director of EPEA Inter-

nationale Umweltforschung GmbH, Hamburg, Germany, and co-founder of MBDC; both firms embrace intelligent, aesthetic, and eco-effective design and seek to optimize products within the Cradle to Cradle framework.

Douglas Brinkley
Douglas Brinkley is a professor of history at Rice University and a contributing editor at *Vanity Fair. The Chicago Tribune* has dubbed him "America's new past master." Six of his books have been selected as *New York Times* Notable Books of the Year. His book *The Great Deluge: Hurricane Katrina, New Orleans and the Mississippi Gulf Coast* won the Robert F. Kennedy Book Award. He lives in Austin and Houston, Texas, with his wife and three children.

Willie Calhoun, Jr.
A retired FAA inspector of non-federal airports, Willie Calhoun is a product of George Washington Carver, Sr. High School and Southern University of New Orleans. He is a lifelong resident of the Lower Ninth Ward and is also a Baptist minister. He founded the New Life Intracoastal Community Development Corporation during the 1990s to encourage community development and to create affordable housing in the area. Since Katrina, he has been diligently working to help his community recover.

Richard Campanella
Tulane geographer and mapping scientist Richard Campanella is the author of three critically acclaimed books, including the award-winning *Geographies of New Orleans* (2006) and *Time and Place in New Orleans* (2002). His fourth book, *Bienville's Dilemma: A Historical Geography of New Orleans* was published in 2008. Campanella's research at the Tulane/Xavier Center for Bioenvironmental Research has appeared in the *Journal of American History, Architectural Education, Technology in Society, Photogrammetric Engineering,* on NPR and PBS, in *The New York Times,* and elsewhere. He and his wife Marina live in the Upper Ninth Ward.

Alice Craft-Kerney

Executive director of the Lower 9th Ward Health Clinic and a New Orleans native, Alice Craft-Kerney, RN, BSN, is a product of Orleans Parish public schools. She graduated with a bachelor's degree in biology from Southern University of New Orleans and a bachelor's of science degree in nursing from LSUHSC School of Nursing. She is executive director of the Lower 9th Ward Health Clinic founded by herself and other community members as a result of inadequate primary healthcare in the Lower Ninth Ward post-Hurricane Katrina.

Mary Croom-Fontenot

Executive director of All Congregations Together (ACT), a native New Orleanian, and resident of the Ninth Ward, Mary Croom-Fontenot is a graduate of the New Orleans public school system and received her bachelor's degree from Southwestern Louisiana University. A mother of three daughters and sister of five, she found the conditions of the Lower Ninth Ward to be deplorable after Hurricane Katrina, and therefore felt compelled to use her strong leadership to empower people to improve their quality of life and the Lower Ninth Ward.

Pam Dashiell

Pam Dashiell is a long-time civic and environmental justice activist in the Lower Ninth Ward. She directs the Lower Ninth Ward Center for Sustainable Engagement and Development (CSED) and chairs the board of the Holy Cross Neighborhood Association. Pam is sustainability program coordinator for the Louisiana Bucket Brigade, an advisor to the Gulf Coast Fund, member of the Lower Ninth Ward Stakeholders Coalition, and serves on the boards of the Alliance for Affordable Energy, and Smartgrowth Louisiana.

Tom Darden, III

Tom Darden is the executive director of Make It Right. Mr. Darden received a BA with honors from the University of North Carolina at Chapel Hill. He then worked as a development consultant in Washington, DC, evaluating former manufacturing and mining sites in the DC metropolitan market, including the site of the discovery of the largest dinosaur bone unearthed on the east coast of North America. Darden focused efforts on reclaiming the mine while establishing a conservation easement in order to preserve the archeologically significant site. In 2003, he joined a startup wireless telecommunications firm in Raleigh, N.C., which he helped grow from five employees to over twenty-five in two years. Darden left in 2005 to found Arbor Equity, a real estate firm committed to sustainable development. Mr. Darden has relocated to New Orleans to oversee the Make It Right project.

Hervé Descottes

Hervé Descottes co-founded the lighting design and consulting firm L'Observatoire International in 1993. The firm collaborates on such disparate spatial expressions as architecture, urban, landscape, and fine art projects. Descottes has received the Award for Collaborative Achievement in Design from the American Institute of Architects (AIA), and the Award for Excellence in Design from the Art Commission of New York City.

Tim Duggan

Tim Duggan, ASLA, joined Make It Right (MIR) after working five years in Kansas City for BNIM Architects. While at BNIM, Tim assisted in a variety of sustainable design projects ranging from streetscape to public art and urban renewal projects, small-scale site design to large, comprehensive master-planned communities. He is also a well-rounded, motivated landscape designer who embraces sustainable design approaches for each new landscape he helps shape. Tim's design process has evolved from his traditional landscape architecture and planning education, to his extensive international experience and education. He integrates a balanced approach for each of his projects and is an avid proponent of basic sustainable design principles that produce sound creative solutions. He brings to the table an extensive understanding of innovative stormwater management techniques such as rain gardens, wetlands, and bioswales.

Kristin Feireiss

Dr. h. c. Kristin Feireiss, editor, curator, architecture critic, architecture historian, in 1980 founded, and since then directs the Aedes Architecture Forum in Berlin, one of the most successful institutions internationally for communicating architecture culture, urban design, and similar topics. From 1995 to 2001 she was director of the Netherlands Architecture Institute (NAI) in Rotterdam and commissioner for the Dutch Pavilion at the Venice Biennale in 1996 and 2000. She is editor of numerous international publications, such as *Blank: Architecture, Apartheid and After, Informal City: Caracas Case*, and several thematic publications and monographs, many of which have received awards. She innovated the Rotterdam Biennale, the Zumtobel Group Award for Sustainability Humanity in the Built Environment, is consultant in architecture and urban space for public and private clients, and serves on juries for projects such as the Olympic Green, Beijing, or the Mariinsky Theatre, St. Petersburg. In 2001, she was honored for her commitment to the communication of architecture and the strengthening of bilateral relations with the Order of Merit of the Federal Republic of Germany. In 2009, she founded an international educative network platform, the Aedes Network Campus Berlin.

Bryan Flaig

Bryan Flaig has practiced architecture at GRAFT Los Angeles since 2005. He acquired his master's of architecture degree at the Southern California Institute of Architecture (SCI_Arc), previously studying at the University of Virginia's School of Architecture. He has taught within SCI_Arc's graduate program as well as at Columbia University's Graduate School of Architecture and Planning.

Holly Fling

Holly Fling, LEED-AP, is an associate with Cherokee, where she supports corporate strategy efforts and the sustainable planning of redevelopment projects. She analyzes corporate sustainability initiatives, supports deal due diligence, and designs and implements Cherokee's data management system. Ms. Fling's previous work experience includes wildlife management and wetlands restoration in the Florida Everglades. She received a bachelor of arts from Harvard University and a master of environmental economics and policy from the Nicholas School of the Environment at Duke University, where she was a Doris Duke Conservation Fellow.

Jay Gernsbacher

Founder of Center Staging, Inc., Jay Gernsbacher, a New Orleans native, incorporated the company in 1993. Center Staging, Inc. is one of the leading event production companies in the Gulf South region and has been instrumental in providing production support services for many of New Orleans' signature events. Jay's input was the final design and fabrication of the base and roof structures, the assembly of the labor team to deliver, install, maintain, and remove the Pink Project over its life span.

GRAFT

GRAFT is a full-service design firm with the collective professional experience that encompasses a wide array of building types including fine arts, educational, institutional, commercial, and residential facilities. The firm has been awarded the Honor Award 2005 from the AIA in Los Angeles, the Contract World Award in 2004 and 2005, the Hospitality Design Award 2005, along with numerous other international awards and prizes. GRAFT has founded offices in Los Angeles, Berlin, and Beijing.

Katherine Grove

Architect Katherine Grove, AIA, LEED-AP, is a director and project manager with William McDonough+Partners, where she has collaborated on a range of institutional, commercial, mixed-use, and residential projects. Grove has served as project manager for the new American University School of International Service, the Sarah Heinz House, and the Cave Avenue Co-Operative Housing.

Kim S. Haddow

Kim S. Haddow is the director of communications for the Make It Right Foundation where she oversees the Foundation's strategic communications planning, branding, message development, earned and paid media, website, and e-communication channels. Prior to joining Make It Right, Haddow served as the Sierra Club's national communications director and worked as the head of her own media consulting and advertising agency. Before starting her own business, she spent eight years at Greer, Margolis, Mitchell, Burns, a consulting firm where she worked on 22 gubernatorial, senatorial and statewide initiative campaigns. Haddow started her career at WWL-AM in New Orleans.

Heimann und Schwantes

A design company founded by Michael Heimann and Hendrik Schwantes in Berlin. Their works, particularly consisting of publication concepts and designs in the fields of art and architecture, have been multiply awarded.

Michael Heimann

Born in Munich, Germany, he studied communication design at the University of Applied Sciences Trier and the Basel School of Design. He worked as junior designer at Interbrand Zintzmeyer & Lux, Zurich, and after that as a designer at kognito Gestaltung Berlin. Together with Dorothea Weishaupt he founded groenland.berlin.basel, a design office specializing in book design. From 2005 he ran it as groenland.berlin. In 2007 he founded the design office Heimann und Schwantes with Hendrik Schwantes.

Serge Hoeltschi

Serge Hoeltschi blazed onto the scene in 1994 as one of Switzerland's leading fashion, portrait, and advertising photographers. He pocketed the Gold Lion Award at the 2007 Cannes Film Festival for best commercial director, as well as New York Festival's Gold Award, and has worked with such clients as *Wallpaper*, German *Vanity Fair, GQ,* and Coca-Cola. Now based in Los Angeles, Hoeltschi's saturated images and flawless use of lighting capture the sophistication, simplicity, and sexiness that is the cornerstone of his work.

Gregor Hoheisel

Gregor Hoheisel, Dipl.Ing. Arch, architect, currently residing in Beijing, China, studied architecture in Germany at the Technische Universität Braunschweig. He worked at Gerkan, Marg+Partners in Berlin before he joined GRAFT in 1999 as a principal. In 2002 he moved to Beijing, China, where he currently leads the GRAFT office. GRAFT has succeeded with numerous national and international award-winning projects in the fields of fine arts, educational, institutional, commercial, and residential facilities.

Sarah Howell

Sarah Howell, is an architect and fine artist from Connecticut who practiced in California and New York before moving to New Orleans. As a student at Yale, she developed an interest in sustainable design and historic preservation and that interest eventually led her to John Williams and to the Make It Right project. A LEED Accredited Professional, Sarah's role on the team is to coordinate the architects' efforts toward environmentally responsible building

Linda Jackson

President of the Lower Ninth Ward Homeowner's Association, Linda Jackson has been a Lower Ninth Ward resident for almost 30 years. Prior to Hurricane Katrina, she was a proprietor. Linda coordinates efforts to help homeowners in the community rebuild. She organizes neighborhood watch security for the Lower Ninth Ward through block captains, seeks monetary resources to help reconstruct homes, and advocates throughout the nation, the state, and the City of New Orleans to obtain help in rebuilding. She also informs residents of policy changes through monthly meetings and connects them to legal aid and counseling resources.

Vanessa Johnson-Gueringer

A lifelong resident of the Lower Ninth Ward, Mrs. Johnson-Gueringer has been a member of ACORN since 2001 and, during September 2005, became chair of the Lower Ninth Ward ACORN. Upon returning home after Hurricane Katrina, she was distressed by the lack of interest in rebuilding her community. Her leadership role has allowed her to actively lobby for her community, meet with elected officials, lead protests, and confront political leadership about foul treatment of the community.

Patricia Jones

The executive director for the Lower 9th Ward Neighborhood Empowerment Network Association (NENA). Patricia presently directs the Recovery Center in the Lower Ninth Ward where she manages a staff that has grown from two volunteers to 15 employees. She has 12 years' experience in the nonprofit sector. Prior to Katrina, she ran her own business specializing in bookkeeping and tax preparation. Since Katrina, Patricia has partnered with many to navigate a strong comeback for the Lower Ninth.

Nina Killeen

Born and raised in New Orleans, and after living in Miami, Italy, and New York (each for only 2 years), she returned to New Orleans to raise three children. She has spent most of her adult life in the field of film production. She served as one of the founding team members of Make It Right, and as co-producer of the Pink Project.

LaToya King

LaToya King is a senior associate with the Make It Right Foundation, focusing on development, fundraising, and operational activities. Prior to Make It Right, Ms. King was an associate with Cherokee, focusing on deal analysis, due diligence, and asset management and the Fannie Mae Foundation, underwriting debt investments for the development of affordable housing. She began her career as an analyst and underwriting manager with Bank of America in the Community Development Banking Group. Ms. King received a BBA from Howard University and an MBA from the Kenan-Flagler Business School at the University of North Carolina at Chapel Hill.

Ajamu Kitwana

Ajamu Kitwana is director of Homeowner Services for Make It Right. Homeowner Services include outreach to Lower Ninth Ward residents, homeowner counseling for program participants, and affordable home financing. Mr. Kitwana coordinates the work of the MIR team, Lower Ninth Ward community partners, and subcontractors for the provision of these services. Mr. Kitwana has a BS in civil and environmental engineering and an MS in environmental engineering, both from Stanford University.

Lars Krückeberg

GRAFT principal Lars Krückeberg, MArch, Dipl.Ing. Arch, Architect BDA, studied architecture at the Technische Universität Braunschweig, Germany, at the Universitá degli Studi di Firenze, the German Institute for History of Art, Florence, Italy, and he received his master's degree at the Southern Institute of Architecture, Los Angeles, CA. In 1998 he established GRAFT in Los Angeles together with Wolfram Putz. Graft has succeeded with numerous national and international award-winning projects in the field of fine arts, educational, institutional, commercial, and residential facilities. Lars Krückeberg is a member of the German Chamber of Architects (BDA).

M. Alejandra Lillo

M. Alejandra Lillo, MArch, received her first professional degree and license in architecture at the University of Mendoza, Argentina, later pursuing a master's degree in architecture at the University of California Los Angeles. As a designer, project architect, and project manager she has worked on numerous international award-winning educational, institutional, commercial, and residential projects while practicing in Canada and the U.S. In 2007 she became partner at GRAFT, leading the Los Angeles office.

Lighthouse for the Blind in New Orleans

The Lighthouse for the Blind in New Orleans is a not-for-profit agency that has been in existence for almost 100 years and is the manufacturer of the Pink bags made from 100-percent recycled scrap materials from the Pink Project. The Lighthouse employs people who are blind or visually impaired, helps them find employment in the community, and provides a wide range of services to visually impaired adults and children. All Lighthouse activities are aimed at promoting individual independence and self-reliance.

Jennifer Lo

Since graduating from the University of Texas at Austin in 2004, Jennifer Lo has worked on a variety of architectural projects, most of which included residential work. She moved to New Orleans in 2006 to take an active role in the rebuilding of New Orleans and is a part of the Make It Right team at the office of John C. Williams Architects. She is coordinator of the local architectural design sector of MIR as well as a facilitator in the development of international designs.

George Long

George Long of George Long Photography and Gallery is a hardworking commercial and event photographer with a great attitude. His heart and soul have resided in New Orleans for over 30 years. Find his book, *Katrina Days: Life in New Orleans after Hurricane Katrina,* featured on his website www.georgelong.com.

Edwin López

A PhD candidate in the Department of Sociology at the University of California, Santa Barbara, Edwin López is currently conducting a critical global ethnography of New Orleans residents and organizers who are working to rebuild their lives in the wake of Hurricane Katrina. He also serves as a volunteer for the Common Ground media collective.

Anthony Manno

Marine Tops and Covers' usual course of work is to fabricate marine-related soft goods, from soft-tops for sport fishing boats to industrial covers and specialty items for commercial and military use. Anthony's background also includes a long stint overseeing the fabrication of large tent tops and sky boxes for major golf tournaments, which made him just the right person for the Pink Project. Anthony was responsible for the fabrication of the pink base and roof covers, fabricating over 325 various pieces that ultimately came to represent 150 houses, the initial goal of Make It Right in the Lower Ninth Ward.

William McDonough

Architect and designer William McDonough, FAIA, Int. FRIBA, has been recognized as a "hero for the planet" by *Time* magazine. He and German chemist Michael Braungart co-authored *Cradle to Cradle: Remaking the Way We Make Things.* McDonough founded the architecture and community design firm William McDonough + Partners, and co-founded McDonough Braungart Design Chemistry (MBDC), a product and process design consultancy. McDonough is a venture partner with Vantage Point Venture Partners in San Bruno, California.

Vera McFadden

President of the Lower 9th Ward Neighborhood Council and resident since 1951, Mrs. McFadden is the secretary at Dr. Martin Luther King, Jr. Charter School for Science and Technology, where she worked pre- and post-Katrina. Through her activities with the Lower 9th Ward Neighborhood Council, Mrs. McFadden is an outspoken advocate for her neighborhood, helping it to recover.

Carol McMichael Reese

Carol McMichael Reese is associate professor and the Christovich Professor in the Tulane School of Architecture. Her books and articles focus on contemporary architecture and urban planning in the Americas. She is a co-organizer, with Michael Sorkin and Anthony Fontenot, of

Charles E. Allen, III

Ken Alston

Claudia Baulesch

Stefan Beese

Carrie Bernhard

Dr. Michael Braungart

Doug Brinkley

Willie Calhoun, Jr.

Richard Campanella

Alice Craft-Kerney

Mary Croom-Fontenot

Tom F. Darden, III

Pamela Dashiell

Hervé Descottes

Tim Duggan

Kristin Feireiss

Bryan Flaig

Holly Fling

Jay Gernsbacher

Katherine Grove

Michael Heimann

Serge Hoeltschi

Gregor Hoheisel

Sarah Howell

Linda Jackson

Vanessa Johnson-Gueringer

Patricia Jones

Nina Killeen

LaToya King

Ajamu Kitwana

Lars Krückeberg

Alejandra Lillo

Jennifer Lo

George Long

Edwin López

Anthony Manno

William McDonough   Vera McFadden   Carol McMichael Reese   Virginia Miller   Lionel Milton   Trevor Neilson

Neiel Norheim   Terry Parker   Brad Pitt   Wolfram Putz   Malik Rahim   Ricky Ridecós

John Sader   Verena Schreppel   Hendrik Schwantes   Ware Smith   Charlie Varley   Jason Villemarette

Sam Whitt   Christopher Whittaker   Thomas Willemeit   John C. Williams   Joyce Williams   Daniel Winkert

Mavis Yorks

Brandon Young

Project New Orleans, which has produced a website and exhibition documenting plans for the post-Katrina rebuilding of the city. In October of 2009, Project New Orleans will host a national conference at Tulane to analyze the city's recovery process.

MGX Lab

MGX Lab is an innovation and incubation think tank providing its partners high-return brand acceleration through experiential design solutions across all media. They employ a 360-degree approach in order to optimize the consumer experience at all touch points. Their team is comprised of veteran entrepreneurs with backgrounds in architecture, industrial design, publishing, advertising, brand identity, graphic design, animation, mobile, and interactive development.

Virginia Miller

Virginia Miller is co-owner of Beuerman Miller Fitzgerald, a full-service public relations and marketing firm with a worldwide client base, and services that range from public relations, media, and government affairs to consumer and business-to-business advertising, crisis communication, litigation support, and reputation management. A native of Washington, DC, and a graduate of Tulane University, Ms. Miller, in addition to her work on behalf of Make It Right, serves on the boards of The Horizon Initiative, The Innocence Project and provides pro bono services for many others, including the Lighthouse for the Blind and arts and social service organization Young Aspirations / Young Artists (YA / YA).

Lionel Milton

The Pink House painting was commissioned by the Make it Right NOLA foundation and painted by New Orleans artist Lionel Milton. Born and raised in the Lower Ninth Ward, Lionel was inspired by the Crescent City's unique music he grew up around as well as the deep-rooted people of the city. Lionel's art has become a well-recognized figure by companies and collectors throughout the country who seek his artistic style that uniquely and vibrantly demonstrates a raw urban energy with ubiquitous appeal and broad demographic charm. His infectious style and imagery have also crossed from design into television, art direction, licensing, pub-

lishing, and illustrations. You can see more of Lionel's work at his website www.elleone.com.

Trevor Neilson

Trevor Neilson is a senior advisor to the Jolie-Pitt Foundation, and is president of the Global Philanthropy Group. Trevor served as executive director of the Global Business Coalition on HIV/AIDS, director of special projects for the Bill & Melinda Gates Foundation, and in the White House during the Clinton administration. He helped Bono form DATA (Debt Relief, AIDS, Trade Africa) and serves on its policy board. He is also an advisor to APCO Worldwide, the Wikimedia Foundation (Wikipedia), the Genocide Intervention Network, and Global Action for Children.

Neiel Norheim

From its inception, Neiel Norheim has been the project manager for Make It Right, developing and leading the process for GRAFT. He received his bachelor's degree of architecture from the California Polytechnic State University San Luis Obispo with a minor in sustainability, studying one year in Europe (International Studies Program, Copenhagen, Denmark). After working as a designer for Coop Himmelblau, he joined GRAFT in 2005 as a lead designer and project manager. He is also a design professor for the architecture program at Pasadena City College.

Terry Parker

Terry Parker has been employed at John C. Williams Architects for 13 years, is experienced in project coordination, and is currently providing construction administration for New Orleans City Park, Pan American Stadium, and the New Orleans Fairgrounds New Slot Facility Addition. Recently completed construction administration for a new dormitory at the New Orleans Fairgrounds. Terry assists in project coordination and management for the Make it Right project.

Brad Pitt

Brad Pitt is the founder of Make It Right, co-chair of the Jolie-Pitt Foundation, and an award-winning actor and film producer. He is also a co-founder of Not On Our Watch, an organization focused on driving global attention and resources towards putting an end to mass atrocities around the world.

Wolfram Putz

GRAFT principal Wolfram Putz, MArch, Dipl.Ing. Arch, Architect BDA, studied architecture in Germany at the Technische Universität Braunschweig, the University of Utah, Salt Lake City, and received his master's degree at the Southern Californian Institute of Architecture, Los Angeles, CA. After working for Gerkan, Marg und Partners he founded GRAFT with Lars Krückeberg in 1998 in Los Angeles. GRAFT has succeeded with numerous national and international award-winning projects in the field of fine arts, educational, institutional, commercial, and residential facilities. Wolfram Putz is a member of the German Chamber of Architects (BDA) and associated member of the American Institute of Architects (AIA).

Malik Rahim

Raised in New Orleans' Algiers neighborhood, Malik Rahim founded and operated the Algiers Development Center and Invest Transitional Housing. He is co-founder and outreach organizer of Housing is a Human Right in San Francisco, California, and co-founded Common Ground Relief in September 2005 with Scott Crow and Brandon Darby. Since Hurricane Katrina, nearly 13,000 volunteers have gutted over 3,000 homes in the Ninth Ward of New Orleans through their efforts.

Rehage Entertainment (RE:)

Since its 1992 inception RE: has become one of the country's leading entertainment companies. The New York- and New Orleans-based group creates and executes a wide range of events throughout the U.S. offering production, design, artist booking, marketing, and sponsorship services. The company's annual events include the EIF Revlon Run/Walk For Women™ in Times Square, the ESSENCE Music Festival® (New Orleans), and Women's Health "Are You Game?" (Chicago and New York City). In addition, RE: developed its own critically acclaimed signature brand, the Voodoo Experience® (New Orleans) in 1999. For more on RE:, please visit www.rehage.com.

Ricky Ridecós

Born and raised in Buenos Aires, Ricky Ridecós is a Los Angeles-based photographer. Ranging from the representational to the ethereal images captured within this book, Ricky's photographs have appeared in a variety of publications, including *Interior Design, Elle Decor,* and *Living Design,* as well as Taschen's acclaimed Architecture Now! series. Ricky is honored to participate in the Make It Right project.

Jon Sader

Jon Sader is the construction director at Make It Right. Sader is a third-generation contractor and developer from Michigan with experience ranging from custom homes, commercial structures, municipal infrastructures, and multimillion dollar projects throughout the Midwest. Sader brings with him a vast amount of expertise in site-built, panelized, and modular construction, and is dedicated to the concept of environmentally safe, affordable housing.

Verena Schreppel

Verena studied product design at the University of Fine Arts in Hamburg and in Madrid. She has worked as a designer in Germany and the U.S. before founding Studio Verena Schreppel in 2005. As a consultant she has operated in the fields of architecture and marketing for numerous enterprises and joined GRAFT supporting the Make It Right project in its communication and organization. Currently managing this publication.

Hendrik Schwantes

Born in Stuttgart, Germany, studied photography and communication design at the University of Applied Sciences Hamburg. He worked as a designer at Lars Müller Publishers, Baden, Switzerland. Afterwards he started his own practice in Berlin in 2004 and was lecturer at Berlin University of the Arts. In 2007 he founded the design office Heimann und Schwantes with Michael Heimann.

Ware Smith

Ware Smith is the director of external affairs for Make It Right. Joining as the second employee of Make It Right in June of 2007, Smith served to help organize and implement the strategic plan leading to the large-scale development of Make It Right. Since public launch in December of 2007, which generated widespread attention to the project, Smith is in charge of managing external communications, including incoming general inquiries, donor relations, website messaging and content,

as well the coordination of Make It Right merchandising. In addition, Smith is responsible for writing grants and proposals with potential benefit to project goals. Smith received a BA from the University of Virginia and spent a year in France studying marketing and advertising.

Charlie Varley

Charlie Varley is a British photojournalist currently based in New Orleans, where he lives with his wife and young son. Represented by SIPA Press in New York and Paris, Charlie has traveled the world capturing images from the sublime to the surreal, from celebrities and presidents to war and peace. His work is published worldwide in books, newspapers, magazines, TV, and the World Wide Web. For more information, please visit www.varleypix.com.

Jason Villemarette

Founder of Fire on the Bayou and the videographer for the Pink Project. Fire on the Bayou is a full-service production company based in New Orleans that specializes in creative storytelling. It was formed in 2001 by founder Jason Villemarette, a native New Orleanian, who was introduced to the filmmaking process by participating in a award-winning community documentary called *Desire.* Fire on the Bayou offers all production services from concept to production and editorial finishing. Recent projects include national, regional, and local commercials in addition to nationally syndicated documentaries and television shows.

Sam Whitt

Mr. Whitt is a lawyer and business executive with more than 20 years of experience in a wide range of business and legal matters. Mr. Whitt is special counsel at Nexsen Pruet, a Carolinas law firm and general counsel to Southern Capitol Ventures, a venture capital fund. He is a founding member of Clover Energy, LLC, a private equity fund focused on renewable energy. Mr. Whitt previously served as the executive director of the Cherokee Gives Back Foundation, a foundation dedicated to improving the lives of the world's poor. He currently serves on the board of directors of the Make It Right Foundation, Airimba Wireless, Inc., and RCHS Foundation.

Christopher Whittaker

Volunteer videographer and photographer/production assistant for the Pink Project, Christopher Whittaker is happy to have been born and raised in New Orleans. Spending most of his life working in production he had been attending U.N.O for two years in the pursuit of a film/communications degree when Katrina hit. Christopher Whittaker will continue to work in production until his dream of producing powerful projects is completed. "Dream as though you will never die."

Thomas Willemeit

Dipl.Ing. Arch, Architect BDA, GRAFT principal Thomas Willemeit studied architecture at the Technische Universität Braunschweig and the Bauhaus Dessau, masterclass in architecture and urban planning. He worked on competitions for Prof. Gerber and Associated and Studio Daniel Libeskind before becoming principal at GRAFT in 2001. Besides his successful career in the architectural field, he won numerous national prizes as a violin player and a chorister and was a scholar of the German Music Council. Thomas Willemeit is a member of the German Chamber of Architects (BDA).

Joyce Williams

Joyce Williams is the office manager for Make It Right. In addition to traditional administrative and office management duties, Ms. Williams helps with resident intake and answers questions for inquiring MIR program candidates. Ms. Williams has been a resident of New Orleans for 47 years. She attended the University of New Orleans and Sidney Collier Vocational Technical School where she received certified training in business administration and financial correspondence. Her professional experience includes educational development, finances, human resources, and business management. Ms. Williams enjoys working with MIR as an opportunity to enrich her community.

John C. Williams

John C. Williams, AIA, is the principal architect and owner of John C. Williams Architects, LLC, which he started 25 years ago in New Orleans, LA. Williams Architects works on planning, architecture, and interior design projects. Williams Architects has been honored with awards from the American Institute of Architects, the New Orleans Historic District Landmarks Commission, and the Vieux Carré Commission. John is a leader in sustainability for post-Katrina rebuilding in the New Orleans region.

Daniel Winkert

An architect and planner who has spent the past 22 years learning and practicing architecture in New Orleans, Mr. Winkert has devoted his work to the betterment of the city and to the environment, working on advancing local sustainable building practices, neighborhood involvement, and social service nonprofit work. A LEED Accredited Professional, Mr. Winkert is the project architect for John C. Williams Architects on the Make It Right project.

Brandon Young

A New Yorker, Brandon Young, an alumnus of the Prep for Prep and the Browning School, moved to North Carolina to attend the UNC Chapel Hill. While studying economics and social entrepreneurship he connected with Cherokee Gives Back through the Carolina Entrepreneurship Initiative, joining the Make It Right team as an intern in June 2007, serving as analyst, and then IT manager after deciding to continue working with MIR during the fall semester of his senior year. In 2008, Young returned to Chapel Hill where he continued to assist MIR from out of state.

Mavis Yorks

Mavis Yorks of Common Ground Relief has been passionate about photography since receiving her first camera at age 15. She strives to create images that show the enduring spirit and dignity of the voiceless, abused, or ignored. In 2008 she returned from a year donating her skills to a relief organization in the fertile human soil of New Orleans. In 2006 she was co-producer of the acclaimed documentary *When Pigs Fly,* released in 2007. Dutch by birth but international in vision, she has lived on four continents. She currently resides in Sarasota, Florida.

The Times-Picayune

The newspaper originated in 1837 as *The Picayune. The New Orleans Times,* which had begun publication before the Civil War, combined with *The Times-Democrat* in 1881. That newspaper merged with *The Picayune* in 1914 to form *The Times-Picayune. The New Orleans Item* was founded in 1877, and *The New Orleans States* made its debut three years later. Both were afternoon papers. *The States* bought *The Item* in 1958, becoming *The States-Item. The Times-Picayune* and *The States-Item* merged in 1980 and eventually became *The Times-Picayune.* A picayune was an old Spanish silver coin worth about 6¼ cents. The original newspaper, *The Picayune,* sold for that price.

Architect Contacts

Adjaye Associates
www.adjaye.com
415 Broadway, 3rd Floor
New York, NY 10013
United States of America

Atelier Hitoshi Abe
www.a-slash.jp
459 S. Holt Avenue
Los Angeles, CA 90048
United States of America

Bild Design
www.bildit.com
8521 Zimple Street
New Orleans, LA 70118
United States of America

Billes Architecture
www.billesarchitecture.com
1055 St. Charles Avenue, Suite 220
New Orleans, LA 70130
United States of America

BNIM
Berkebile Nelson Immenschuh
McDowell Architects
www.bnim.com
106 West 14th Street, Suite 200
Kansas City, MO 64105
United States of America

buildingstudio
www.buildingstudio.net
322 Lafayette Street
New Orleans, LA 70130
United States of America

concordia LLC
www.concordia.com
201 St. Charles Ave., Suite 4318
New Orleans, LA 70170
United States of America

Constructs LLC
www.constructsllc.com
40 Fourth Circular Road
Contonments, Accra
Ghana

ELEMENTAL
www.elementalchile.cl
Av. Los Conquistadores 1700 Piso 25-A
7530128 Providencia
Chile

Eskew+Dumez+Ripple
www.studioedr.com
365 Canal Street, Suite 3150
New Orleans, LA 70130
United States of America

Gehry Partners, LLP
www.gehrypartners.com
12541 Beatrice Street
Los Angeles, CA 90066
United States of America

GRAFT
Los Angeles, Berlin, Beijing
www.graftlab.com
3200 N. Figueroa Street
Los Angeles, CA 90065
United States of America

KieranTimberlake
Associates LLP
www.kierantimberlake.com
420 North 20th Street
Philadelphia, PA 19130
United States of America

Morphosis Architects
www.morphosis.net
2041 Colorado Avenue
Santa Monica, CA 90404
United States of America

MVRDV
www.mvrdv.nl
Dunantstraat 10
3024 BC Rotterdam
The Netherlands

Pugh+Scarpa Architects
www.pugh-scarpa.com
2525 Michigan Avenue, F1
Santa Monica, CA 90404
United States of America

Shigeru Ban Architects
www.dma-ny.com
330 W. 38th Street, Ste. 811
New York, NY 10018
United States of America

Trahan Architects
www.trahanarchitects.com
445 North Boulevard, Suite 570
Baton Rouge, LA 70802
United States of America

Waggonner & Ball Architects
www.wbarchitects.com
2200 Prytania Street
New Orleans, LA 70130
United States of America

William McDonough+Partners
www.mcdonoughpartners.com
700 East Jefferson St.
Charlottesville, VA 22902
United States of America

References

Carol McMichael Reese
From Field of Disaster to Field of
Dreams: The Lower Ninth Ward

Campanella, Richard. *Geographies of New Orleans, Urban Fabrics Before the Storm.* Lafayette, LA: University of Louisiana, 2006.

———. *Time and Place in New Orleans: Past Geographies in the Present Day.* Gretna, LA: Pelican, 2002.

Colten, Craig. E. *Transforming New Orleans and its Environs: Centuries of Change.* Pittsburgh: University of Pittsburgh, 2002.

———. *An Unnatural Metropolis: Wresting New Orleans from Nature.* Baton Rouge: Louisiana State University, 2005.

Landphair, Juliette. "'The Forgotten People of New Orleans': Community, Vulnerability, and the Lower Ninth Ward." *Journal of American History* 94 (December 2007): 837–45.

Spain, Daphne. "Race Relations and Residential Segregation in New Orleans: Two Centuries of Paradox," *Annals of the American Academy of Political and Social Science* 441 (January 1979): 82–96.

Richard Campanella
Urban Transformation in
the Lower Ninth Ward

Bureau of Governmental Research. *Wards of New Orleans.* New Orleans: City of New Orleans, 1961.

Campanella, Richard. *Bienville's Dilemma: A Historical Geography of New Orleans.* Lafayette, LA: Center for Louisiana Studies, 2008.

Campanella, Richard. *Geographies of New Orleans: Urban Fabrics Before the Storm.* Lafayette, LA: Center for Louisiana Studies, 2006.

Campanella, Richard. *Time and Place in New Orleans: Past Geographies in the Present Day.* Gretna, LA: Pelican Publishing Company, 2002.

Carter, Sam R. *A Report on Survey of Metropolitan New Orleans Land Use, Real Property, and Low Income Housing Area.* New Orleans: Works Projects Administration, Louisiana State Department of Public Welfare, and Housing Authority of New Orleans, 1941.

City Planning and Zoning Commission. *Major Street Report.* New Orleans: City Planning and Zoning Commission, 1927.

Colten, Craig E. *An Unnatural Metropolis: Wresting New Orleans from Nature.* Baton Rouge and London: Louisiana State University Press, 2005.

Cunningham, Robert, David Gisclair, and John Craig. "The Louisiana State-wide LIDAR Project" and LIDAR elevation data at www.atlas.lsu.edu.

D'Iberville, Pierre Le Moyne, Sieur. *Iberville's Gulf Journals,* edited and translated by Richebourg Gaillard McWilliams. University, AL: The University of Alabama Press, 1991.

Dabney, Thomas Ewing. *The Industrial Canal and Inner Harbor of New Orleans: History, Description and Economic Aspects of Giant Facility Created to Encourage Industrial Expansion and Develop Commerce.* New Orleans: Board of Commissioners of the Port of New Orleans, 1921.

The Daily Orleanian, 1849–1850 Drainage Advisory Board. *Report on the Drainage of the City of New Orleans.* New Orleans: T. Fitzwilliam & Co. Printers, 1895.

Friends of the Cabildo. *New Orleans Architecture,* 8 vols. New Orleans and Gretna, LA: Friends of the Cabildo and Pelican Publishing Company, 1971–97.

Hennick, Louis C., and E. Harper Charlton. *The Streetcars of New Orleans.* Gretna, LA: Firebird Press Book / Pelican Publishing Company, 1965; reprinted 2000.

Labbé, Ronald M. and Jonathan Lurie. *The Slaughterhouse Cases: Regulation, Reconstruction, and the Fourteenth Amendment.* Lawrence, KS: University Press of Kansas, 2003.

Marshall, Bob. "City's Fate Sealed in Hours: Timeline Maps Course of Post-Katrina Deluge." *The Times-Picayune,* May 14, 2006, A–1.

Périer and De La Chaise. Letter to the Directors of the Company of the Indies, November 3, 1728. *Mississippi Provincial Archives 1704–1743: French Dominion,* vol. 2. Ed. Dunbar Rowland and Albert Godfrey Sanders (Jackson, MS, 1929), 2:592.

Sewerage and Water Board of New Orleans. *Report on Hurricane "Betsy," September 9–10, 1965.* New Orleans: Sewerage and Water Board, October 8, 1965.

U.S. Army Engineer District, New Orleans. *Hurricane Betsy, September 8–11, 1965, Serial No. 1880.* New Orleans: Corps of Engineers, November 1965.

U.S. Army Engineer District, New Orleans. *Hurricane Betsy, September 8–11, 1965: After-Action Report.* New Orleans: Corps of Engineers, July 1966.

U.S. Census Bureau. "Census 2000 Full–Count Characteristics (SF1)," compiled by Greater New Orleans Community Data Center.

U.S. Census Bureau. "Profile of Selected Social Characteristics, 2000, Census 2000 Summary File 3 (SF 3) Sample Data."

U.S. Census Bureau. "Louisiana 1910 Census: Orleans Parish (Part)." Digital database of 1910 Census population schedules. North Salt Lake City, UT: HeritageQuest, 2003.

U.S. Census Bureau. *Population 1910: Reports by States, with Statistics for Counties, Cities, and Other Civil Divisions, Alabama–Montana.* Washington, DC: Government Printing Office, 1913.

U.S. Census Bureau. *Population and Housing Statistics for Census Tracts: New Orleans, LA.* Washington, DC: U.S. Government Printing Office, 1942.

U.S. Census Bureau. *Population and Housing, 1960: Census Tracts: New Orleans, LA.* Washington, DC: U.S. Government Printing Office, 1961.

Credits

Editor's Acknowledgments

Authors
Charles E. Allen, III
Carrie Bernhard
Doug Brinkley
Richard Campanella
Tom Darden, III
Tim Duggan
GRAFT
Patricia Jones
Nina Killeen
Ajamu Kitwana
William McDonough
Carol McMichael Reese
Trevor Neilson
Brad Pitt
Jon Sader

Interview partners
Denise and Elder Larry Baham
Willie Calhoun
Alice Craft-Kerney
Mary Croom-Fontenot
Pam Dashiell
Charles and Thirawer Duplessis
Linda Jackson
Sharon Johnson
Vanessa Johnson-Gueringer
Gertrud Leblanc
Vera McFadden
Malik Rahim

Photographers
Claudia Baulesch
Richard Campanella
CIMSS (Cooperative Institute for
    Meteorological Satellite Studies)
Rob Decosmo (GRAFT)
FOX
Getty-Images
Megan Grant
    (Rehage Entertainment)
Serge Hoeltschi
Alexei Lebedev (MIR)
Jennifer Lo
    (John C. Williams Architects)
George Long
Ricky Ridecós
Ware Smith (MIR)
Verena Schreppel (GRAFT)
The Times-Picayune
Charlie Varley
Mavis Yorks

Book designers
Michael Heimann
Renate Huth
Hendrik Schwantes
Haig Walta

Lithography
Markus Hannes
Michael Henckus

Architects
Adjaye Associates
Atelier Hitoshi Abe
Bild Design
Billes Architecture
BNIM
buildingstudio
concordia LLC
Constructs LLC
Elemental
Eskew+Dumez+Ripple
Gehry Partners, LLP
GRAFT
Kappe Architects/Planners
KieranTimberlake
Morphosis Architects
MVRDV
Pugh+Scarpa Architects
Shigeru Ban Architects
Trahan Architects
Waggonner & Ball Architects
William McDonough+Partners

Donors
Aedes Architecture Forum
GRAFT
Heimann und Schwantes
MIR
max-color
Brad Pitt
The Times-Picayune

GRAFT

Heimann und Schwantes

max-color

The Times-Picayune

Make It Right Foundation Sponsors

The Ellen DeGeneres Show helped
to raise almost $1.3 million from their
studio audiences and fans.

Make It Right Foundation donors
$50,000 and above as of 5/21/09:

Idol Gives Back Foundation
Jolie-Pitt Foundation
Bush Clinton Katrina Fund
Stephen Bing
Jenna King (The King Family)
AARP
Universal City Studios LLLP
Peter B. Kellner
Brown Cat, Inc.
Capital One Services, Inc.
Colin Johnson
Ellen Howe Foundation
Ferrell/Paulin Family Foundation, Inc.
Frank and Gale Robitaille
George Clooney
J. Kerry Clayton
James W. Buffett Trust
John Langan
Mike Novogratz
Payton's Play It Forward Foundation
Richard & Dorinda Medley
Susan Haugerud
The James R. Burroughs Family
  Foundation
The Steven A. and Alexandra M.
  Cohen Foundation Inc.
The Wonder Trust
W.K. Kellogg Foundation
W. Ware Smith Jr.
Potter, Inc.
BRITA
By-Tour Inc.
David Spade
Energizer
Greenworks Natural Cleaners
Kellogg's Corporate
  Citizenship Fund
SC Johnson, A Family Company
The Clorox Company
Fact Frame Trustees, Ltd
Louisiana Disaster
  Recovery Foundation
Samsung Electronics America, Inc.
Better Than Ezra Foundation
Denise Rich
Donna Karan Weiss
Dwight Anderson

Jack Selby
Letitia Emilie Rieck
Maroon 5
New York Football Giants, Inc.
Phil Lesh
Slazer Enterprises LLC
The Supreme Master Ching Hai
Tim & Andrea Collins /
  The Ripplewood Foundation, Inc.
Wolfe Rudman

Pink Project donors and volunteers
Acorn
Alcoa
All Congregations Together
ARUP
Ashmead Group
Battery World
Beuerman Miller Fitzgerald
Bush-Clinton Katrina Fund
C2C Holdings / ReProduct
Champagne Electric
Cherokee
City of New Orleans
Clinton Global Initiative
Common Ground Relief
Donna Karan
Enterprise Corporation
  of the Delta (ECD)
GalCan Electric
Getty Images
Graft
Gulf South Solar
Holy Cross
  Neighborhood Association
Home Depot
Home Front Communications
Jane Rosenthal
  and Craig Hatkoff
Jay and Tracy Snyder
Kee Klamp
L'Observatoire International
Lady Cynthia Willard-Lewis
Lower 9th Ward Health Clinic
Lower 9th Ward
  Neighborhood Council, Inc.
Lower 9th Ward Neighborhood
  Empowerment Network
  Association (NENA)
Lower Ninth Ward
  Center for Sustainable
  Engagement and Development
McDonough Braungart
  Design Chemistry (MBDC)

McGlinchey Stafford
MGX Labs
ModSpace
NeighborWorks America
New Life Intracoastal Community
  Development Corporation
New Orleans
  Criminal Sheriff's Office
New Orleans Police Department
New Orleans Office of Council
New Orleans Office of Judge
Ospraie Management, LLC
Parsons Brinckerhoff
Peter B. Kellner
Piper Griffin
Rehage Entertainment
Sherman & Sterling
Solar Electric Light Fund (SELF)
STD LLC Waste
  and Debris Services
The Beatrice Snyder Foundation
The Lower Ninth Ward
  Homeowner's Association
The Ripplewood Foundation
Tipitina's
Trey and Jenny Laird
Twitchell Corporation
Universal Visual
Virgin
…100 anonymous donors

© Prestel Verlag, Munich · Berlin ·
London · New York, 2009
© for the texts by the authors, 2009
© for the works reproduced is
held by the architects and artists,
their heirs or assigns, 2009
© for the images, see Credits, p. 485

Prestel Verlag
Königinstrasse 9
80539 Munich
Tel. +49 (0)89 24 29 08-300
Fax +49 (0)89 24 29 08-335

Prestel Publishing Ltd.
4 Bloomsbury Place
London WC1A 2QA
Tel. +44 (0)20 7323-5004
Fax +44 (0)20 7636-8004

Prestel Publishing
900 Broadway, Suite 603
New York, N.Y. 10003
Tel. +1 (212) 995-2720
Fax +1 (212) 995-2733

www.prestel.com

Prestel books are available
worldwide. Please contact your
nearest bookseller or one of
the above addresses for information
concerning your local distributor.

Library of Congress Control Number:
2008943395

British Library Cataloguing-in-
Publication Data: a catalogue record
for this book is available from the
British Library. The Deutsche Bibliothek
holds a record of this publication in
the Deutsche Nationalbibliografie;
detailed bibliographical data can be
found under: http://dnb.ddb.de

Project management
GRAFT, Berlin, Los Angeles, Beijing

Design and layout
Heimann und Schwantes, Berlin

Copyediting
Jonathan Fox, Barcelona

Origination
max-color, Berlin

Production
Nele Krüger

Printed and bound
appl druck GmbH & Co. KG, Wemding

Printed in Germany on acid-free paper

FSC
Mix
Produktgruppe aus vorbildlich
bewirtschafteten Wäldern und
anderen kontrollierten Herkünften
Product group from well-managed
forests and other controlled sources
Zert.-Nr. SGS-COC-004238
www.fsc.org
© 1996 Forest Stewardship Council

ISBN 978-3-7913-4276-4